RHODES
IN ANCIENT TIMES

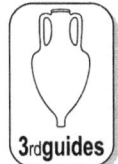

Terra-cotta "Melian" relief from Camiros

τὸν δ'οὖν Τληπόλεμον κοινῇ μετὰ τῶν ἐγχωρίων
τριμερῆ ποιῆσαι τὴν Ῥόδον, καὶ τρεῖς ἐν αὐτῇ
καταστῆσαι πόλεις, Λίνδον, Ἰηλύσον, Κάμειρον·

Diodoros Siculus, *Library of History*, Book IV.58.7-8

"The City of the Rhodians lies so far superior to all others in its harbours and roads and walls and improvements in general, that I am unable to speak of any city to equal it."

Strabo (IVX, 2-13)

"And in the Hereford Chart about 1300 A.D. Rhodes is depicted with a column stretching from coast to coast and leaving little room for anything but a legend to the effect that it was a happy island with a very tall column."

Cecil Torr, *Rhodes in Modern Times*

Cecil Torr in his garden at Yonder Wreyland
(from the author's personal album)

RHODES IN ANCIENT TIMES

by

Cecil Torr

first published 1885

A new edition with additional material edited by
Gerald Brisch

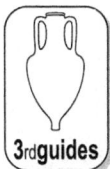

Also available in the Archaeopress 3rdguides Series:

Cecil Torr, *Rhodes in Modern Times*
J. Theodore Bent, *The Cyclades, or Life Among the Insular Greeks*
Christopher Wordsworth, *Athens and Attica*

Rhodes in Ancient Times, first published by Cambridge University Press, 1885

This edition © Archaeopress and Gerald Brisch 2005

3rdguides is an imprint of

Archaeopress
Gordon House, 276 Banbury Road
Oxford OX2 7ED, UK

All rights reserved. No part of this publication may be reproduced, stored in a retrieval system, or transmitted, in any form or by any means, electronic, mechanical, photocopying, recording or otherwise, without the prior permission of the publishers.

ISBN 0 9539923 6 5

Printed and bound in Great Britain by
Marston Book Services Ltd, Oxfordshire

3rdguides series editor: Gerald Brisch

Acknowledgments
Brenda Stones, Keith Bennett, Constance Rivemale
Cover photograph © Nick Nacc (The Temple of Pythian Apollo, Ancient Acropolis, Rhodes)
The two photographs of Cecil Torr © The Lustleigh Society, Lustleigh, Devon

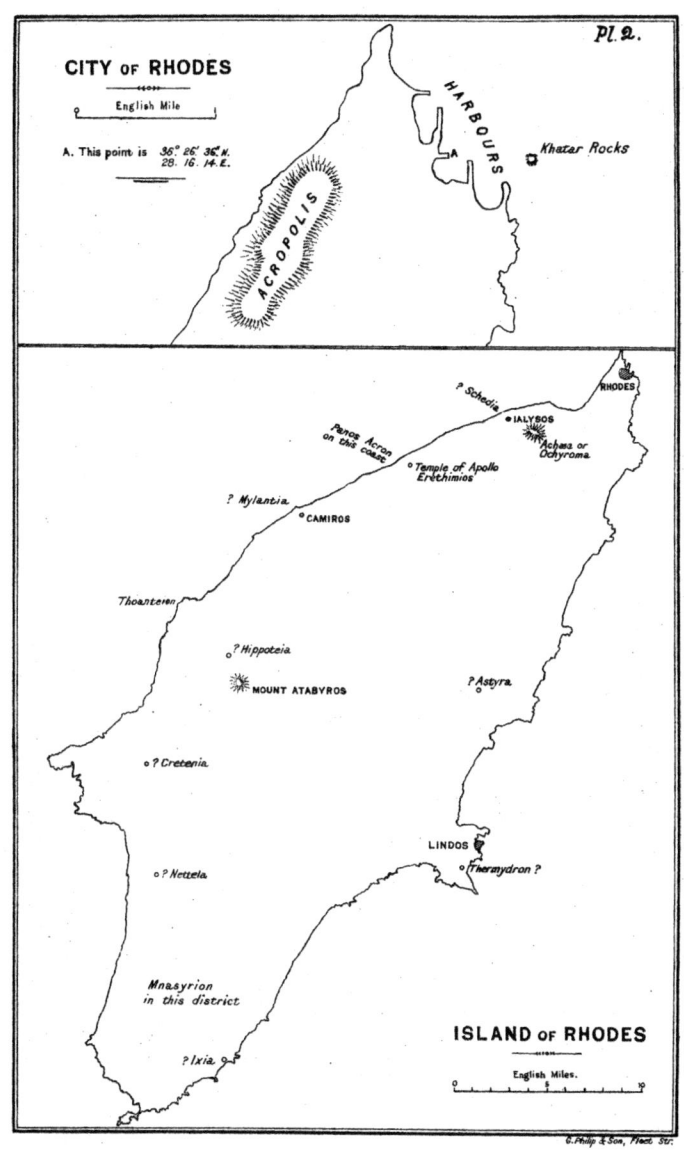

Plan of the City and Island of Rhodes [Plate 2]

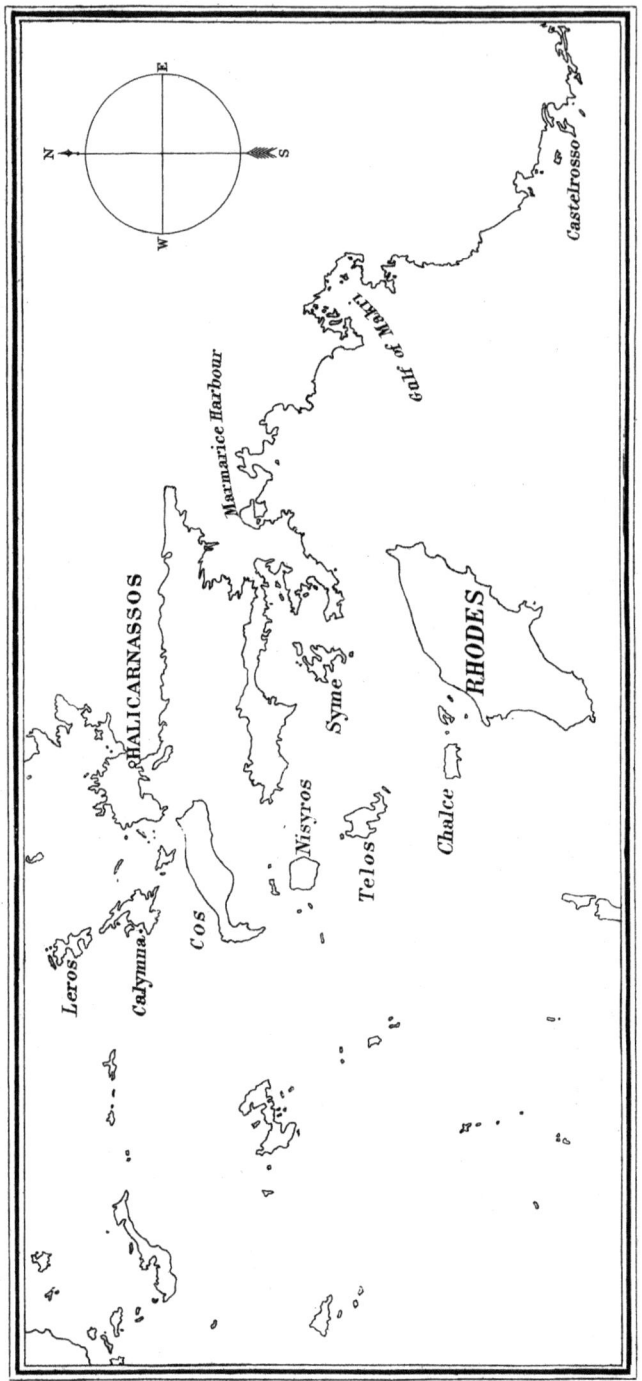

Map of the neighbourhood of Rhodes

Contents

	Page
Illustrations	II
Preface	III
Introduction - Cecil Torr	VI
Chronology	XIX

Cecil Torr, *Rhodes in Ancient Times*

Preface	ii
Note on References	v
Contents	vi
List of Plates	vii
Chapter I – Topography	1
Chapter II – Public Affairs	7
Chapter III – At Sea	36
Chapter IV – On Shore	62
Chapter V – The Gods	86
Chapter VI – Art	110
Chapter VII – Learning	142
Chapter VIII – Legends	166
Index	183

Bibliography & Sources	191
Sidetrack 1: Digging Rhodes: an archaeological guide to 19th-century exploration	198
Sidetrack 2: Rhodes, the Olympic Games and Athletic Fame	204
Sidetrack 3: Cecil Torr and Rhodes	208
Sidetrack 4: Rhodes – an island chronology To March 7, 19482	211

Illustrations

(Torr's own Plate references are in square brackets)

Terra-cotta "Melian" relief from Camiros [Plate 5]...*half-title verso*

Cecil Torr in his garden at Yonder Wreyland (from the author's personal album)...*faces title-page*

Plan of the City and Island of Rhodes [Plate 2]...*opposite title-page verso*

Map of the neighbourhood of Rhodes...*follows above*

Gold box, from Camiros, actual size [Plate 1]...*p.221*

Bronze weapons, from Ialysos, one-third of actual size [Plate 3]...*p.222*

Bronze figure of a bull, from Rhodes and probably from Mount Atabyros, extreme height 6¼ in. [Plate 4]...*p.223*

Terra-cotta hydria, from Camiros, extreme height 13½ in. [Plate 6]...*p.224*

Cecil Torr on holiday in the Scilly Isles in 1907 (from the author's personal album)...*p.226*

Preface - *Rhodes in Ancient Times*

First impressions are hard to shake. Today, by the time your ship has rounded the tip of Rhodes and drifted past the Tower of St Nicholas, where perhaps the Colossus stood, and tied up beneath the medieval walls of the Old Town, your impressions of the place have already probably been fixed. Under these solid fortifications, it is clear, you have disembarked fairly and squarely in the world of the Knights of St John, those soldier-surgeons who retreated here in 1309 from Palestine, by way of Cyprus, and established themselves in some style for 200 years, until ousted by Suleiman the Magnificent in 1522; and Rhodes as a great theatre of influence in the Eastern Mediterranean then closed her eyes for the second and last time.

But you never know, from the deck, something - a pointing minaret - might lead your eyes up to the hills beyond, to see on the summit the outline of a few reconstructed columns. And with this glimpse of the Italian-period reconstruction of the Acropolis of ancient Rhodes you can start a sea journey back, a millennium say, to another period in the island's story: a less easy to imagine period when Rhodes was one of the most enterprising maritime city-states in the known world.

Traces of this influence in the town of Rhodes now are few: that Acropolis, the foundations of a Temple of Aphrodite, the lower courses of certain sections of walling, domestic architectural remains preserved under modern apartment blocks, Durrell's "Marine Venus" in the museum, the permanent display of mundane household objects in the Grandmasters' Palace.

If, however, you had been standing on your ship and rounding the tip of Rhodes in 250 BC, you would have been staring wide-eyed at a fantastic city, laid out in generous blocks and sweeping down to her sea walls from the terraces of the Acropolis. (As much again stretched away out of sight inland; a far larger area than that encircled by the medieval Knights' walls.) Everywhere you looked there would have been statues in bronze and marble. The harbours teemed with trading vessels that freighted prestigious Rhodian amphorae to and from Africa and Egypt, Libya, Greece, Italy, Spain, the Black Sea...

In *Rhodes in Ancient Times* (1885), the author's first book on the island (he was to inspect the Knights in 1887 in *Rhodes in Modern Times*), Cecil Torr goes to all the ancient sources he can find and illustrates the irresistible rise of the island in the millennium before Christ. Rhodes awoke, and ever after her fortune depended on her position at the heart of a nexus of embryonic trade routes - a position exploited by the Minoans and Mycenaeans in the Bronze Age before - and her fame depended on a long line of skilled autocrats and admirals who, through the centuries, were forced to steer a self-interested course between the very great and dangerous powers of the times – Persia and the acquisitive states on the mainland opposite, Macedonia, Syria, and ultimately Rome.

Geographically modest, about 1400 square kilometres only, Rhodes always punched much above her weight. But in the end she backed a losing Roman contender and that was that. Augustus effectively sidelined the island as a cultural and trading centre of any significance and she went to sleep again, until touched by the Imperial purple of Byzantium, 800 or so years later.

This new edition of *Rhodes in Ancient Times* is reproduced as Cecil Torr planned the first 1885 printing; the author's layout and punctuation are adhered to as much as possible. The Greek fonts, textual marks and details are retained, as, of course, are all Torr's studiously researched footnotes and references. (Any one of which can divert for hours or days.) Spellings and personal names are unchanged, as are the island's 19th-century toponyms. The place-names correspond phonetically, with a few exceptions, to the majority of locations readers will find in their preferred guides. The original illustrations are reproduced, and all of Torr's outline maps, although they fall here on different pages from their positions in his volume. These maps are more for interest than practical use. Readers are recommended to have modern ones to hand as you read or stroll, as well as a good gazetteer for the hundreds of ancient sites referred to.

The introduction that follows (with some slight changes) first appeared in the 2003 edition of *Rhodes in Modern Times*.

Given Torr's fastidious footnotes, it was pleasing to find him, as I did first, mentioned as a footnote himself in Lawrence Durrell's *Reflections on a Marine Venus*. The original blue-cloth volumes that Durrell encourages us to read - by "the sour Torr" - *Rhodes in Ancient Times* and *Rhodes in Modern Times* are now collectors' items and not borrowable from libraries. I have been lucky enough to spend some years on Rhodes, and the opportunity to be involved with new editions of these histories is a happy way of saluting the sunny place, χαίρε...

Gerald Brisch
April 2005

Oxford – Rhodes

Cecil Torr

'I have a letter of 14 February 1911 from Henry Montagu Butler, the Master of Trinity, but headmaster at Harrow at the time when I was there; and in this letter he says, "You and Arthur Evans are, I think, the chief antiquarians of our Harrow generation..."' (*Small Talk at Wreyland*, III, p.111)

There cannot be many British visitors, strolling the reconstructions at Knossos this summer, who have not heard of Arthur Evans. By contrast if, 375 kilometres north-east of the Minoan capital by ferry, you stop and interrogate the tour groups blocking the 'Street of Knights' in Rhodes' Old Town about Cecil Torr, chances are you will be met with quizzical stares.

But, who knows, one visitor over the crowds of a summer week might very well be a scholar of early nautical history, or ancient Greek music, or icons in the British Museum, or, then again, might perhaps remember a character from a Lawrence Durrell book (as, on reflection, I did) about an enigmatic antiquarian from Devon, who, in the 1880s, wrote two monumental books on the island of Rhodes, in the Greek Dodecanese.

Although Torr was every bit as well-travelled and gifted as Durrell and Evans, if you were to imagine the three of them (Durrell anachronistically, of course) setting out together on a metaphorical dash to some form of celebrity, then it was inherent in our subject's nature that he would drop out early on – but not through laziness, I should stress from the start.

Cecil Torr was born on 11 October 1857, the son of Augusta Elizabeth and John Smale Torr, as Queen Victoria was enjoying the twentieth of her sixty-four years as monarch. John Torr was a solicitor, of Galsworthian means, with property in Surrey and London's Bloomsbury. Cecil's grandparents were comfortably-off landowners on the edges of Dartmoor, at Wreyland (Lustleigh) in North Devon.

In tune with his time, Cecil was educated privately at home before being sent to Harrow, to the Grove, when it was the Rev. T.H. Steel's, in 1872. A privileged child, at ten he was taken for a holiday to France, crossing the Alps for the first time two years later. These early trips fostered his instinctive feel for, and interest in, the arts, travel, and classical antiquity, which, once developed, he indulged for the next fifty years in a series of annual trips abroad. In 1876, Cecil became a monitor at Harrow before going up to Trinity College, Cambridge; he graduated BA in 1880 and MA in 1883. (In a rather old-fashioned move, in 1880 he took both Part I of the Mathematical Tripos and Part I of the Classical Tripos. He was awarded Senior Optime status (2:1) in the former, but only a Third in the latter.)

His travels and developing analytical mind had already laid the foundations for his considerable scholarship in the classics, but his university results surprised and, perhaps, unsettled him. With no particular disposition towards mathematics, he wrote later in *Small Talk at Wreyland*, "Looking back on my years of Harrow and Cambridge and judging them by the results, I find that Classics have supplied me with a mass of interesting and amusing facts to think about..." (*Small Talk*, II, p.77).

'Amusing' is a curious word, if entirely in character. It is 1880, Cecil is 22, wealthy, down from Cambridge, and very much set to play his part in Victorian Britain's establishment. He has a distinguished future ahead of him and could have selected from a wide field of disciplines at a time when the new sciences were aggressively challenging entrenched academic thought: "The old Classical men were just as cross with [the new approach to] Archaeology. They had learned to understand the Ancient World by years of patient study of its literature; and here were upstarts who could understand the Ancient World (perhaps better than they did) by merely looking at its statues, vases, coins and gems." (*Small Talk*, III, p.33). But, financially secure, Torr now seems to take something of a 20th-century turn by appearing to 'amuse' rather than 'apply' himself: never frivolous, but rather disinclined. Torr's individualistic path is marked out; he tips his straw hat to Lawrence Durrell and Arthur Evans, and, having written a short series of bravura monographs, quietly retires.

Violet Markham, in her book *Friendship's Harvest* (1956), gives this pen-portrait of her old friend (and, so doing, surely gets a little ink on her own fingers): "An eccentric and a solitary man; a mass of contradictions; a highly trained brain which he put to little use. Unfortunately, as a bachelor, comfortably off and with no family ties or charges, he lacked the will for the laborious work the quality of his scholarship demanded. Constitutionally he was lazy. Further, he was incurably whimsical, not to say crotchety..."

A childhood accident had left Torr with a lateral curvature of the spine and a consequent slight stoop. He was unfortunate, too, in losing his father when he was 21, his mother at 30, and his brother just after he was 40. Unmarried, he developed into a solitary figure with just a few close friends. He seems to have taken pleasure in argument and debate, and could be a formidable opponent, channelling any aggression into long, scholarly squabbles and, unsurprisingly, even longer games of chess. A Unitarian, he was not always on the best of terms with the local church establishment, and he had a notorious blast against the (English) Order of St John of Jerusalem, in which he had first become interested when writing *Rhodes in Modern** *Times* (*Small Talk*, II, p.43-5), and which he considered was founded on falsified historical evidence.

You certainly need to get your facts straight with Torr, but it is his aim for clarity and accuracy, as much as his crotchetiness, which make him adversarial, and even 'frightening' to Lawrence Durrell: "... history for Torr was a serious business... From a commanding position on Exmoor [sic] he consulted 'every known authority'... We are all very much afraid of Torr. Read him and you will see why." (*Reflections on a Marine Venus*, 1953, pp.100-1)

At the core of Torr's resolute intellectual grasp is a genius for detailed evidence gathering, penetrating observation and insight. In 1923 he addressed a local society: "Many years ago I looked through the works of about 200 Greek and Latin authors, in search of information about ancient ships. Of course, I had read the best of them before; but I should never have read the others except for information. I felt I could not speak with much

---

* The 'modern' reader should not be misled. Torr is not setting out to sample the nightlife of late 19th-century Faliraki – then just a tiny fishing community off the long, clean beach. As well as referring, of course, to the notion of the modern historical period, Torr has in mind a logical pendant to his *Rhodes in Ancient Times* of a few years earlier.

authority on ships or anything else unless I knew the evidence from end to end."

And it is just these qualities that inspire such trust as you read him. True, his style is often dry: he seems to relish the finer differences between Rhodian shipping (He published a highly regarded monograph on ancient ships in 1894.). Durrell again: "Not the shadow of a smile disturbs the dry exposition of the scholarly Englishman who has given us the best historical monograph on [Rhodes]." But now and then Torr chuckles to himself in the way some academics will: "There also lived at Rhodes a certain Idæos, who wrote some three thousand verses on his own account about his native island and then augmented and improved the Homeric poems by setting a line of his own between each two of Homer's; Euodos, an epic poet of Nero's time, a perfect marvel at Latin verse; and Pitholeon, who wrote his poems in a mongrel dialect of Greek and Latin: happily their works have perished." (p.148)

After Cambridge, Torr opted for his father's profession, albeit a different branch. While inheriting the London and Devon properties of his grandfather and father (deceased respectively 1870 and 1878), Cecil was admitted as a member of Inner Temple on 7 November 1879, and was duly called to the bar on 21 June 1882. The Admissions Stamp Duty Register (ADM/4/22) describes him thus: "Cecil Torr (aged 22) of Trinity College, Cambridge, the younger son of John Smale Torr, late of 38 Bedford Row, Bloomsbury, London, solicitor, deceased". Although a member of Inner Temple, he chose to have chambers at Lincoln's Inn, first at 16 and then 19 Old Buildings, where he appears to have stayed for the whole of his undemanding legal career. He is listed in the *Law Lists* as being chambered there from 1883 to 1928 (his last entry).

These details in red tape belie the fact that Torr practised little and had less incentive so to do, other than to exercise his talent for the impartial arts. (Something of his qualities as an adversary is revealed in his protracted 1890 dispute with the English Order of the Knights of St John, as alluded to above. The dispute makes amusing reading, and resonates still.[1]) By 1888, the thirty-one year old Torr had stepped into the combined rôle of immaculately dressed country squire, old-fashioned Grand Tourist, and scholar. The previous year he visited Olympia to see Praxiteles' famous Hermes, "and felt it justified the trouble, though Olympia was not a very accessible place then". For the next twenty years he was regularly out of the country on long expeditions – mostly to Europe, the Eastern Mediterranean and the Asia Minor littoral – which provided him with most of the material and the inspiration for his best-known scholarly works.

And here we can solve a puzzle for Durrell, who confides: "I have not been able to discover whether [Torr] visited Rhodes." (*Reflections on a Marine Venus*)

Torr, the great traveller, the Grand Tourist, had visited Rhodes of course. Besides one or two clues in the text, the historian confirms his stay on the island in several references in *Small Talk at Wreyland* (II, p.48), but without, sadly, telling us the actual dates (as he so often did on other journeys): "I have been to see the remains of two of the Seven [Wonders], the Pyramids at Memphis and the Temple of Diana at Ephesos and the sites on which two others stood, the Zeus at Olympia and the Colossos at Rhodes..."

---

[1] Those intrigued by Torr's initial six-month campaign against the Order are referred to *The Atheneæum*, Nos. 3245, 4/1/1890; 3248, 25/1/1890; 3267, 7/6/1890; 3268, 14/6/1890.

At twenty, Torr visited Athens for the first time, observing that the Acropolis still had its medieval ramparts, and later (1888) remarked that the same site was then being formally excavated and that the old ramparts had disappeared: "The results were of the highest interest; but the charm was gone." (*Small Talk*, II, p.31)

On his first tour of the eastern Mediterranean (1880), he had just graduated from his classics course at Trinity and was putting famous places to faces. The following year (1881) he cruised down the Turkish coast to Chios and Patmos and was back again in Athens, in 1882, on his way to or from a lengthy expedition to the Holy Land before being called to the bar in June. He was twenty-five.

In 1883 he found himself on Sicily, and interested in Rhodian colonies: the Rhodians being great colonists, settling the Mediterranean as far as Spain. There is a site tantalizingly called Rodi, near Milici/Longane on the northeast of Sicily, but Torr spent time at Taormina (40 years before another Lawrence) and climbed Etna. The major Rhodian colony on Sicily is at Gela, on the south coast, founded, jointly with a Cretan force, about 700 BC. (The Cretans, and before them the Minoans, were always influential to Rhodes. There is a Minoan 'settlement' excavated at Trianda (ancient Ialysos), halfway between the airport and Rhodes town, Santorini's cataclysmic ash layers there being just hours, or days, later than those at Knossos itself.)

As well as the great events in Rhodes' past, very little of the minutiae escapes Torr. For example he manages to trace the celebrity chefs of the times: "Timachidas of Rhodes was the author of a huge epic poem entitled Dinners, and Parmenon of Rhodes wrote the School of Cookery" and "Lynceus of Samnos in an epistle, written about 250 B.C., compares the delicacies of Rhodes and of Athens."

Then, as now, seafood was highly praised and the fishmongers obviously had well-stocked displays including anchovies, swordfish, perch, and a species of shark (alopex). "A popular saying advised a gourmet who could not afford a Rhodian alopex to steal one even if he died for it... Varro and Pliny thought the swordfish the greatest delicacy of the island."

For desert, Lynceus "...liked the Rhodian 'escharites', a sweet cake that made drinkers sober and restored to gourmands their appetites. Martial, however, thought they were like rock-cakes... The peach tree, when introduced from Egypt, proved sterile and tantalized the people by merely flowering... The wild figs were admired... and also the custom of eating them before dinner instead of after. The figs had a fine flavour and were known in Rome... The dried figs known as 'brigindarides' were a local speciality."

For more than two millennia Rhodes has had a thriving wine and spirits industry. Lynceus favoured a Rhodian grape called 'hipponios' that ripened in July. "The Rhodian wine was in repute at Athens and at Rome, and was widely exported. Some of it was sweetened with boiled must, but most of it was pure: and a delicate flavour was imparted by just the right quantity of seawater... Cato economized by flavouring his homemade wine in this way, and flattered himself that it passed for Rhodian... The Rhodians frequently drank theirs mulled with myrrh, cinnamon, mint, etc., with divers beneficial results."

In *Small Talk at Wreyland* (II, pp.43-46), Torr sums up the five years of scholarship that led to his first historical monographs:

"Many years ago I wrote a couple of volumes on the history of the island of Rhodes...At first I only thought of writing about the Rhodian colonies in

Sicily, but the subject led me on to Rhodes itself, and then to the adventures of the Knights after they had quitted Rhodes; but these were not included in the book."

By the end of 1883, *Rhodes in Ancient Times* had appeared to general acclaim ("About religion, art, architecture, &., there is much to be said, and Mr Torr has taken much pain to say it completely." – *Spectator*) The book's reception, and Torr's shift of interest to Byzantine Rhodes, lead the historian next to a preparatory volume *Rhodes under the Byzantines* (1886), before deciding to expand it. Torr knew the Venetian authorities, but it is unclear from his travel accounts whether he ever visited Malta to inspect the Knights' documents and records, then in the Valletta Public Record Office. Nevertheless, his combined researches resulted, a year later, in *Rhodes in Modern Times*.

Steaming away from Rhodes, further monographs were to follow: *Ancient Ships* (1894), *Memphis and Mycenae* (1896), *On the Interpretation of Greek Music* (1896), and *On Portraits of Christ in the British Museum* (1898). However, the turn of the century saw a drop in Torr's academic output and the consensus of opinion among his peers was that this gifted scholar never fulfilled his considerable potential: his great ship opus remained unfinished. For whatever reasons, and Torr was 43 in 1900, he gradually spent less time in London, and abroad, and was less motivated towards classical studies. The approach of the First World War coincided with the last journey he was to take out of England – to Venice, "by way of Reims, Laon, and Amiens", in 1913.

Abandoning travel for Torr was a marked change in a habit that stretched back fifty years and which must have had real significance for him; it foreshadowed a general withdrawal to Dartmoor. In

1914 he disposed of his London property and settled permanently on his rural estate at Wreyland, near Lustleigh, in Devon.

Lustleigh is a small, fragmented village close to Moretonhampstead, on the north-eastern edge of Dartmoor (about 15 miles southwest of Exeter) with access to the valley "in which the West Teign, or Bovy River flows". In White's *Devonshire Directory* of 1859, it contained in its parish "311 souls, and 2,239 acres of land, half of which is open commons and waste, on the eastern side of Dartmoor. On the common called Lustleigh Cleve, is a fine range of rocks and crags; and in the vicinity is a logan stone, and some other Druidical remains..." In the village is the 13th-century church of St John the Baptist (appropriate for the great scholar of medieval Rhodes), standing on a rise in the centre of the village and overlooking the village green and its knot of thatched cottages. A stroll from the centre of the village, across a small clapper bridge, takes you to the hamlet of Wreyland, in effect a smaller village within Lustleigh proper. Here there are further lovely thatched houses, some dating from the 14th century. This ancient manor was owned in the 19th century by Torr's grandfather, John Torr (1790-1870), and his wife, Susanna (1782-1866). When the estates became his, Torr found obvious satisfaction in his responsibilities as patrician, and he was a dedicated advocate and supporter of the local community of which he was, in effect, squire. As a landlord he was extremely conscientious and proud of his beautiful, ancestral lands. Hard working and practical in things agricultural, he was known for being kind and generous, despite his eccentricities. Here, in terms of his studies and interests, over a slow half a century, he exchanged the wider sweep of world history for a panelled study that gave on to a large cottage garden in a remote English hamlet. You can hear the grandfather clock along the landing...

From his study (he called it "the tallet", with its cases of "statues, vases, coins and gems" – souvenirs of his earlier travels), Torr now found time for writing in a different vein. The historical monographs twenty years behind him, his most significant and endearing later work was the expansion of his 1910 *Wreyland Documents* into the three volumes known as *Small Talk at Wreyland* (1918-1923). These have subsequently established the author as a social and local historian of note, with obvious parallels to Cobbett, if not Montaigne (or James Woodforde). Torr's obituary (*The Times*, 20 December 1928) contains a sympathetic review: "(Torr) wrote three books, each entitled *Small Talk at Wreyland*, which are about first of all (though he did not know it) Cecil Torr, next about Wreyland in the past and present, and then about subjects so diverse and so many that few readers (and no reviewer) could resist the fun of seeing how incongruous a list could be made of them. These books are an inexhaustible joy to lovers of the country, of learning, of the arts, and of human nature; and besides the qualities of the squire, the scholar, and the traveller, they are rich in the shrewd senses and the independent humorous thought of this finely intellectual English country gentleman."

Torr's last works were smaller in scale. His miscellaneous papers of the 1920s now contain various typed pieces; there is less evidence of his distinctive hand, short-stroked, with curious serifs on the 'c', 'g', and 's' when younger – becoming more italicised in later life. Quite in character, he proposed and published his own route for the great Carthaginian in *Hannibal crosses the Alps* (1924) – a subject of interest to him ever since his trip in March 1891 to Tunisia, where he visited Kairouan and, surely, the site of Carthage itself. (The second edition contains a waspish, and typical, attack on unwise critics of his thesis.) Other publications followed of more local appeal: *An Address to the Moretonhampstead Literary Society* (1923), *Some remarks on an account of the so-called church house at Lustleigh by the Rev. Herbert Johnson* (1925), *Survey of Wreyland, 19 August 1566* (1927), *Bovey Tracey church-rates and poor-rates 1596-1729* (1928), and *French prisoners of war on parole in Devonshire &c 1794-1812* (1929). Addicts may track all these down in the Westcountry Studies Library, Exeter.

From his island garden (and what a contrast to Torr's), Lawrence Durrell speculates: "Perhaps [Torr] thought it wiser to stay out of this sunlit landscape whose wine and fruit could only lead a man to laziness..." (*Reflections on a Marine Venus*) There is a pleasing irony here. Laziness again. Lazy? – as Violet Markham gossiped – or just disinclined?

Setting out to record even a vague likeness of Cecil Torr calls for daring. (Rather look for him in the pages of *Small Talk*, or his monographs; the two snapshots included in this volume are typically contrasting – see facing title-page and p.226.) Torr has few competitors when it comes to investigative flair or genius for research and, even were his biographer not to stray too far into surmise and conjecture, it is slightly reassuring to know that he is not around to take issue, as he surely would have: he died, one winter, in Devon. His final papers include some typed pages, the opening lines of yet another book, or article, or address: "the world has many Peter Pans: they do not quite grow up, but seldom stop their growth at the right time".

There are no memorials to him in any of the great locations he visited and wrote about – Alexandria, Jerusalem, Rome, or Rhodes – no 'Cecil

Torr was here' plaque on the 'Street of Knights', but you *will* find him, of course, in their academic libraries. For something less permanent, there is a line in the modest Unitarian graveyard in Cross Street, Moretonhampstead, a country-lane stroll from Lustleigh – U42: CECIL TORR of Yonder Wreyland born 1857 died 1928.

Gerald Brisch
April 2003

Oxford – Rhodes

Chronology

(The figure in parenthesis after the year records Torr's age at the time. The titles of Torr's major published works are shown in italics. See also the bibliography on p.191)

1782		Grandmother, Susanna, born
1790		Grandfather, John Torr, born
1819		Father, John Smale Torr, born
1819		Mother, Augusta Elizabeth, born
1857		Cecil born (11 October 1857)
1866	(9)	Grandmother dies (aged 84)
1867	(10)	First visit abroad, Paris and France
1869	(12)	First crosses the Alps, via Splügen
1870	(13)	Grandfather dies (aged 80)
1872	(15)	Enters Harrow. Trip to Netherlands, Antwerp (August)
1873	(16)	Crosses Alps (September)
1874	(17)	Visits Leipzig (August) and Dresden
1875	(18)	First visit to Rheims (March)
1876	(19)	Becomes a monitor at Harrow. Visits Rome (September). Goes up to Trinity College, Cambridge
1878	(21)	Father dies (aged 59)
1879	(22)	Admitted as member of Inner Temple (November)
1880	(23)	Graduates BA from Trinity. First visit to Athens and Constantinople (Spring)

1881	(24)	In Greek waters. Visits Chios and sees Patmos from his steamer
1882	(25)	Called to the bar as a member of Inner Temple (June). Begins extensive tour of E. Mediterranean and Holy Land: Athens, Alexandria, Jerusalem via the Damascus Gate, Jericho, Jordan River, Lebanon (March), Asia Minor, Mt. Sipylos (Niobê), Asia Minor (April), and home to London via Corfu and Trieste (May)
1883	(26)	Awarded MA from Trinity, first entry in *Law Lists*. Sicily (Taormina), Mt. Etna (September). Returns via Alps and St Gotthard Tunnel (October)
1885	(28)	*Rhodes in Ancient Times*
1886	(29)	*Rhodes under the Byzantines*
1887	(30)	Visits Spain and the Alhambra, Granada (September), Mother dies (aged 68), *Rhodes in Modern Times*
1888	(31)	Extensive tour of Greece: from Athens to Sounion, Thebes and Boetia (Spring)
1889	(32)	To St Petersburg
1891	(34)	Sees Kairouan (modern Tunisia/ Carthage) (March)
1892	(35)	Visits Rome (April)
1894	(37)	Travels to Lourdes (September), *Ancient Ships*
1896	(39)	*Memphis and Mycenae, On the Interpretation of Greek Music*
1897	(40)	To Italy and Naples (September). Death of his brother
1898	(41)	Journey to Sienna, Ancona, Loreto (August)
1907	(50)	Visits the Scilly Isles
1909	(52)	To Venice
1913	(56)	Last journey abroad. Venice, and back

1918 (61) *Small Talk at Wreyland – Vol. 1*
1921 (64) *Small Talk at Wreyland – Vol. 2*
1923 (66) *Small Talk at Wreyland – Vol. 3*
1924 (67) *Hannibal crosses the Alps*
1928 (70) Last entry in *Law Lists*
1928 (71) Cecil Torr dies (17 December, aged 71), obituary in *The Times*, 20 December

RHODES

IN ANCIENT TIMES

BY

CECIL TORR, M.A.

WITH SIX PLATES

PREFACE.

MUCH light has been thrown in late years on the ancient condition of Rhodes. Some three hundred and fifty inscriptions have been found in the island since Hamilton found the first in 1837, and these have been published in collections of inscriptions and in the various archæological journals. Large numbers of statuettes, vases, coins, gems, etc. have also been found there within the last thirty years, chiefly in the excavations on the sites of Ialysos and Camiros and of some town near the modern village of Siana; and the finest of these may be seen in the British Museum, the Louvre, and the Berlin Museum. But no complete statement has yet been attempted of the results derived from these new materials as well as from those previously accessible.

Apparently the only modern works dealing with the subject are these. *Meursius, Rhodus*, 1675, contains about two-thirds of the passages from the classics that bear on the subject, and also one inscription found at Brindisi. These passages are heaped together without regard to their relative value, and sometimes with amusing forgetfulness of their contexts; and the references are very vague. *Paulsen, Commentatio exhibens Rhodi descriptionem Macedonica ætate*, 1818, is thorough: but it is very brief and deals mainly with political affairs. *Rost, Rhodus*, 1823, is careless and fragmentary. *Menge, Vorgeschichte von Rhodus*, 1827, is accurate but slight. *Heffter, Die Götterdienste auf Rhodus im Alterthume*, 1827–1833, and *Specielle Geographie der Insel Rhodus,* 1830, are thorough: but their subjects are just those on which the inscriptions have since thrown most light. *Rottiers, Description des monuments de Rhodes,* plates 1828, text 1830, contains some remarks on the ancient history of the island, but the plates are almost all of its mediæval ruins. *Hamilton, Researches in Asia Minor, Pontus and Armenia,* 1842, *Ross, Reise auf die griechischen Inseln des ägäischen Meeres,* vols. iii. and iv., 1845 and 1852, and *Newton, Travels and Discoveries in the Levant,* 1865, contain the first accurate accounts of the ancient remains and inscriptions in Rhodes. Hamilton travelled there in 1837; Ross in 1843 and 1845; and Mr Newton resided there for the greater part of 1853. *Guérin, Ile de Rhodes,* 1856, deals mainly with the island itself and only incidentally with its ancient history. *Berg, Die Insel Rhodus,* 1862, touches lightly on the ancient history: but the text is throughout subordinate to the illustrations, many of them very good. *Lüders, Der Koloss zu Rhodus,* 1865, exhausts its subject and much else. *Schneiderwirth, Geschichte der Insel Rhodus,* 1868, deals mainly with political affairs and treats them very thoroughly: but relies entirely upon the classics for material. *Salzmann, Nécropole de Camiros,* 1875, contains sixty chromolithograph plates of objects found in the excavations at Camiros between 1858 and 1865. The text was not published owing to Salzmann's death. *Biliotti et Cottret, L'Ile de Rhodes,* 1881, briefly sketches the ancient condition of the island. The chapters on the topography and ruins are creditable; but it is to be feared that many of M. Biliotti's facts have been sacrificed to the Abbé Cottret's eloquence. *The Admiralty Charts* of *Rhodes Island* and of *Mediterranean Archipelago* (south sheet) are admirable maps of the island itself and of its neighbourhood. Heffter promised a history of Rhodes, but did not keep his promise. And a great work on the island by Professor Hedenborg was said to be ready for the press five and twenty years ago; but he is dead and it has not appeared.

The illustrations of this volume have been taken, as far as possible, from antiquities found at Rhodes which have not previously been published.

I gladly acknowledge the kind encouragement and advice that I have received throughout the course of my work from Mr A. S. Murray of the British Museum. It is only just to add that his advice has often been neglected, and that he is not responsible for the faults of this book.

CECIL TORR.

19, OLD BUILDINGS,
                LINCOLN'S INN.

NOTE ON REFERENCES.

Inscriptions are cited by number from the following collections:–

B.	Boeckh, Corpus Inscriptionum Græcarum.
F.	Foucart, Inscriptions inédites de l'Ile de Rhodes, in the Revue Archéologique for 1865, 1866, and 1867.
K.	Kirchhoff and Koehler, Corpus Inscriptionum Atticarum.
L. B.	Loewy, Inschriften griechischer Bildhauer.
L. U.	Loewy, Unediertes aus Rhodos, in the Archäologisch-epigraphische Mittheilungen aus Oesterreich for 1883.
N.	Newton, The collection of ancient Greek inscriptions in the British Museum.
R. A.	Ross, Archäologische Aufsätze, Inschriften von Lindos.
R. H.	Ross, Hellenica.
R. I.	Ross, Inscriptiones Græcæ Ineditæ.
W.	Le Bas and Waddington. Inscriptions Grecques et Latines recueillies en Grèce et en Asie Mineure.
W. F.	Wescher and Foucart, Inscriptions recueillies à Delphes.

Inscriptions are cited by the page and by the year or volume from the following periodicals:–

A. Z.	Archäologische Zeitung.
B. C. H.	Bulletin de Correspondance Hellénique.
J. H. S.	Journal of Hellenic Studies.
M.	Mnemosyne.
M. I. A.	Mittheilungen des deutschen archäologischen Institutes in Athen.
Rev. A.	Revue Archéologique.

CONTENTS.

		PAGE
I.	TOPOGRAPHY	1
II.	PUBLIC AFFAIRS	7
III.	AT SEA	36
IV.	ON SHORE	62
V.	THE GODS	86
VI.	ART	110
VII.	LEARNING	142
VIII.	LEGENDS	166
	INDEX	183

LIST OF PLATES.

[The page numbers here refer to the original 1885 edition. For this volume see page II.]

PLATE I ...*to face Title.*

A. Gold box, from Camiros, actual size. **A.a.** Its lid, with relief of Eros. Pollux says (ix. 7) that in the game of ἱμαντελιγμός one player made a noose with two cords, and the other had to disentangle the cords by a thrust from a little stick without letting the stick be caught in the noose. See Becq de Fouquières, *Les jeux des anciens,* 2nd Ed. pp. 294 ff. **A.b.** Its foot, with relief of Thetis. **B.** Gold reel, provenance unknown, actual size. **C.** Chalcedony intaglio, from Camiros, actual size. On it, a stork with antlers. See Aristotle, Poetics, xxvi. 10, on does with antlers in paintings. **D.** Alabaster box, from Camiros, two-thirds of actual size. The gold box, A, with another exactly like it now in the Louvre, and the gem, C, were found in the alabaster box, D, in the tomb at Camiros which contained the vase painted with Peleus and Thetis published by Mr Newton in the *Fine Arts Quarterly Review* for 1864, III. p. I.

PLATE 2... *to face page* 1

Plan of the City and Island of Rhodes.

PLATE 3...*to face page 58*

Bronze weapons, from Ialysos, one-third of actual size. The knives **A** and **B** and the sword blade **D** have nails for attachment of handle. The knife **F** retains its ivory handle.

PLATE 4 ...*to face page 76*

Bronze figure of a bull, from Rhodes and probably from Mount Atabyros, extreme height 6¼ inches. Part of the tail and the lower part of the left fore leg and of both hind legs are restored in the drawing. Bronze figure of Helios, provenance uncertain, extreme height 5¼ inches.

PLATE 5...*to face page 112*

Terra-cotta "Melian" relief, from Camiros, actual size. Faint traces of black, white, red, yellow and blue paint.

PLATE 6...*to face page 118*

A. Terra-cotta hydria, from Camiros, extreme height 13 ½ inches. Dull orange coloured clay, decoration in black with white and purple accessories, details marked by incised lines. **A. a.** Its upper frieze. A terra-cotta amphora, from Camiros, extreme height 23¾ inches, bears the panels **B.a.** and **B.b.** on either side. The panels are orange coloured with decoration and details as in A: the body of the vase is black. For other vases with Heracles and Geryon, see Klein, *Euphronios, pp.* 28 ff. and Mr Cecil Smith in the *Journal of Hellenic Studies* for 1884, pp. 176 ff. For other vases with Heracles and Cycnos, see Mr Percy Gardner in the *Journal of Philology* for 1877, pp. 215 ff. and Plates A and B.

The above plates, except the second, are from drawings by Mr Robert Elson from antiquities in the British Museum.

I.

TOPOGRAPHY.

THE Island of Rhodes lies in the Mediterranean off the south-western angle of Asia Minor. Its greatest length is from N.E. by N. to S.W. by S. and is about 49 English miles: its greatest breadth at right angles to this is about 21 English miles.

A chain of mountains runs along the length of the island with many spurs on either side. A mountain about the middle of the chain rises 4070 feet above the sea, and overtops the rest by some 1300 feet: this must be the Atabyros of the ancients, for it was the highest mountain there[1]. On the top are the ruins of the temple of Zeus Atabyrios, and a little lower down in a hollow are those of another temple, probably of Athene.

The City of Rhodes stood at the north end of the island. There a long point of land runs out toward the mainland, some twelve miles distant. The harbours were on the eastern side, of this point, about a mile from the end. On the western side also about a mile from the end rose the Acropolis, a long hill running nearly parallel to the shore and shewing an abrupt front to it, while descending gradually on the other side in terraces toward the harbours. The northern was the Little Harbour, and the southern the Great Harbour. Each opened to the north, and had the shore on the west and south and a mole on the east. The mole of the Little Harbour was about 500 yards, and that of the Great Harbour about 300 yards in length. The Greek masonry remains in the lower courses of each. A spit of land sheltered the Little Harbour from northerly winds, while the Great Harbour was exposed to them. As the harbour Acanias was exposed to northerly winds[2] it may have been the Great Harbour under another name. In late times a rhetorician talks of three harbours: one fitted for receiving ships coming from Ionia, another for ships from Caria, another for ships from Egypt, Cypros and Phœnicia[3]. This third harbour was probably to the south of the others, and like them open to the north with the shore on the west and south and a mole on the east. Some remains suggest that this mole ran to the Khatar Rocks about 600 yards out. Starting from the east side of the point just north of the harbours the city walls crossed to the west side and followed the coast to the north end of the Acropolis: they next ran along the seaward edge of the hill and then leaving its south end made a wide circuit across the point reaching the east side some way to the south of the harbours. At the south end of the Acropolis, its highest point, the walls are of poorer work and later date than elsewhere. The finding there of a dedication[4] to Zeus Atabyrios has probably fixed the site of his temple. Mithridates tried to surprise it because the wall near it was weak[5]. No other site within the city has been fixed. The temple of Isis was near the walls by the sea[6]. The temple of Dionysos and the Deigma were in the lowest part of the city near the sea, the temple of Asclepios was a little higher up, and the Theatre higher again and near the walls[7]. The positions of the other public buildings are unknown. There are remains of a stadium, of several temples and other buildings, of roads and a bridge, and of many tombs.

Lindos stood near the middle of the east coast of the island. A promontory there breaks at the end into several small bays: two of these formed the harbours and the city lay between them. The harbour to the north is exposed to S.E. gales, the worst on that coast, but the small harbour to the south is well sheltered by high rocks. An abrupt hill rising some six hundred feet from the sea at the end of the city was the Acropolis. At its highest point and on the very edge of the cliff toward the sea are the ruins of a temple marked by its position[8] as that of Athene Lindia; and near them those of another temple, perhaps of Zeus Polieus. The entrance to the Acropolis seems to have been by a passage carried up through the hill from an opening at its base toward the city. On the southern slope of the hill are some rock-cut seats belonging to a theatre; and close by the ruins of another temple. There are many tombs in the rising ground on the other side of the city.

The cities of Rhodes and Lindos still exist: their harbours have saved them. The other ancient places in the island have perished, and the sites of few of them are known with certainty.

Ialysos was on the west coast, about nine miles from the north end of the island[9]. By the shore are the remains of a mole: perhaps at the ancient harbour, Schedia[10]. On the other side of the city rose its Acropolis, Ochyroma[11], a long level hill nearly two miles from the sea. There is a pillar bearing a decree[12] of the men of Ialysos that the decree itself and certain other matters be engraved on three stone pillars, and the pillars be set up, one in the temple, of Alectrona, another at the entrance for people coming from the city, and the third on the way down from the city Achæa. This pillar was found on the slopes of Ochyroma some way from any ruins, and apparently in its original place: so it must be the third of these. The city Achæa is thus Ochyroma under another name. Ergeias[13] hints this when he plays on the word Ochyroma (ὀχύρωμα) in talking of "the very strong (ὀχύρωμα) city called Achæa."

Camiros was also on the west coast about twenty miles from the north end of the island. A little cape close by is probably Mylantia[14], and the ruins of a mole by its side mark the ancient harbour. From this harbour the city ran inland rising with the ground along a series of terraces to the Acropolis, the highest point of the hill and about half a mile from the shore. The tombs are on the landward side of this hill and in the valley below. There is a pillar bearing a decree[15] of the men of Camiros that the pillar be bought and certain matters be engraved thereon, and the pillar be set in the temple of Athene and fastened there with lead. The finding of this pillar in some ruins on the Acropolis has fixed the site.

A hoard of coins of Astyra was found among some ruins between the modern villages of Archangelo and Malona. As these coins bear Rhodian types, this Astyra was probably in or near the island, and this may be its site. The harbour Thermydron was near Lindos[16]. Ixia or Ixiæ was to the south of Lindos[17], and had a harbour[18]. Some considerable ruins, including a mole in the bay between capes Istros and Vigli, may mark its site. Mnasyrion was also in the south of the island[19]. Netteia was probably near the modern village of Apolakia, for an inscribed pillar[20] that once stood in a temple at Netteia was found not far from there. The late excavations near the modern village of Siana shew that there was a large and wealthy town there from early times. This may be Cretenia: it lay below Mount Atabyros[21]. Places called Hippoteia and apparently Angyleia and Roncyos are mentioned in an inscription[22] found near the modern village of Embona as if they lay near its original site, which was presumably in that neighbourhood. Near the modern village of Tholo are remains of a temple shewn by inscriptions[23] found there to be that of Apollo Erethimios; and close by are traces of a small theatre. Cyrbe was in the district of Ialysos; and in the plain, for it was overwhelmed by a flood[24]. Near the city of Rhodes was the sacred plain called Elysion[25]; and perhaps the fountains Esos and Inessa[26]. The Thoanteion was the headland just opposite the group of islands round Chalce[27]. The headland of Pan was on the coast between Ialysos and Camiros[28].

The names of some other places may be inferred from their ethnics which occur in inscriptions. The places whose ethnics were Argeios, Brasios, Bulidas, Camyndios, Cattabios, Clasios, Ladarmios, Œiates, Pagios and Pedicus, were in the territory of Lindos; as also was Netteia, whose ethnic was Nettidas[29]. The places whose ethnics were Amios, Amnistios, Astypalæeus, Brycuntios, Brygindarios, Casareus, Diacrios, Dryites, Erinaeus, Istanios, Neopolites, Pontoreus, Rynchidas and Sibythios were probably not in the territory of Lindos; but there is nothing to shew the position of any of these, except that Rynchidas may be the ethnic of Roncyos.

RHODES.

[1] Strabo, p. 655.
[2] Aristotle, p. 973.
[3] Aristeides, p. 341.
[4] N. 346.
[5] Appian, de bel. Mith. 26.
[6] Ib. 27.
[7] Diodoros, XIX. 45, XX. 98.
[8] Strabo, p. 655.
[9] Strabo, p. 655.
[10] Dieuchidas, Fr. 7.
[11] Strabo, p. 655.
[12] N. 349.
[13] Ergeias, Fr. I.
[14] Stephanos, s.v. Μυλαντία.
[15] N. 351.
[16] Apollodoros, II. 5.
[17] Strabo, p. 655.
[18] Stephanos, s.v. Ἰξίαι.
[19] Strabo, p. 655.
[20] J. H. S. II. p. 354.
[21] Stephanos, s.v. Κρητηνία.
[22] B. C. H. IV. p. 138.
[23] R. I. 276, 277. R. H. 43, 44.
[24] Diodoros, V. 57.
[25] Etymologicum Magnum, s.v. Ἠλύσιον.
[26] Vibius Sequester, de fontibus.
[27] Strabo, p. 655.
[28] Ptolemy, Geographia, V. 2.
[29] N. 357. K. I. 226, 235, &c.

II.

PUBLIC AFFAIRS.

THE Rhodians, when history began, were Greek by race. Earlier settlers in the island had been absorbed or expelled, and the whole people called themselves Dorians and claimed Argos for their parent state[1]. In most of the Ægean islands there was but a single city; but in Rhodes there were three, and it was called the island of three cities – τρίπολις νᾶσος – just as Crete was called the island of a hundred cities. These Rhodian cities were Lindos, Ialysos and Camiros. There were large towns as well, as the ruins and remains of that age shew; but the three cities alone governed the island and its possessions. With Cos and Cnidos they formed a religious league, the Doric Pentapolis, holding a temple in common on the Triopian Cape. Halicarnassos had once belonged to this league, then the Doric Hexapolis; but it had been expelled in very early times, and the other Dorian cities near had always been excluded[2]. From this religious league arose a political alliance mainly directed against the alien states on the mainland, but there is no trace of joint action here like that of the twelve Ionian cities further north that formed the Ionic Dodecapolis[3].

The Greek cities on the mainland were taken by Cyros in 546 B.C. Rhodes and the other islands has as yet nothing to fear, for the Persians could not then command the Phœnician fleet and had none of their own[4]. But this security did not endure for many years, and Rhodes was among the conquests of Dareios[5]. There was a Persian party in the island; as was natural among a rich commercial society of merchants, who valued security above liberty, and wealthy men, like Timocreon, with a taste for court life. Leaders of this party were exiled, but there is no record of resistance to the Persian fleet in 490 B.C.[6]. The Persians levied troops for the present and took hostages for the future[7]; and ten years later there were Rhodian seamen in the fleet of Xerxes on its way to Salamis[8]. After the battle Themistocles came down to Rhodes with the Athenian fleet, and restored its independence[9].

The Greek islands were soon after united against Persia in the Confederacy of Delos. At first it was an alliance of independent states with Athens at their head; but as time went on most of the allies found foreign service irksome, and instead of fitting out ships paid their cost over to the Athenians who supplied them: and thus they put themselves at the mercy of the Athenian fleet. When the Peloponnesian War broke out in 431 B.C. nearly all the islands of the Ægean, and Rhodes among them, had fallen into the Athenian Empire[10]. So firm was the grasp of Athens on Rhodes that on the Sicilian Expedition (415 B.C.) she forced the Rhodians to serve not merely against their Dorian kinsmen of Syracuse but against their own colonists, the men of Gela[11].

The struggle between Athens and Sparta proved for the Rhodians mainly a question of democracy and oligarchy. In the age of the despots Cleobulos had ruled at Lindos and Damagetos at Ialysos[12]; but that was long past, and probably democracy had now been established for many years. There was, indeed, a strong oligarchic party in the island; but at the beginning of the war Athens had driven Dorieus and others of its leaders into exile[13]. Thus when Chios, Cnidos, and many other states of the Ægean revolted from Athens in the summer after the disaster at Syracuse, Rhodes for the time remained faithful. But in the autumn (412 B.C.) Dorieus came down to Cnidos with twelve ships and put pressure on the Rhodian merchants by capturing the trading vessels that touched at the island on their way from Egypt. The Athenians soon stopped this, and then cruised off the coast with twenty ships to keep the enemy in check. But by the end of the year their squadron had been beaten off, and a Spartan fleet of ninety-four ships had assembled at Cnidos. The oligarchic party in the island asked the aid of this fleet; and the admirals were ready to give it, as they hoped to raise men and money at Rhodes under an oligarchy. So in the early days of 411 B.C. the fleet appeared off Camiros. The populace knew nothing of the negotiations and took to flight from their supposed enemies. The people of the three cities were, however, soon after called together, and the arguments or the ships of the Spartans persuaded them formally to revolt from Athens. The Athenians at their headquarters at Samos had heard what was doing and came down with their fleet to stop the revolt. They appeared in the offing when it was just too late, and after a stay at Chalce went back to Samos. Rhodes paid dearly for her new oligarchy. The Spartans levied 32 talents (£7,680) on the island, and though their fleet stayed idle there for nearly three months, they did not even protect the coast. The Athenians were allowed to make Chalce, an island within five miles of Rhodes, their base of operations; and from there they came over to ravage the country, once landing in force and defeating the Rhodians in battle when they came out to protect their fields. At last the Spartan fleet moved off, and the Athenian followed it[14]. The Rhodians being thus left to themselves tried to revolt from Sparta; but Dorieus came down with thirteen ships to keep them in order, and stayed till the winter[15]. After that there was no further attempt at revolt. In 407 B.C. Alcibiades ravaged the island and carried off vast supplies for the Athenian forces. On taking over the Spartan command that same year Lysander requisitioned ships at Rhodes, and the year after his successor did the like. Lysander was again there with the whole Spartan fleet just before Ægospotamœ (405 B.C.), and at the end of the war in 404 B.C. Rhodes remained in the power of Sparta[16].

Meanwhile the ancient cities of Lindos, Ialysos and Camiros had joined in founding (408 B.C.) the city of Rhodes, and had surrendered to it the government of the island[17]. Though the cities had always acted in concord, they had been separate states – for example, they had separately joined the Confederacy of Delos, for there was a dispute about the tribute payable to Athens by Lindos[18] – and they remained separate states, each with its senate and commons, in the days of the Roman Empire. The Rhodians, who had hitherto been at the mercy of the strongest fleet in the Ægean, found formidable means of defence in the fortifications of the great city; and the rapidly increasing wealth and power that enabled them to found it soon allowed them to have a policy of their own.

After the war the annoyances inflicted by Sparta through the oligarchy led the Rhodians to set the example of revolt in 395 B.C. A Spartan fleet of 120 ships was lying in the harbours of the great city; but this was driven out, and Conon who came up with an Athenian fleet from

Caunos was allowed to enter. Next year Conon utterly defeated the Spartans off Cnidos, and thereby freed the Rhodian democracy from any danger from abroad. The revolt had been so unexpected that a convoy of corn coming from Egypt for the Spartans had sailed into harbour without suspicion and been captured[19]. Some coins shew that an alliance, presumably for maintaining independence, was now formed between Cnidos, Iasos, Ephesos, Samos and Rhodes. The leaders of the oligarchic party who were expelled at the revolt found their way to Sparta, and urged on the government the danger of allowing a great island like Rhodes to be ruled by a democracy pledged to Athens. A Spartan squadron was at length sent over – the first that had ventured across the Ægean since the defeat at Cnidos: but when it arrived off Rhodes (390 B.C.) the admiral found the democrats carrying all before them ashore and afloat, and cruising with a squadron twice as large as his own. After a time the Spartan squadron was made up to 37 ships and then gave some support to the oligarchic party. The Athenians were alarmed, and next year Thrasybulos was sent out with forty ships. He did not go straight to Rhodes, thinking he could not easily damage the oligarchic party, as they held a fort and had the Spartan squadron there to help them; while the democrats held the cities and had defeated their opponents in battle, and so could be in no need of support[20]. – There is another version of these events. The year before the Spartan ships came over, the oligarchic party had risen against the democracy and seized the great city, while the democrats retired to a fort. The oligarchy had then defeated the democrats in battle with great loss and proscribed the fugitives; and after that had sent to Sparta for aid as a rising was expected[21]. The former version is on the better authority. – The fleet under Thrasybulos came down to Rhodes after his death (389 B.C.) and gave some aid to the democrats, but the Spartan squadron was off the island most of that year, and returned again the next[22]. The Peace of Antalcidas in 387 B.C. must have put an end to this civil war: its result is not known, but the oligarchy was in power a few years later. The Persian party of a century before was not yet wholly extinct, for it was believed at Athens in 380 B.C. that if the Persians got a really firm hold on the Greek cities on the mainland ceded to them at the Peace of Antalcidas, Rhodes would throw in her lot with them[23]. But when the new Athenian Confederacy was formed in 378 B.C. the Rhodian democrats at once expelled the oligarchy and joined Athens[24].

This Confederacy, like that of Delos a century before, began in alliance on equal terms but soon tended to Athenian empire. Rhodes was now too powerful to submit. Thus when Epaminondas hoped to make Thebes a naval power (363 B.C.), the Rhodians readily assented to his plans[25]. At last Byzantion, Chios, Cos and Rhodes formally seceded (357 B.C.) from the Confederacy on the pretext that Athens had designs on them. Mausolos of Halicarnassos for his own ends urged them on, and supported them against Athens[26]. The Athenians at once made war on the seceding states, and sent out an expedition to Chios where the allied forces had assembled. There was an action on shore without result, but the Athenian fleet was repulsed in an attack on the harbour and the expedition retired. After this the allies with their fleet of a hundred ships sailed about as they pleased, plundering the Athenian islands. At length Athens made an effort to finish off the war, and fitted out sixty ships to join sixty others already at sea. These went up to besiege Byzantion, but the allied fleet followed and overtook them in the Hellespont. A general action was stopped by a storm. One of the Athenian admirals tried to attack, but the other two did not support him as they thought the sea too rough; and the affair ended in nothing. The pugnacious admiral was then incautious enough to fight a battle for a rebel Persian satrap against the king's forces. It was soon rumoured that the king would reply by joining the allies with a fleet of 300 ships. The Athenians therefore thought it well to make peace, and recognised the secession of the states. The war had lasted three years[27].

Mausolos used the influence acquired through his support during the war to establish an oligarchy at Rhodes[28]. But when he died and was succeeded by his widow, Artemisia, the Rhodians with unwarranted contempt for a woman as a ruler ejected this oligarchy and tried to seize Halicarnassos. Artemisia by a stratagem seized Rhodes instead[29]. She reinstated the oligarchy, and secured it by executing the democratic leaders and stationing a Carian garrison in the Acropolis. The Athenians in spite of the late war gave the Rhodians at least diplomatic aid; partly out of sympathy with democracy, but chiefly in their own interest. They thought that if the Egyptian revolt against Persia prospered, Artemisia would hand over Rhodes to Egypt; and if the revolt failed, the island would remain an outpost for her suzerain the Persian king: and Rhodes in the power of either Persia or Egypt would be a standing menace to Greek freedom. Besides, they fancied that if Athens shewed herself in earnest, neither Artemisia nor the Persian king would care to fight[30]. It is not known when or how Artemisia's troops were driven out: but the fact is certain, for her successor, Idrieus, had to seize the place afresh a year or two later (346 B.C.)[31]. But in a few years Rhodes was again free and had no more troubles from this source, for Caria and Persia itself were soon after crushed by Macedon.

On the first advance eastward of the Macedonians, Rhodes joined Athens and other Greek cities in forcing Philip to raise the siege of Byzantion (340 B.C.)[32]. Six years later when Alexander the Great marched through Asia Minor, the Persian fleet (then commanded by a Rhodian admiral) kept the islands from him. But during the siege of Tyre ten Rhodian ships came to assist him[33], and upon its capture in 332 B.C. Rhodes formally submitted[34]. A Macedonian garrison was placed in the city. Alexander next year promised to withdraw it[35], but it was still there when he died. On hearing of his death in 323 B.C. the citizens expelled it, and declared themselves again independent[36]. Alexander had greatly advanced Rhodes, and her most famous age now began: she was no longer merely an equal of Chios or Byzantion, but the first naval power of the Ægean[37].

In the wars between Alexander's successors it was no light thing to maintain independence or even neutrality. The Rhodians easily repelled an attack by Attalos[38]; but they had more to fear from Antigonos, the strongest and nearest of these kings. At first they declined to join him in attacking Cassander, though allowing him to have ships built at Rhodes: but when he made the freedom of the Greek cities a pretext for the war, they became his allies (312 B.C.), and fitted out ten ships of their own; and in the end some degree of freedom was given to Athens[39]. But they could not risk a war with Ptolemy, for the bulk of their revenue came from dues on the trading vessels running to Egypt, and most of their supplies were drawn thence. So when Antigonos sent his son Demetrios Poliorcetes to ask their alliance against Ptolemy they refused it, saying their policy was universal neutrality. While observing this policy in their public acts, they betrayed their sympathy with Egypt; and Antigonos, fearing they would join Ptolemy during the war, forced a crisis by sending a squadron to plunder the Rhodian trading vessels on their way to Alexandria. The traders, however, refused to be plundered, and beat off his men of war. Upon this he charged the Rhodians with beginning a war without provocation, and prepared to invade them. They did not want to fight. They decreed various honours to Antigonos, and sent envoys to point out that they had treaties of amity with Ptolemy. Then, finding that Demetrios was actually marching against them, they granted the alliance. But Demetrios now required them to give a hundred of their chief men as hostages and admit his fleet to their harbour. This suggested some design on the city and negotiations were broken off. Still, even after he had landed on the island, they treated again before the fighting began; but without result[40]. On finding war inevitable, they allied themselves with Ptolemy of Egypt, Cassander of Macedon and Lysimachos of Thrace, who had been for some years in alliance against Antigonos[41]. The political relations of Rhodes with Rome seem to have begun about this time[42].

Demetrios Poliorcetes landed in the spring of 304 B.C. without opposition, and established a camp and harbour near the great city. His assaults were at first mainly directed against the harbours. The city was for a time in grave peril, but at last the Rhodian sailors inflicted such damage on the floating siege-engines that attacks by sea were abandoned and with them all hope of starving out the garrison. After this the Rhodian cruisers cut off the invaders' supplies, while provisions were thrown into the city by Ptolemy, Cassander and Lysimachos, and reinforcements came in from Egypt and Crete. Some months were now spent in building the Helepolis and other engines for the assaults by land. With these the walls were breached, and the decisive action was fought in the very streets of the city. But at the end of a year Rhodes was still untaken[43].

Mediation had already been attempted by Cnidos and then by Athens and many other Greek states. But now Antigonos directed Demetrios to make peace; and Ptolemy, who was the mainstay of the defence, advised the Rhodians to accept any reasonable terms. A treaty was soon made on the mediation of the Ætolian League, or else of Athens. The terms were these: Rhodes to be an ally of Antigonos against all his enemies except Ptolemy, and (probably) except Cassander and Lysimachos: a hundred hostages for this to be chosen by Demetrios from the citizens, but no one holding office to be named: Antigonos to respect the independence and revenues of Rhodes, and to place no garrison in the city[44].

The Rhodians had now proved their power, and they used it skilfully. Though most states were seeking alliance with them, they bound themselves to none: even with Rome their treaty was merely of friendship and equality[45]. They were thus at liberty to take either side in a dispute, and strong enough to turn the scale in most wars. Few states failed to conciliate their favour with gifts, and become in some sense their tributaries[46]. When the city was shattered by a great earthquake about 227 B.C. the immense gifts sent by Ptolemy of Egypt, Seleucos of Syria, Hiero and Gelon of Sicily, Prusias, Mithridates and the other sovereigns of Asia Minor, Antigonos of Macedon and by independent cities without number shewed the width of Rhodian influence[47]. But it was not the policy of this commercial people to take any active part in the quarrels of other states: they seldom fought unless their home or their trade was threatened; and not then if the danger could be averted by diplomacy. They interfered in 220 B.C. in the interests of trade when the Byzantines began to levy dues on the exports from the Black Sea to Greece. War was not declared till remonstrances, backed by preparations for war, had failed. Even then the Rhodians employed very few ships, and no troops. But they incited Prusias of Bithynia, who had grievances against the Byzantines to advance on the Bosporos. Byzantion met this by an alliance with Attalos of Pergamos and with Achæos, an independent sovereign in Asia Minor who could invade the dominions of Prusias or the Rhodian possessions on the mainland. The Rhodians thereupon fell back on negotiations and left Prusias to carry on the war alone. Meanwhile they obtained from Ptolemy the release of Andromachos, the father of Achæos, who was then a prisoner at Alexandria; and so won over the strongest ally of Byzantion. The negotiations soon after ended in a treaty binding the Byzantines not to levy the dues[48]. Some years later, when Eumenes of Pergamos tried to blockade the Hellespont during a war with Pharnaces of Pontos, a Rhodian squadron stopped him without actual fighting[49]. Again, Rhodes supported Sinope, another commercial city, against the kings of Pontos. When Mithridates attacked the place in 220 B.C. the Rhodians voted 140,00 drachmæ

(£5,600) to purchase supplies for the defence[50]; and when Pharnaces captured it in 182 B.C. they sent envoys to the Roman Senate to complain[51]: but in neither case did they fight. Some of the ships fitted out for the war with Byzantion in 220 B.C. were sent to assist Cnossos in Crete against Eleuthernæ, another Cretan city; and Eleuthernæ replied by threatening reprisals and then declaring war against Rhodes[52]. In sending these ships the Rhodians seem to have abandoned their policy of neutrality. It may be that they had a defensive alliance with the Cnossians, and it is notable that the first reinforcement thrown into Rhodes during the great siege came from Cnossos[53]: but probably there was a question of piracy. Sixteen years later seven pirate ships were fitted out by the Cretans, and Rhodes made war on behalf of the trading world[54]. Piracy in general the Rhodians put down in their own interest[55], and they also stopped pillaging by belligerents. When Demetrios of Pharos began plundering the Cyclades in 219 B.C., they drove him off without involving themselves in the war[56].

The advance of Macedon under Philip V seemed to the Rhodians to threaten more than their trade. They fancied that if that great monarchy became closely involved in the politics of Greece proper, it would be a standing menace to their liberty. So, when the Macedonians marched down into southern Greece in 208 B.C. Rhodes joined Chios, Athens and Egypt in sending envoys to arrange a peace. For over two years these Rhodian envoys urged peace on Philip, following him about on his marches, and getting from him nothing but civil and evasive answers. They also met the Romans, who were now in active war with Macedon. At last they gained their point: Philip made peace (205 B.C.) with his Greek enemies, and soon after with the Romans[57]. The Rhodians suspected the king's sincerity, and readily believed his admiral Heracleides when he appeared at Rhodes as a suppliant saying he had been dismissed for dissuading his master from a war against Rhodes, and gave up despatches from Philip to the Cretans urging them to carry through their war with the Rhodians. But as soon as the wind suited his purpose, Heracleides set fire to the dockyard and went off in a boat. Philip disclaimed the act, but did not dismiss his admiral[58]. In 201 B.C. the Macedonians crossed into Asia Minor and began to seize the independent cities. Rhodes and Pergamos at once reported this at Rome. The Senate replied that it would attend to the matter, but referred the military question to the consuls; and nothing was done[59]. Meanwhile Philip had taken Cios; and while his envoys at Rhodes were proclaiming that as a proof of goodwill to the Rhodians their master would not harm the Cians, news came in that he had razed the city and sold the people into slavery[60]. After this Rhodes did not hesitate, and Pergamos and Byzantion soon joined her in declaring war against Macedon. It was now known that Philip was allied with Antiochos of Syria for the conquest of Egypt and the division of its possessions[61]: so great Rhodian interests were at stake.

Macedonian squadrons attacked Chios and Samos while Philip with the main body of his fleet blockaded Pergamos, thinking the allies would come too late to save the city, if they came at all. But Theophiliscos the Rhodian admiral, who was almost the only man that felt himself a match for Philip, prevailed on the allies to sail at once instead of waiting till their preparations were complete; and the blockade was raised. The Macedonian fleet slipped away to join the squadron at Samos before the engagement, but it was overtaken in the Straits of Chios and forced to fight there. The allies, though vastly outnumbered, were stronger in ships of the largest size and far superior in seamanship; and they had the best of the action. Thinking, however, that Attalos the king of Pergamos had been killed when his ship went ashore, they lost heart and did not follow up their advantage. Still, they destroyed half Philip's fleet, while their own loss was slight[62]. The remains of the Macedonian fleet went south, followed by the Rhodians alone, and another action was fought off Lade near Miletos. The Rhodian ships sheered off one by one, and their station at Lade was left in the hands of the enemy[63]. While the Rhodian fleet retired to Cos, Philip marched through Caria, seizing the Rhodian cities on the mainland. But the approach of winter forced him to recross the Hellespont. Here the allies made their fatal blunder in failing to cut off his retreat with their fleets: they might then have secured the liberty of Greece without aid from Rome. After allowing him to retire to Thrace to prepare for another campaign, they could merely sail over to Ægina and induce the Athenians to join them in the war. After this the Rhodian fleet went round the islands and brought them all over to the alliance except three which were held by Macedonian garrisons; and then went home for the winter. Next spring (200 B.C.) Philip secured the passage of the Hellespont by taking Abydos. The Rhodian fleet moved up to Tenedos to observe; but a single ship from this fleet and 300 men from Attalos were all the reinforcements sent to the unfortunate city, though the allies could easily have raised the siege[64]. The Rhodians were now hesitating about the war, and readily listened to an embassy from the Achæans in the interests of peace. They had reported at Rome the designs of Philip and Antiochos on Egypt and its possessions[65]; but Rome had so far contented herself with blunt speeches to Philip from her ambassador. When a Roman squadron at last arrived in the Peiræus, they sent up only three ships to join it. But when this squadron had taken Philip's stronghold of Chalcis in Eubœa, and Roman ambassadors had arrived at Rhodes to advocate war[66], they shewed more spirit and sent up twenty ships to join the Romans. These were used as a squadron of observation on the Macedonian fleet during 199 B.C., but went home early for the winter as there was no fighting. Next year Flaminius arrived in Greece and the war was pushed on with more vigour. The twenty Rhodian ships joined the Pergamene and Roman squadrons; and the fleet thus formed, after some successes in Eubœa, took Cenchreæ, the port of Corinth, while Corinth was itself besieged[67]. During the siege most of the Achæan cities declared against Philip, and in the winter he was treating for peace. But the negotiations fell through, and in 197 B.C. Flaminius utterly defeated him at Cynoscephalæ. The Rhodians had meanwhile retaken their cities on the mainland captured by Philip in 201 B.C. Their general Pausistratos invaded Caria with about 3000 mercenaries and defeated the Macedonians, who were in nearly equal force, at Alabanda, taking the phalanx in flank and inflicting great loss. But he did not follow up his victory, and spent time in occupying outlying posts and villages instead of marching at once on Stratoniceia, the chief fortress of the country. He thus gave time for the garrison to recover from its panic and the remains of the Macedonian forces to come in, and found the place too strong for him[68]. Peace was concluded in 196 B.C., but a year later a Rhodian squadron went to help the Roman and Pergamene in putting down Nabis of Sparta, who was still holding out[69].

In the abortive negotiations for peace before Cynoscephalæ Philip offered to restore to the Rhodians the Peræa – the tract comprising their ancient possessions on the mainland – but refused the rest of their claims. These were for the evacuation of the Carian cities and of Sestos and Abydos on the Hellespont: for the freedom of all the markets and ports in Asia Minor: and for the restoration to Byzantion of its subject state Perinthos[70]. When the negotiations wore referred to Rome the Rhodian envoys went further and supported the general demand of the Greeks that Philip should give up 'the three fetters' Chalcis, Corinth and Demetrias[71]. This support by the Rhodians of claims that did not concern them very closely and their refusal of the restoration of the Peræa alone mark their altered policy: no longer merely to secure the city and its trade, but to protect and afterwards to govern the Greek cities of Asia Minor. By the treaty of peace in 196 B.C. the Carian cities that Philip had occupied were granted to the Rhodians who now held most of them. But the Romans did nothing to carry out the treaty as regards Stratoniceia, which the Rhodians had not yet taken, and it was Antiochos of Syria who obtained the place for Rhodes[72].

During the war (197 B.C.) Antiochos had moved up along the south coast of Asia Minor with his fleet to support Philip and had taken many of the coast towns. The Rhodians saw the danger of allowing his forces to unite with the Macedonians, and their envoys told him in his camp before Coracesion that he must not pass the Chelidoniæ by sea or by land; and that their fleet and army would stop him if he tried. These islands were chosen as an ancient boundary fixed by Athens and Persia. This bold message was put in civil terms, and the king gave a civil answer that he purposed no injury to them or their allies, offering at the same time to renew the treaties between Syria and Rhodes. Just then news came of the defeat of the Macedonians at Cynoscephalæ, so the Rhodians saw no further need for the present of opposing the advance of Antiochos. They merely helped the cities threatened by him, sending information of his movements to some and auxiliaries to others[73]. The war did not begin in earnest till 192 B.C. At first the Rhodians had little share in it: their squadron was too late for the defeat of the Syrian fleet by the Roman and Pergamene off Cyssos in 191 B.C. and merely joined in blockading the enemy at Ephesos[74]. They sent out thirty-six ships under Pausistratos in good time next year. These were surprised in harbour at Samos through the treachery of the Syrian admiral Polyxenidas, a Rhodian exile; and only seven ships escaped, while Pausistratos himself was killed. Twenty fresh ships were sent out in a few days, and these joined the Romans at Samos, and went with them to make a demonstration off Ephesos. Polyxenidas did not respond, and there seemed so little chance of further fighting that some of the Rhodian ships were detached to act as convoys[75]. A descent on Patara, the metropolis of Lycia, was now planned, with the double object of capturing the ships fitting out there for Antiochos, and of setting free the Rhodian forces employed in defending their possessions on the mainland against the Lycians. Some Roman and Rhodian ships came down from Ephesos, picked up others at Rhodes and sailed for Patara. A storm prevented them from making the harbour and they ran for shelter to Phœnicos: there they had a struggle to keep off the citizens and some Syrian troops, and so went on to Telmessos. After this miscarriage the design on Patara was given up. Later on the main body of the Roman fleet was brought down to seize the place; but after getting as far as Loryma, just opposite Rhodes, the admiral found an excuse for going back[76]. Meanwhile the Syrians had laid siege to Pergamos. The Roman and Rhodian fleet moved up to Elæa to support the city, and then to Adramyttion when that place was threatened: but the Syrians retired, and the fleet returned to Samos. During this siege Antiochos offered to treat for peace, and the Rhodians were ready to come to terms, but Eumenes of Pergamos utterly refused and the matter ended[77]. The fleet coming up from Syria under Hannibal was now expected. The Rhodian ships at Samos went home to wait for it; but were sent on with the others, thirty-six in all, first to Phaselis, which was untenable for fever, and then to the mouth of the Eurymedon. Hannibal soon came up with forty-three ships, most of them larger than his opponents'. In the action the Rhodians at first fell into confusion in forming, but as soon as they were fairly engaged, the better build of their ships and their seamanship told, and more than half the enemy's fleet was disabled. They could not follow up their victory as most of their rowers were weak after the fevers. Hannibal went on to Patara, and a Rhodian squadron lay off there to prevent a junction with Polyxenidas. The Romans would have nothing more to do with Patara, though the Rhodian admiral was ordered to use all his influence to bring them there[78]. The operations round Ephesos soon after ended in the decisive action off Myonnesos. The Syrian fleet of eighty-nine ships under Polyxenidas engaged the allied fleet of eighty ships, – twenty-two of them Rhodian and the rest

Roman. At first the Syrians were likely to outflank the Romans, but the Rhodians threw part of the enemy's line into confusion, and then the Romans broke through and took it in the rear. In the end nearly half the Syrian fleet was sunk, burnt or taken. The Rhodian squadron next went to the Hellespont to help in transporting the Roman troops into Asia, and then went home[79]. Scipio soon after defeated Antiochos with a loss of fifty thousand men at Magnesia. Polyxenidas, seeing that the war was over, retired from Ephesos and sailed as far as Patara; but hearing there that a Rhodian squadron was cruising near Megiste, he left his ships and continued his retreat overland[80]. By the treaty of peace Antiochos gave up his fleet, and the Syrian ships at Patara, to the number of fifty, were burnt there by the Romans[81].

After the defeat of Antiochos Rhodian envoys arrived in Rome and were received with honours second only to those granted to Eumenes of Pergamos. The Rhodians asked for the independence of the Greek cities in Asia Minor, intending to be first their patrons and afterwards their sovereigns; while Eumenes, who was already the sovereign of some of them and had designs on the rest, of course opposed this. They also asked for the independence of Solœ, with a view to getting a hold on Cilicia; but did not press the claim. The Senate, by way of compromise, granted Lycia and Caria as far as the Mæander to the Rhodians and the rest of the dominions of Antiochos west of Mount Tauros to Eumenes: and confirmed the independence of all the Greek cities of Asia Minor that had paid tribute to Antiochos except those that had previously been tributaries of Pergamos. Ten commissioners went over to Asia Minor to settle the details[82]. The treaty of peace made upon their report in

189 B.C. excepted Telmessos from the grant of Lycia to Rhodes, the Romans having meanwhile seized the place and given it to Eumenes[83]. When the Carians and Lycians were thus handed over to Rhodes, their relations with her were not clearly settled; and while they sent envoys suggesting an alliance, she sent commissioners to regulate their affairs[84]. A war followed; and when the Lycians were beaten they complained at Rome of Rhodian oppression. The Senate pointed out to the Rhodians that by the records of the ten commissioners the Lycians were to be their friends and allies, and not their slaves. On hearing this the Lycians took up arms again and seem to have been fighting for the next three years. The Rhodians thought the Senate had been misled and sent envoys to Rome to argue the point[85].

Rhodes now became somewhat estranged from Rome. The growth of Roman power in the East clearly threatened Rhodian independence, and a strong party in the island held that the true policy for the Rhodians was to support the other states of the East against Rome, and if necessary to oppose her themselves. Thus when Perseus, the young king of Macedon, married Laodice of Syria, the bride was escorted to her new home by the Rhodian fleet, which had been fighting a few years before against the Macedonians and Syrians: and then there were ostentatious manœuvres of the whole of this fleet as a hint to the Romans[86]. The estrangement of Rhodes from Pergamos, the firm ally of Rome, had begun in the contest for Asia Minor. Then the attempt of Eumenes to blockade the Hellespont during his war with Pharnaces was an interference with commerce that a Rhodian squadron had checked almost by force. Moreover, Pergamene troops ostensibly sent to assist the Rhodians against the Lycians had been plundering in the Peræa[87]. At last when Eumenes brought on the war between the Romans and Perseus in 171 B.C., his sacred embassy to the festival of Helios at Rhodes was turned back[88], and he was violently attacked by a Rhodian envoy before the Roman Senate. In this attack the envoy shewed too much sympathy with Perseus, and another was sent to protest the fidelity of Rhodes to Rome. But the Roman legates who were then in the island to renew the treaties of friendship, reported that the people were wavering[89]. A strong partizan of Rome, however, just then became head of the Rhodian government, and determined its policy for a time. Further legates who came from Rome to secure the assistance, or at any rate the neutrality, of a fleet of forty ships then fitting out at Rhodes, went back convinced that the people could be trusted. Envoys sent by Perseus to suggest that the Rhodians might arrange terms of peace and if necessary enforce them, were dismissed with an answer that though Rhodes desired peace she could not endanger her friendship with Rome. Five Rhodian ships were sent to the Roman admiral when he asked for them. His request had not been forwarded by the proper official, and the anti-Roman party fixed on this irregularity to cast doubts on the authenticity of the despatch: not doubting it themselves, but wishing to shew the Romans that Rhodes would not go out of her way to help them. The ships soon returned as there was no fighting[90]. As the war dragged on and was more and more mismanaged by the Roman commanders, the Rhodians declared themselves more plainly; and it became notorious in Rome that parties were now nearly evenly balanced in the island. But the Senate ignored this, and confirmed the treaty of friendship with the Rhodians in 169 B.C. without remark, and also gave them leave to export corn from Sicily. But the Consul Quintus Marcius very curiously hinted to a Rhodian envoy at his camp that Rhodes might arrange a peace, as she was the power from whom an offer of mediation could best come; and privately asked him to mention the matter at home. Rhodes soon after offered to mediate between Egypt and Syria, who were now at war, but nothing was then done as to Rome and Macedon[91]. The Consul's request came to the ears of the anti-Roman party and confirmed their opinion that Rome was unequal to the task before her. They went so far as to inform Perseus, who was now in alliance with Genthios of Illyria, that they were ready to join him in the war. Envoys from these kings were received with marked honour at Rhodes; and after a stormy debate on their proposals for an alliance against Rome, the anti-Roman party carried the day. Rhodian envoys were sent to Perseus and the Consul at the seat of war and to the Roman Senate[92]. Before the Senate they spoke as a superior power, saying they had determined to put an end to the war in the interests of commerce and would attack any state that declined their mediation[93]. The Consul was even more angry than the Senate when the Rhodians arrived with their message a few days before the battle of Pydna, but he merely said he would answer in a fortnight[94]. After his victory the envoys who were still in Rome were sent for by the Senate. Their chief calmly said they had desired peace in the best interests of Rome, and now had only to congratulate the Romans on their glorious victory. They at once retired without waiting for an answer, but the Senate replied by a despatch pointing out the facts[95].

The blunder of the Rhodians lay less in their action against Rome than in the time of taking it. Had war followed then, they could perhaps have destroyed several Roman fleets before they submitted; but they might have checked the eastward advance of the Romans for many years, had they joined Perseus while he was still successful. It was believed at Rome that the suggestion of mediation to the Rhodians by the Consul Quintus Marcius was intended simply to make them commit themselves[96]. Some Roman legates now refused to touch at the island on their way to Egypt, and went to Loryma on the mainland instead. The Rhodians at last persuaded them to come over, and on a hint from one of them ordered the execution of all who had spoken or acted against Rome during the war. Many had anticipated this decree by flight or suicide, but it was carried out as far as might be[97]. At Rome a Proctor would have proposed to the people a war against Rhodes, had not a Tribune of the Plebs very irregularly pulled him down from the rostrum. This Tribune then introduced to the Senate some further envoys from Rhodes who had previously been refused audience and ordered to leave the city. The senators who had served in the war were bitterly opposed to Rhodes, and she would have fared badly had not Cato taken her part. He reminded them that Rhodes had not actually taken up arms, and could not in any case be blamed for protecting her independence[98]. In the end the Senate cancelled the treaty of friendship with the Rhodians and ordered them to evacuate those parts of Caria and Lycia granted them after the war with Antiochos. Their admiral came over next spring (167 B.C.) to negotiate a treaty of alliance now that a treaty of friendship was out of the question, for they thought it necessary to determine their relations with Rome even at the cost of fettering their policy for the future. Meanwhile they put down a revolt of Caunos, Mylassos and Alabanda, fearing that if they lost Caria and Lycia their other possessions would revolt or be seized by the neighbouring states; but the negotiations at Rome for the treaty hindered them from crushing the rebels[99]. An order for the evacuation of Caunos and Stratoniceia was then obtained from the Roman Senate by those cities, and the Rhodians who were still anxious for the success of the negotiations, obeyed. The alliance was refused for the present, but was granted a year later (164 B.C.) chiefly through the influence of Tiberius Gracchus. Rome had deprived the Rhodians of Caunos and Stratoniceia as well as of the territory she had herself granted them twenty-five years before; and also of all return for their sacrifices in putting down the revolts in Lycia and for the money spent there. She had also damaged them indirectly by proclaiming Delos a free port to divert trade from the island. None of these measures were withdrawn, though a year later the Rhodian claims to private property in Lycia and Caria were allowed by the Senate and the city of Calydnos was permitted to exchange Caunos for Rhodes as its sovereign. But the power of the island was not broken, though it suffered in repute[100].

Rhodes had been on good terms with Crete during the war between Perseus and the Romans, sending envoys in 168 B.C. to the several Cretan cities as well as to the assembled Cretans to renew their treaties of friendship. A dozen years later, Rhodes declared war against the Cretans as pirates: but some reverses reduced her to despondency, and she sought foreign aid. The Achæans were inclined to assist her, but could do nothing without the consent of

Rome. The Romans would do nothing decided, and the most that the Rhodian admiral could obtain from the Senate (153 B.C.) was an offer of mediation. Meanwhile the Rhodians had probably dropped the war, for some of the ships they had fitted out for it went in 154 B.C. to assist the Pergamene fleet against Prusias[101].

The reputation of Rhodes was restored by her resistance to Mithridates. The king easily occupied the whole of Asia Minor (88 B.C.) but his progress southward by sea was stopped at Myndos by the Rhodians. His fleet was the stronger, but the ships were badly built and the sailors no match for their opponents; and he was completely defeated[102]. When the Romans were shortly afterwards massacred throughout Asia Minor by his order, the few that escaped found refuge at Rhodes. The great city was at once prepared for a siege, and was soon attacked. The Rhodian fleet was almost surrounded when it went out to oppose the landing of the enemy and had to retire without fighting; and in the small engagements that occurred during the siege it gained only slight advantages. Following the example of Demetrios, Mithridates pitched his camp close to the city and made his first attacks by sea. The citizens repulsed these and destroyed the floating siege-engines: they baffled an attempt to surprise the harbours and the Acropolis by a night attack: and at last they forced the king to raise the siege[103]. Next year Rhodes supplied Lucullus with three ships when he went round to stir up the allies of Rome, and then with some part of the fleet with which he gained successes in 85 B.C. off Lectum and again off Tenedos[104]. At the peace (84 B.C.) the Rhodians received some reward from Sulla for their fidelity to the Romans[105]: probably the confirmation of their title to Caria and Lycia, for Caunos was in revolt against Rhodes soon after[106]. When Mithridates renewed hostilities with the Romans, twenty Rhodian ships served against him at the siege of Heracleia[107].

Rhodes next became involved in the party politics of Rome. The leaders of the Civil War were well known in the island; but the people merely desired to be on the winning side and did not follow either party very eagerly. Pompey was popular for his campaign against the pirates in 67 B.C., in which many Rhodians had served under him[108]; and when he raised forces in the East in 49 B.C. to oppose Cæsar, Rhodian ships formed one of the squadrons of his fleet. This squadron was wrecked in the Adriatic, and Cæsar then gained some favour by sending the survivors of the crews safe home[109]. There were also Rhodian troops among Pompey's forces at Pharsalos. After the battle Pompey himself escaped from Lesbos on Rhodian ships[110]; but when some of his party came to Rhodes, the people sent them off, thinking it was high time to change sides. When Cæsar crossed to Egypt soon after this, it was with ten Rhodian ships[111]. One of these deserted on the way, but the rest did all the hardest fighting at the capture of Alexandria. Their admiral was afterwards lost with his ship in an action off the Canopic mouth of the Nile, but the others went on with Cæsar to his African campaign[112]. After Cæsar's death the Rhodians fitted out ships for Dolabella in 43 B.C., but refused any to Cassius; saying, when he pressed his demand, that they would be no parties to a civil war and had merely intended the ships with Dolabella as an escort. Upon this Brutus and Cassius determined to crush Rhodes before they marched on Rome: partly to secure their advance from the Rhodian fleet, and partly to fill their military chest. The populace thought they could resist Cassius as well as

Demetrios or Mithridates, but the more sensible people dreaded a contest with Romans. After abortive negotiations at Myndos, where Cassius was fitting out, the Rhodians attacked the Roman fleet there. At first their seamanship gave them the advantage; but they were far inferior in the number and size of their vessels, and at length retired with a loss of five ships. In another action when the enemy approached the island they lost two more ships. The great city was then invested by sea and land; and its capture was inevitable, for there had not been time to provision it. It was believed that some of the leading men, knowing that resistance was hopeless, agreed to open the gates. At all events, the Romans suddenly appeared in the middle of the city. Cassius kept his troops in order, and beyond executing some fifty of the citizens and proscribing a few more, did no harm to the city or the people: but he seized all gold and silver, clearing the temples and the treasury and even the wells and tombs in which valuables had been hidden. He left 3000 legionaries to hold the city, and then went on his way to Philippi[113]. After the battle this garrison was withdrawn: Cassius Parmensis had carried off all the Rhodian ships he could man and burnt the rest, and it no longer mattered what side Rhodes might take[114].

The Rhodians never recovered from this blow. Antony granted them several islands as some compensation for their losses: but these they governed so harshly that he revoked the grant[115]. Under the Empire Claudius withdrew their independence in 44 A.D. because they had crucified Romans, but in 53 he restored it[116]; and after that it was several times forfeited for intrigues against Rome and then regained by services in war[117]. At last Vespasian placed Rhodes among the Roman provinces[118].

1 Thucydides, VII. 57.
2 Herodotos, I. 144.
3 Dionysios of Halicarnassos, IV. 25.
4 Herodotos, I. 143, 174.
5 Æschylos, Persæ, 891.
6 Timocreon, Fr. 3.
7 Herodotos, VI. 99.
8 Diodoros, XI. 3.
9 Timocreon, Fr. I.
10 Thucydides, I. 99, II. 9.
11 Ib. VII. 57.
12 Pausanias, IV. 24; Plutarch de εἰ Delph. 3.
13 Xenophon, Hell. I. 5; Pausanias, VI. 7.
14 Thucydides, V. II. 35, 41, 42, 44, 55, 60.
15 Xenophon, Hell. I. 1; Diodoros, XIII. 38, 45.
16 Ib. Hell. I. 5, 6, II. 1; Diodoros, XIII. 69, 70.
17 Diodoros, XIII. 75.
18 Harpocration, s. vv. ἀπειπεῖν, &c.
19 Diodoros, XIV. 79.
20 Xenophon, Hell. IV. 8.
21 Diodoros, XIV. 97.
22 Ib. XIV. 99. Xenophon, Hell. V. 1.
23 Isocrates, p. 75.
24 Diodoros, XV. 28. K. II. 17.
25 Ib. XV. 79.
26 Demosthenes, p. 191.
27 Diodoros, XVI. 7, 21, 22.
28 Demosthenes, p. 191.
29 Vitruvius, II. 41.
30 Demosthenes, pp. 190-201.
31 Ib. p. 63.
32 Diodoros, XVI. 77.
33 Arrian, Anabasis, II. 20.
34 Quintus Curtius, IV. 5; Justin, XI. 11.
35 Ib. IV. 8.
36 Diodoros, XVIII. 8.
37 Diodoros, XX. 81.
38 Arrian, de rebus successorum, 39.
39 Diodoros, XIX. 57, 58, 77.
40 Ib. XX. 46, 81, 82.
41 Diodoros, XX. 84.
42 Polybios, XXX. 5.
43 Diodoros, XX. 82-88, 93-98.
44 Ib. XX. 95, 99; Plutarch, Demetrios, 22.
45 Polybios, XXX. 5; Dio Cassius, Fr. 161; Livy, XLV. 25.
46 Diodoros, XX. 81.
47 Polybios, V. 88-90.
48 Ib. III. 2, IV. 46-52.
49 Ib. XXVII. 6.
50 Polybios, IV. 56.
51 Ib. XXIV. 10; Livy, XL. 2.
52 Ib. IV. 53.
53 Diodoros, XX. 88.
54 Ib. XXVII. 3.
55 Ib. XX. 81.
56 Polybios, IV. 16, 19.
57 Ib. V. 24, 100; Livy, XXVII. 30, XXVIII. 7.
58 Polybios, XIII. 4, 5; Polyænos, V. 17.
59 Livy, XXXI. 2.
60 Polybios, XV. 23.
61 Livy, XXXI. 14.
62 Polybios, XVI. 2-9.
63 Ib. XVI. 15.
64 Livy, XXXI. 14-17.
65 Appian, de reb. Macedon, 3.
66 Polybios, XVI. 35.
67 Livy, XXXI. 18, 22, 28, 46, 47, XXXII. 16, 23.
68 Ib. XXXIII. 18.
69 Ib. XXXIV. 26.
70 Polybios, XVII. 2, 6; Livy, XXXII. 33, 35.

PUBLIC AFFAIRS. 35

71 Polybios, XVII. 2, 6; Livy, XXXII. 33, 35.
72 Appian, de reb. Macedon, 6.
73 Polybios, XXXI. 7; Livy, XXXIII. 18, 30.
74 Polybios, XVIII. 24; Livy, XXXIII. 20.
75 Livy, XXXVI. 45; Appian, de reb. Syria, 22.
76 Livy, XXXVII. 9-14; Appian, de reb. Syria, 24, 25.
77 Ib. XXXVII. 15-17.
78 Polybios, XXI. 8; Livy, XXXVII. 18-22.
79 Livy, XXXVII. 22-24; Appian, de reb. Syria, 22, 28.
80 Ib. XXXVII. 29-31; Appian, de reb. Syria, 27.
81 Ib. XXXVII. 45.
82 Ib. XXXVIII. 39.
83 Polybios, XXI. 14, XXII. 1-7; Livy, XXXVII. 52-56; Diodoros, XXIX. 11; Appian, de reb. Syria, 44.
84 Polybios, XXII. 26, 27; Livy, XXXVIII. 38, 39.
85 Polybios, XXIII. 3.
86 Ib. XXVI. 7, 8; Livy, XLI. 6, 25.
87 Polybios, XXVI. 7.
88 Polybios, XXV. 5, XXVII. 6.
89 Appian, de reb. Macedon, 9.
90 Livy, XLII. 14, 19, 26.
91 Polybios, XXVII. 3, 4, 6; Livy, XLII. 45, 46, 56.
92 Polybios, XXVIII. 2, 14, 15, 19; Appian, de reb. Macedon, 15.
93 Ib. XXIX. 2, 4, 5; Livy, XLIV. 23, 29.
94 Livy, XLIV. 14; Diodoros, XXX. 24; Dio Cassius, Fr. 159.
95 Livy, XLIV. 35.
96 Polybios, XXIX. 7; Livy, XLV. 3.
97 Polybios, XXVIII. 15.
98 Livy, XLV. 10; Dio Cassius, Fr. 160.
99 Aulus Gellius, VI. 3; cf. Sallust, Cataline, 51.
100 Polybios, XXX. 4, 5; Livy, XLV. 20-25; Dio Cassius, Fr. 161.
101 Polybios, XXX. 19, XXXI. 1, 7, 16, 17.
102 Ib. XXIX. 4, XXXIII. 11, 14, 15.
103 Memnon, Fr. 31; Appian, de bel. civ. IV. 71.
104 Appian, de bel. Mith. 24-27.
105 Plutarch, Lucullus, 2, 3.
106 Appian, de bel. Mith. 61.
107 Strabo, p. 651.
108 Memnon, Fr. 50.
109 Florus, III. 6.
110 Cæsar, de bel. civ. III. 5, 26, 27.
111 Appian, de bel. civ. II. 71, 83.
112 Cæsar, de bel. civ. III. 102, 106.
113 Aulus Hirtius, de bel. Alexand. 11-15, 25; de bel. Afric. 20.
114 Appian, de bel. civ. IV. 60-74; Dio Cassius, XLVII. 33.
115 Appian, de bel. civ. V. 2.
116 Ib. de bel. civ. V. 7.
117 Dio Cassius, LX. 24; Suetonius, Claudius, 25.
118 Tacitus, Annales, XII. 58.
119 Eutropius, VII. 19; Suetonius, Vespasian, 8.

III.

AT SEA.

IN the lists of powers holding the Thalassocratia, the sovereignty of the seas, Rhodes stands sometimes fourth and sometimes fifth, holding it for twenty-three years about 900 B.C.[1] This probably means that the power standing next below Rhodes in the lists began to be reckoned among the sovereigns of the seas twenty-three years after Rhodes was itself first reckoned among them. This Thalassocratia could be claimed on many grounds, and it is not clear on what grounds it is here assigned to Rhodes. More is learnt from the statement that before the Olympic games were founded (? 884 B.C.) the Rhodians for years together sailed far from home for the safety of mankind, voyaging as far as Spain and founding divers colonies[2]. The use of naval power for putting down piracy and for trade and colonization gave a claim to the Thalassocratia.

Little is known of the Rhodian colonization of this age in the West. There was Rhodos, Rhode, or Rhoda at the northeast corner of Spain[3]. Rosas inherits the name, but the site of the old town is toward the headland at San Pedro de Roda. It was doubted in ancient times whether it was founded by Rhodes or by the neighbouring city of Emporion, itself a colony of the Phocæans of Massalia (Marseilles). The place fell into the hands of the Massaliots, and the belief that it was founded by them may have arisen after that. There was also Rhode, Rhoda, or Rhodanusia somewhere near Massalia itself[4]. It was also doubted whether this was a colony of Rhodes or of Massalia. It was said that the city had its name from Rhodes and gave it to the Rhodanos (the Rhone); but it seems more likely that the river gave the name to the city, and that the name then suggested Rhodes as the parent state. The Rhodians also founded Parthenope among the Opici[5]. This Parthenope would be Neapolis (Naples). That city, however, was commonly held to be a colony of Cumæ, and it may be that these settlers founded the neighbouring Palæopolis. On the other side of Italy, Salapia, just to the south of the Lago di Salpi by the Gulf of Manfredonia, was founded by colonists from Rhodes and Cos under a certain Elpias in one ancient account; but in another Diomed founded it together with Canusium and Arpi, of which it was the port[6]. Lastly, the Rhodians under Tlepolemos after the return from Troy planted colonies in the parts about Sybaris on the Gulf of Taranto and in the Balearic Islands[7]. Other states joined Rhodes in sending out some later colonies; and it may be that in these early migrations the colonists were of several stocks and that each stock afterwards claimed for itself alone the honour of founding the city.

The Rhodian colonization in Sicily belongs to a later age and is well known. Their chief colony was Gela; for a time the most powerful city in Sicily and itself the founder of Camarina and Acragas. When Greek colonists first came to the island they planted five Greek cities there in little more than five years. These were all upon the eastern coast. There was a pause for nearly forty years, and then a body of Dorians from Rhodes and Crete founded Gela (Terranova) about the middle of the south coast (690

B.C.). Antiphemos the Rhodian and Entimos the Cretan were reverenced together as joint founders; but the Rhodians probably had the greater share in the colony, for the Acropolis was called Lindice after Lindos, which was the city of Antiphemos and his followers. The name Gela was taken from the river close by[8]. In the Sicilian Expedition of 415 B.C. both Rhodians and Cretans fought for Athens against the Geloans who were fighting for Syracuse: the Rhodians from necessity, the Cretans for pay[9]. Further to westward on the south coast, Acragas, afterwards Agrigentum and now Girgenti, was founded by the Geloans in 582 B.C., and the Dorian customs that their fathers had brought from Rhodes were established in the new city[10]. The statement that Acragas was colonized directly from Rhodes is on less authority[11]. But the famous bronze bull of Phalaris recalls certain bronze kine that bellowed on mount Atabyros in Rhodes; while Phalaris himself seems to have been born at Astypalæa near Rhodes, and to have been building a temple to that great god of Lindos, Zeus Polieus, when he seized the supreme power at Acragas[12]: and no doubt many Rhodians came over to help the Geloans in peopling their new colony. Camarina also lay on the south coast, but to the east of Gela. Its ruins are not far from Vittoria. It was at first a colony of Syracuse, but the colonists revolted against their parent state and were expelled. Hippocrates, the despot of Gela, acquired the place in 492 B.C. in exchange for the Syracusan prisoners taken at the Heloros, and planted there a colony of Geloans. Seven years later these colonists were transported to Syracuse, which had been seized by Gelon, the successor of Hippocrates; and Camarina was destroyed. But on the fall of the Gelonian dynasty in 465 B.C. Camarina was refounded by Gela, and probably peopled with its former colonists who had now been expelled from Syracuse. This Gelon, the greatest sovereign of the age, and Hiero, the brilliant despot of Syracuse, were descended from a native of Telos near Rhodes who had come over to Gela with Antiphemos[13]. The city of Inessa on the southern slopes of Etna, commonly called a colony of Syracuse, was said to take its name from the fountain at Rhodes[14]. About 580 B.C. a body of colonists from Rhodes and Cnidos sailed for Sicily and landed at the western end of the island. They found Selinos at war with Egesta, and took part with Selinos. Many of them were killed when the Selinuntines were defeated in battle; whereupon the rest agreed to go home again, and sailed off round the north coast of Sicily. On their way they touched at the island of Lipara, and were welcomed there by the Children of Æolos. These now numbered only five hundred, and the new comers joined them in founding their city afresh. The Cnidians probably outnumbered the Rhodians in this colony, for the leader was a man of Cnidos, and when he fell in the battle three of his kinsmen succeeded him[15].

Passing over a vague statement that in Macedonia there dwelt a race of Cypriots and Rhodians[16], no records remain of any other distant colonies of Rhodes but Apollonia and Naucratis.

Apollonia, now Sizeboli, on the Roumelian coast of the Black Sea, was founded in 609 B.C. by Milesians and Rhodians[17]. Probably few of these colonists came from Rhodes, as the place is also called a colony of Miletos alone. The ruins of Naucratis have lately been found near Teh el Bârûd in the Delta of the Nile. The city seems to have been founded in the reign of Psametik I. (666-612 B.C.) by a body of Milesians[18]. It was never a colony in the usual sense, but merely a trading station: Miletos had no exclusive claim on the place and was not among the nine cities that were presidents of the market and founded the chief temple there, the Hellenion. Four of the nine cities were Doric: Rhodes, Cnidos, Halicarnassos and Phaselis[19]. As to these four: Cnidos and Halicarnassos belonged to the Doric Hexapolis; Phaselis was a colony of Lindos; and Rhodes must mean Lindos, for Ialysos and Camiros had little to do with Egypt. It is said that the Rhodians levied custom dues at the island of Pharos off Alexandria till Cleopatra made the island part of Egypt by building the Heptastadion, the great mole joining it to the mainland[20]. The Heptastadion, however, was built before then, and the whole story is very doubtful. A little island in the eastern harbour of Alexandria with a palace and a port was called Antirrhodos, as if a rival of Rhodes[21].

On the coast of Asia Minor, Solœ in Cilicia was commonly called a colony of Rhodians from Lindos and of Argives[22]. But when the Rhodians asked the Roman Senate for its independence in 189 B.C. they merely said that its people were like themselves colonists from Argos[23]. The place afterwards decayed, and Pompey refounded it in 67 B.C. as Pompeiupolis[24]. Its ruins are near Mersina. Phaselis on the eastern coast of Lycia, now Tekrova, was a colony of Rhodians from Lindos. It was founded in 690 B.C. at the same time as Gela; and the colonists were led by Lacios, the brother of Antiphemos, who led the Rhodians to Sicily. The Delphic Oracle, it is said, bade Lacios sail toward the sunrise; and when Antiphemos laughed at this, the Oracle bade him sail toward the sunset and found a city of Laughter (Gela). The report that the migration to Phaselis was from Argos probably refers only to the worship of Apollo[25]. A few miles south of Phaselis were Corydalla, a city of the Rhodians[26], and Gagæ, a Rhodian colony. The island of Megiste, now Castel Rosso, off the Lycian coast seems from the types of its coins to have been very closely connected with Rhodes: but this only after 408 B.C. when the great city was founded. It is not clear whether Corydalla and Megiste were true colonies of the Rhodians or merely places held by them. The southern seaboard of Caria was called the Rhodian Peræa. It had a coast line of about 175 miles from Dædala on the Lycian frontier at the Gulf Glaucos, now the Gulf of Makri, to Mount Phœnix on the tongue of land just opposite Rhodes[27]. This tongue of land was sometimes called the Rhodian Chersonese[28]. Rhodes bought the city of Caunos, which lay in the Peræa, from Ptolemy's generals[29], presumably just after its capture by the Egyptians in 309 B.C.; and probably took the rest of the district about the same time. The city of Stratoniceia in Caria was acquired by the Rhodians shortly before their war with Antiochos[30]; and after his defeat in 189 B.C. the rest of Caria south of the Mæander and the whole of Lycia except Telmessos was granted to them by the Roman Senate[31]. They did not have undisturbed possession, but under the Roman Empire they still held Caria and some part of Lycia[32]. In the south of Caria there were some Rhodian colonies[33]. Further north Teos in Ionia is spoken of as a city of the Rhodians[34]; and Æantion in the Troad is said to have been founded by them[35].

In the Ægean the Rhodians justified their claim to the Thalassocratia by venturing before all others to an island that was upheaved between Therasia and Thera (Santorin) in 196 B.C. and founding a temple there[36]. They also occupied Nisyros when the colonists from Cos who dwelt there had perished in a plague[37]. Under Antony they held the more distant islands of Andros, Tenos and Naxos for a short time[38]. Under the Roman Empire they governed Chalce (Karki) and the other islands off the west coast of Rhodes; Casos and Carpathos (Scarpanto) further to the south; and Syme, Nisyros, Calymna, Leros and others to the north off the coast of Asia Minor[39].

Lindos was the parent state of Gela, of Phaselis and of Solœ; and of these three alone among the Rhodian colonies is the parent state known. Ialysos and Camiros, with poorer harbours and more fruitful territories, had less reason to seek fortune abroad. The Rhodians had to extend their territory in Asia Minor inland to obtain supplies for the great city when it had outgrown the resources of the island[40]; but the rest of their settlements were by the coast where their maritime genius could have free play. Bold voyages to distant parts of the Mediterranean in very early times and constant warfare with pirates are implied by this widespread colonization, but the naval power of Rhodes did not rise till the new city was founded (408 B.C.) and culminated two centuries later.

In the Catalogue of the Ships Rhodes[41] sends only nine out of 1186 sent by all the Greeks, while Syme sends three, and Nisyros, Carpathos, Casos, Cos and Calymna send thirty between them. Thus at the date of the Catalogue Rhodes could have been no stronger than the neighbouring islands; and these must all have been weaker than the Greek states in Europe. When the fleet of Xerxes was numbered at Doriscos on its way to Salamis in 480 B.C. there were present 307 trieres sent by the Greeks of Asia and the islands; but of these the Dorians of Asia and the islands, including Rhodes, sent only thirty[42]. Thus

Rhodes and her neighbours were still weak. It is said that Xerxes prepared the trieres and the Greeks merely manned them[43]. Rhodes may, however, have sent some of the three thousand smaller vessels of the fleet. When the Peloponnesian War broke out in 431 B.C. Rhodes was paying money to Athens instead of supplying ships[44]; but she may have supplied ships herself in the earlier years of the Confederacy of Delos. Two Rhodian pentecontors served with the Athenians on the Sicilian Expedition in 415 B.C., but these were small vessels[45]. – The lists of the money payments to Athens are so much broken that very few of the sums paid by the Rhodians are quite certain. In 454 B.C.[46] the Lindians paid something over 840 drachmæ, while the Œiatæ of the Lindians paid 55. The Lindians paid 1000 in 449 B.C.[47], and the Ialysians the same sum in 450 B.C.[48] and 447 B.C.[49] The Lindians paid 600 in 445 B.C.[50]; and the same sum was paid by the Lindians and by the Camires in 443 B.C.[51], by the Lindians in 442 B.C.[52], and by the Lindians, by the Ialysians, and by the Camires in 441 B.C.[53] The Pedieis from Lindos paid 1 drachma 4 obols in 445 B.C. and 441 B.C. The Lindians again paid 1000 in 436 B.C.[54]; and also in 428 B.C.[55], although the Ialysians and the Camires paid only 600 that year. The Pedieis paid something over 80 in 428 B.C. In a list of uncertain date, but apparently later than 425 B.C.[56], the Lindians paid as much as 1500 while the Ialysians paid only 500: the Pedieis paid 100 and the Diacriœ in Rhodes paid 200. The Erines, the Brycuntiœ, and the Bricindariœ are named in the lists, and may be the Rhodians with similar ethnics. Thus the direct payments of the Lindians sometimes exceeded those of the Ialysians and the Camires, apart from their indirect payments through the Œiatæ of the Lindians and the Pedieis from Lindos. This may have been the ground of the dispute between Athens and Lindos about these payments[57]. The sums in these lists ranging from 1 drachma 4 obols (16d.) from the Pedieis to 1500 drachmæ (£60) from the Lindians can be only small fractions of the whole sums due. They are out of all proportion to the 32 talents (£7,680) levied by the Spartans on the island a few years later; nor could the Athenians have proposed to exchange these for a 5 per cent. duty on exports and imports[58]. They may be a sixtieth payable to Athene. – In 412 B.C. the Spartan admirals wished to bring Rhodes over to their side, because of the multitude of its seamen[59]. They requisitioned war ships there in 407 and 406 B.C.[60], Lysander thus taking all the ships the cities had[61]. This was after the great city was founded, but the separate fleets of the three cities are not mentioned again. In 390 B.C. the Rhodians had over sixteen trieres at sea[62]. In the Social War of 357 B.C. Rhodes, Cos, Chios and Byzantion had a fleet of a hundred ships: but it is not known how many were sent by each of the allies[63]. The Rhodians sent ten ships to Alexander at the siege of Tyre in 332 B.C.; or rather, the ship called Peripolos and with her nine trieres[64]. They also sent ten ships with Ptolemy on his expedition to Athens in 312 B.C.[65] During the great siege of 304 B.C. they once sent out a squadron of three cruisers, and afterwards three squadrons of three cruisers each; but they did not use the rest of their fleet[66]. Among the gifts to Rhodes after the great earthquake about 227 B.C. were ten penteres fully equipped from Seleucos, and timber for building six others from Ptolemy[67]. In the difficulty with Byzantion in 220 B.C. the Rhodians sent out ten ships, but four of these were supplied by their allies. Later on in the same year they sent three of the six ships with three smaller vessels to aid Cnossos[68]. The allied fleet of Rhodes, Pergamos and Byzantion at the battle of Chios in 201 B.C. numbered 77 ships, 65 of them being larger than trieres: but it is not known how many were sent by each of the allies[69]. Next year three Rhodian tetreres joined the Roman fleet at the Peiræus, and there were twenty Rhodian ships with the Romans during the two following years; and three years later (195 B.C.) eighteen Rhodian ships helped the Romans in putting down Nabis[70]. In 191 B.C., the first year of the naval war with Antiochos, the Rhodians sent out 25 ships. Next spring (190 B.C.) they sent out 36; but these were surprised at Samos and only five escaped. Still they sent out 20 others in a few days; and in the autumn they engaged Hannibal off the Eurymedon with 36 ships – 32 tetreres and 4 trieres – and seem to have had eight ships with the Romans at the same time. A little later they had 20 ships off Patara and 22 others with the Romans at the battle of Myonnesos[71]. Thus the Rhodians had over 70 war ships at sea in 190 B.C.: the greatest number they had at sea in any single year. In late times a rhetorician talks of their fleets of a hundred ships[72]; but there is no trace of them in history. Forty ships were fitted out in 171 B.C. for the war with Perseus, but only five of them went on service[73]: and only five trieres served with Attalos during the war with Crete in 154 B.C.[74] They did not use a large fleet against Mithridates in 88 B.C.[75] Twenty of their ships served against him in the Black Sea in 74 B.C.[76] In the Roman Civil War they fitted out 16 ships for Pompey in 49 B.C., and next year sent ten others with Cæsar to Egypt[77]. They used 33 picked ships against Cassius in 43 B.C. After the great city was taken by him 30 of their war ships were carried off and the rest burnt except the Sacred Ship[78]. At the naval games held by Claudius at the Lake Fucinus, some fifty miles inland from Rome, a contest was given between the fleets of Rhodes and of Sicily; each consisting of twelve, or of fifty, trieres[79].

As to the ships used, trieres, tetreres and penteres are of course ships with three, four and five banks of oars. The dicrotœ seem to be dieres, ships with two banks. In late times there were in the dockyards ships with as many as seven and nine banks[80]. It is not clear that trieres were used by Rhodes before about 400 B.C., when they had been three centuries in use, and tetreres and penteres were first being used. Nor is it clear that Rhodes had any ships larger than trieres till some penteres were given her about 227 B.C. The pentecontorœ were vessels of fifty oars, presumably in one bank. In the legend of Danaos and his fifty daughters, the first ship that came from Egypt to Greece came by way of Lindos and was called the Pentecontoros[81]. Possibly the Lindians introduced this type of ship for long sea voyages. The celoces or celetes, swift vessels also with one bank of oars, were invented by the Rhodians[82]. The triemioliæ were fast vessels without a deck; that is, without a fighting deck from end to end. The aphractœ seem to be of the same class. The Rhodian aphractœ are said to have been bad sea boats[83]. The ship called Peripolos was perhaps the guardship at the great city, and the phylacides cruisers to defend the coast of the island. A Sacred Ship was maintained by most Greek naval powers. The Rhodian traders plying to Egypt must have been well armed, for in 305 B.C. they beat off the war ships of Antigonos[84].

In the Social War of 357 B.C., the first that the Rhodians waged on their own account, they managed to bribe the enemy's admirals not to attack them; and the action at the Hellespont ended in nothing[85]. In later wars they relied on their seamanship; and they were generally successful, though very often opposed by fleets vastly stronger than their own in number and in size of ships. At the great siege of 304 B.C. Demetrios had 200 ships and 170 galleys besides transports, and had the pirates for allies: yet he was at the mercy of the Rhodian cruisers. Three of these suddenly attacked his ships as they were ravaging the coast of the island, sank many of them, ran others ashore and burnt them, and then went safe home. After this three phylacides went to Carpathos, three triemioliæ to Patara and three others round the islands: these sank and burnt his ships with impunity and captured his supplies on their way to the island and the plunder that was being carried off; and they also took many of the pirates and the Arch-pirate, himself[86]. The usual tactics of the Rhodians in action were to run through the enemy's line and break the oars of his ships as they passed; and then turn and ram them in the stern or on the beam, always carrying away something needed for working the ships even if they did not sink them. At the battle of Chios in 201 B.C. the enemy's small craft hampered them in this by crowding round them and spoiling their skilful steering and fast rowing. When thus reduced to ramming stem to stem the Rhodians in some way depressed their prows, and so received the enemy's blow high up while striking him deep. One pentere, however, left her ram fixed in a vessel she thus sank, and herself filled and went down[87]. In the action off Lade a few weeks later the Rhodians suffered severely under the enemy's rams, and sailed out of action one by one to stop their leaks till few were left to fight[88]. At the battle of the Eurymedon in 190 B.C. the enemy were disconcerted by the Rhodian tactics and the sinking of a Syrian ship of seven banks of oars by a single blow from the ram of a Rhodian of much smaller size[89]. At the battle of Myonnesos that same year the anchor of a Rhodian caught in a vessel she rammed; and, as she tried to back off, the cable became entangled in her oars, and she was disabled and taken. At this battle the Rhodians carried braziers of fire hung over their prows; and in trying to avoid these, the Syrian ships exposed their sides to the Rhodian rams[90]. These braziers had alone saved the ships that had escaped at Samos a few months before. The Syrians surprised the Rhodians by night, when lying in harbour there. The Rhodian admiral at once occupied the two cliffs that form the harbours mouth, hoping to keep out the enemy by a cross fire from above. But here he was attacked by troops that had been landed on the other side of the island; and supposing in the dark that these were part of a large force, he re-embarked his men and tried to fight his way out to sea. Five Rhodian ships and two from Cos carried braziers, and the enemy opened to let these pass; but all the rest were lost[91]. The Rhodians were much embarrassed by the swift little vessels of the Cretan pirates in 154 B.C.[92]. But they easily defeated the unwieldy ships of Mithridates in 88 B.C. off Myndos[93]. In the next action, however, the king seemed likely to surround them with his huge fleet, and they thought it prudent to retire without fighting. But their usual tactics again succeeded in a smaller action arising from an attack by a Rhodian dicrotos on one of the king's transports and the arrival of supports on both sides. In the end the Rhodian admiral found himself with six ships opposed to twenty-five of the enemy, and before these he kept giving way; but as they were turning to go back at dusk, he attacked them and sank two by ramming.

And when the king's transports were in difficulties in a storm, a Rhodian squadron came down on them and inflicted great loss[94]. Off Heracleia in 74 B.C. twenty Rhodians began the attack on the Heracleots, thirty in number, and at the first shock three Rhodians and five Heracleots went down[95]. In the Adriatic in 48 B.C. a Rhodian squadron of sixteen ships under Coponius sighted some of Cæsar's ships crossing from Italy to Greece and went in pursuit. When the enemy had just made the harbour, the wind suddenly changed; and the whole squadron went ashore and broke up. This is the only case of the loss of Rhodian war ships through bad weather; and also the only case in which a Rhodian squadron was commanded by a foreign admiral. In one of Cæsar's actions off Alexandria that same year four Rhodians, which had engaged the enemy to give time for the rest of his fleet to get into line, were attacked by some forty ships at once; but they were so well handled that they gave their opponents no chance of ramming them or breaking their oars. In the action off the Canopic Mouth soon after this the admiral's ship was not supported by the rest, either through a blunder or from cowardice, and was surrounded and sunk[96]. The Rhodians once more used their old tactics with success in the action off Myndos in 43 B.C. till Cassius, having 80 ships to 33, closed in on them and confined the fighting to ramming stem to stem, in which they were no match for the heavy Roman ships: and in the second action he followed the same plan[97].

During the sieges there was some fighting by the harbours. In 304 B.C. Demetrios built two towers and two shelters for throwing shot, and floated each of these four engines on two merchant ships. In rough weather, however, they proved unmanageable; and an engine that he afterwards built threefold the former in height and width foundered in a squall before it came into action. Deck-houses with portholes were fitted on the strongest galleys for the long-ranged catapults and the Cretan archers. And to protect the engines from the Rhodian ships a long raft was built with an iron-plated bulwark along it. On the first day of the attack the Rhodians drove the raft and engines out to sea by means of fire-ships. A week later three of their best ships with picked crews rammed the raft to bits, sank two of the engines and damaged many of the enemy's ships. All this was done under a heavy fire, but only one of the three Rhodians was lost. The city walls were raised, as they were overtopped by the floating towers; but they were soon breached by shot from the ships. The citizens held the breach against the enemy's troops, and burnt the boats they had landed in. The Little Harbour was defended by booms and by engines placed on merchant ships near its mouth. There were engines on the mole of the Great Harbour, and a wall across it about half way down. The end of this mole was surprised and held for a fortnight by four hundred of the enemy under shelter of barricades, the citizens recapturing it on a stormy day when the enemy's ships could not support its garrison. Fire balls were thrown from the enemy's fleet into the Rhodian ships with great effect[98]. The booms were again used for the defence in 88 B.C. Mithridates built a huge engine, the Sambuca. It was floated on two ships, and armed with battering rams: boats followed it carrying soldiers with scaling ladders to climb from it to the city walls. But it effected nothing, and at last collapsed[99]. In 43 B.C. the Roman ships were able to attack the walls for they had towers on board that took to pieces and were put up for the siege[100]. Thus the city walls were close to the water at some point in the days of Mithridates and Cassius: apparently not so in the days of Demetrios, for he could only batter with missiles and his storming party had to cross some ground to get to the breach. A change was perhaps made about 227 B.C. after the great earthquake. Later on there was space for merchant vessels touching at the great city to be drawn up on shore and for their crews to pitch tents near them[101]. This was perhaps inside the harbours: there would be no walls there, for command of the harbours gave command of the city. Thus when the Rhodians went over to deliver Halicarnassos from Artemisia in 351 B.C. the ships on returning dressed with laurel as if for their victory were admitted to the harbours without suspicion; and the city was taken. The queen had seized the empty ships when their crews had landed to occupy her city and had sailed back to Rhodes in them with her own troops on board[102]. For this reason again the citizens would not allow Demetrios to bring his fleet into harbour in 304 B.C.[103]. On the other hand, they had driven the Spartan fleet out of harbour in their revolt of 395 B.C.; but this perhaps by surprise[104].

The dockyard was maintained at great cost long after the Thalassocratia had passed from the Rhodians[105]. Intruders into some parts of it were punished with death as at Carthage and elsewhere[106]. When Heracleides set fire to it in 204 B.C. thirteen of the sheds were burnt, each with a triere in it[107]. The sheds were thus like those at the Peiræus: those at Syracuse, and some other places held two trieres each. Besides building for themselves, the Rhodians built ships for Antigonos; but he supplied his own timber[108]. Long afterwards Herod of Judæa had a large triere built at Rhodes[109]. Immense quantities of ship timber were presented to Rhodes after the great earthquake about 227 B.C., and fifty years later Perseus presented more[110]. The presents for the dockyard after the earthquake also comprised iron, lead, pitch, tar, resin, hemp, hair and sailcloth[111]. Once in time of need the Rhodian ladies cut off their hair and gave it for making ropes, just as the ladies of Carthage and Massalia had given theirs[112]. These ropes were long afterwards shewn to strangers who came to Rhodes[113]. The Rhodian commissioners appointed to send stores to Sinope when besieged by Mithridates in 220 B.C. spent the vote of 140,000 drachmæ (£5,600) in sending 150 cwt. of hair, 50 cwt. of sinew, 4 catapults with men to work them, 1000 suits of armour, 3000 pieces of gold and 10,000 jars of wine[114]. Subscriptions for the navy are partly in wine and partly in money in a Rhodian list perhaps belonging to 190 B.C. when a fresh fleet was sent out after the disaster to Pausistratos[115]. In the list 99 drachmæ 4 obols are given for rations for six months, and 265. 3 for some other time. If 1 obol be for some fee and 99. 3 be for rations for six months, 265. 2 would be for rations for 16 months. After the earthquake Ptolemy sent 20,000 artabes of corn as rations for ten trieres[116]. Taking each crew at 200 men, the daily ration at one chœnix, and the Egyptian artabe at 15 chœnices, this corn would last five months. These figures point to commissions for six months and for five months. In the list 151 drachmæ are also given for rations for a year, and 302 for two years. By the treaty with Hierapytna in Crete each Rhodian triere serving there was to be paid 10,000 drachmæ per month[117]. In the list the man who proposed the subscription gave 7000 drachmæ (£280) while the rest gave from 5000 drachmæ (£200) down to 50 drachmæ (£2). Aliens and strangers gave as well as citizens. Many of the subscriptions are for self and son; for self and daughter; for self, children and wife; for self and father: and one child gives for self and grandpapa.

A Rhodian squadron went out every year, the trieres going as far as the Atlantic. The custom remained under the Roman Empire; but then only one or two aphractœ went out, and sailed no further than Corinth[118]. In decrees 'service on ship during war' is distinguished from 'service on ship' simply: this last being perhaps on these yearly voyages[119]. There is no trace at Rhodes of the Athenian trierarchy, the duty of fitting out a ship for the public service, though many voluntary payments for the navy were expected[120]. The democracy had to supply pay for the seamen, and was once overthrown for refusing to hand it over to the trierarchs[121]. Thus a Rhodian is called trierarchos of an aphractos, being apparently its captain[122], and the trierarchos, the master of the trieres, seems an officer like the nauarchos, the master of the ships[123]. The nauarchos was at the head of naval affairs and was of high political rank, having power to make alliances for the state[124]. Other offices were pilot of trieres and master of aphractœ[125]. Rhodian squadrons were commonly of three ships, or of multiples of three ships; and there may have been an officer to command every three, for nothing in their tactics accounts for these numbers. A Rhodian fleet commonly had one commander. At the Eurymedon the fleet had three; but it had been formed from three separate fleets[126].

It was a proverb that ten Rhodians were worth ten ships[127], ἡμεῖς δέκα 'Ρόδιοι δέκα νῆες· and their fine seamanship was acknowledged as much by Romans as by Greeks. There is a story[128] of a Rhodian captain muttering while expecting to lose his ship in a storm, "Well,

Poseidon, you must own I'm sending her down in good trim." And they were fine swimmers. At the battle of Chios in 201 B.C. they lost only sixty men though four of their ships were sunk, while the Macedonians lost 9000 men besides prisoners[129]: and when they went out to burn the siege engines of Demetrios in 304 B.C. they simply swam home if their vessels took fire[130]. It is notable that the Rhodian youths of the noblest families eagerly served under Pausistratos at sea, though he commanded only foreign mercenaries ashore[131]. He perhaps doubted how long the zeal of these sailors would last, for when they assembled in gorgeous armour he took them on board and ordered them to stow their amour there, and then put sentries to see that it remained as security for their return[132]. Just before the siege by Cassius in 43 B.C. the somewhat degenerate Rhodians cruised off the mainland to shew his troops the fetters they had collected for them[133]. The ship's ornaments captured from Demetrios in 304 B.C. were dedicated[134]; and in late times trophies of ships' rams and other spoil stood in many parts of the city, some of it taken from the Etruscan pirates[135]. The Rhodians had put down piracy on their early voyages to the western Mediterranean[136], and these trophies may date from that age. Piracy in the Levant they never put down thoroughly. The pirates there were well organised under an arch-pirate, and made alliances with Demetrios and with Antiochos against Rhodes[137]. With regard to Cretan piracy, Hierapytna agreed with Rhodes to attack the pirates by land and hand over them and their ships to the Rhodians[138]. Cæsar was captured by pirates on his way to Rhodes. His friends were six weeks in getting together his ransom of 50 talents (£12,000), but directly he was free he got some Rhodian ships and took the pirates. The

Romans always sent pirates to the cross; but Cæsar in return for some courtesy these had shewn him, had their throats cut before they were nailed up[139]. When Pompey with the aid of the Rhodians crushed the pirates a few years later (67 B.C.) he could not crucify twenty thousand prisoners; and he settled most of them in the old Rhodian colony of Solœ[140]. Piracy was again familiar in late times, for the plot of a novel written about 200 A.D. turns on the capture of the hero and heroine by a Phœnician pirate triere that had been lying in harbour at Rhodes as a merchant ship and had followed theirs out to sea[141].

Trade was sometimes attracted by dubious means. After the battle of Chæroneia in 338 B.C. an Athenian called Leochares fled to Rhodes, saying that Athens was taken, the Peiræus besieged, and he was the sole survivor. Thinking the power of Athens was really broken, the Rhodians sent out men of war to bring in passing merchant ships; apparently to enforce some right of preemption[142]. So in a case at Athens, in which a ship chartered to carry corn there from Egypt had discharged at Rhodes on the way, Demosthenes congratulates himself in his speech for the charterers that he is not before a Rhodian court, for in that case the owners might be favoured for bringing corn to the island. The owners, it appears, had desired Rhodes as an alternative port to Athens in the charter-party; presumably by the direction of Cleomenes, satrap of Egypt, in whose service they were[143]. This satrap, who had a monopoly of the export of corn from Egypt, must therefore have favoured the trade with Rhodes. A little later most of the supplies of the great city were drawn from Egypt[144]. Merchants touched at the great city on their way from Egypt to Greece; and even before its foundation they came round the north end of the island, probably touching previously at Lindos like the Pentecontoros in the legend. Corn was also imported from Sicily: but after Rome made that her granary, this was only by leave of the Senate and in limited quantities. Thus in 169 B.C. leave was given to import 20,000 quarters[145]. Wine was largely exported from Rhodes both to Egypt and to Sicily, the handles of the jars being found throughout Sicily and at Naucratis and Alexandria. Many of these are stamped like the coins with the head of Helios or the wild rose. They bear the name of some priest of Helios – the dignitary that gave his name to the year at Rhodes – in all cases; and in many cases the name of some month as well. An emblem probably belonging to some magistrate is often added. The stamp would certify the capacity of the jar: it can hardly refer to the vintage, for the names of all the Doric months occur. These handles are found at many other places on the Mediterranean and the Black Sea. Wine and oil were the staple exports from Greece to the Black Sea, while the imports were cattle and slaves, and also honey, wax and pickles. It was to maintain the freedom of this trade that Rhodes, as the chief naval power among the commercial states, went to war with Byzantion in 220 B.C.[146]. Rhodian myrrh oil seems to have been exported to Athens[147]. There was a commercial treaty between Rhodes and Rome as early as 306 B.C.: and among the products of the island exported thither under the Empire were chalk, white-lead, glue, verdigris, sponges, purple, and the saffron unguent[148]. After the great earthquake about 227 B.C. the Rhodians were exempted from all custom dues in Syria and in Sicily[149]. The continuance of this exemption in Syria was secured for them by the Romans under the treaty with Antiochos in 188 B.C.; as were also their real property and rights of action in his dominions[150]. They had long before been encouraged to settle there, for when Antigonos went to war with Rhodes in 304 B.C. he directed that the Rhodian merchants in Syria, Phœnicia, Cilicia, and Pamphylia should be unmolested[151]. The Rhodians occupied a central position for the commerce of the ancient world, and their recognized policy of neutrality brought many foreign merchants to settle in the island[152]. Thus the report of the taking of Athens brought to Rhodes by Leochares was spread over the whole earth by the merchants residing there[153]. And young men were sent there to learn business[154]. It is said that when the Romans offered a general remission of debts after the Civil War, the Rhodians alone refused it[155]: and at Rhodes a son remained liable for the full payment of his father's debts long after he could escape liability at Rome by renouncing the inheritance[156].

Rhodes had close commercial relations with Cnidos, Iasos, Ephesos and Samos soon after 400 B.C., as appears from the issue by these states of coins of a uniform standard and with the same type on the obverse. This standard seems to be the Persian: but the Rhodians, on founding the great city, had issued coins of a new standard, commonly called the Rhodian, of about 60 grains to the drachma. This was soon adopted by Cos, Cnidos, Halicarnassos, Samos, Chios, Cyzicos and other states as far north as Ænos and Byzantion; which thus appear to have been under the commercial influence of Rhodes. In a century and a half this standard fell to about 50 grains to the drachma, and probably became the unit of the cistophoræ, coins that circulated throughout the Levant. A Rhodian talent of 4,500 cistophoræ is mentioned, but the passage is probably corrupt[157]. Early in the IInd century B.C. Rhodes and several other states of the Ægean were striking coins with the types of Alexander the Great and of the Attic standard: a measure necessary for their trade with European Greece now that the Rhodian standard had fallen. These are sometimes a trifle heavier than the corresponding Athenian coins: and in a certain payment made at Tenos shortly before 167 B.C. 100 Rhodian drachmæ seem to have been reckoned equal to 105 Athenian[158]. The Rhodian standard fell still further, for at Cibyra in 71 A.D. a Rhodian drachma was worth only ten sixteenths of a denarius when that coin weighed about 52 grains[159].

The maritime law of Rhodes was adopted by Rome. The response of Antoninus Pius is preserved[160]:- "I rule the land, but the law rules the sea. Let the matter be judged by the naval law of the Rhodians, in so far as any of our own laws do not conflict with that. This same judgment did Augustus give." This last sentence is perhaps doubtful. The comments of Salvinus Julianus, who flourished under Antoninus Pius, are the earliest now extant on the only principle of Roman naval law that is certainly Rhodian. This is the principle of general average[161]:- "that if cargo be jettisoned to lighten the ship, all contribute to make good the loss incurred for the benefit of all." This principle still obtains among all maritime nations; and probably much else of the naval law of to-day has come down from the Rhodians. Nothing is heard of these laws at Rhodes itself. The *Jus Navale Rhodiorum* is a forgery of the Middle Ages.

AT SEA. 59

1. Eusebios, anno 1100. Syncellos, p. 181.
2. Strabo, p. 654.
3. Ib. pp. 160, 654; Pomponius Mela, II. 6; Stephanos, s.v. Ῥόδη.
4. Strabo, p. 180; Pliny, III. 4; Stephanos, s.v. Ῥοδανουσία.
5. Strabo, p. 654.
6. Ib. p. 654; Vitruvius, I. 39.
7. Aristotle, p. 840; Strabo, p. 654; Silius Italicus, III. 364.
8. Thucydides, VI. 3, 4; Herodotos, VII. 153.
9. Thucydides, VII. 57.
10. Ib. VI. 4.
11. Polybios, IX. 27.
12. Pliny, XXXIV. 19; Scholia to Pindar, Ol. VII. 87; Polyænos, V. 1; cf. Epistles of Phalaris, 4, 119.
13. Thucydides, VI. 5; Herodotos, VII. 153-156; Diodoros, XI. 76.
14. Vibius Sequester, de fontibus.
15. Diodoros, V. 9.
16. Epiphanios, contra hæreses, p. 150.
17. Stephanos, s.v. Ἀπολλωνία.
18. Strabo, p. 801.
19. Herodotos, II. 178.
20. Ammianus Marcellinus, XXII. 16.
21. Strabo, p. 794.
22. Ib. p. 671; Pomponius Mela, I. 13.
23. Polybios, XXII. 7; Livy, XXXVII. 56.
24. Strabo, p. 671
25. Athenos, pp. 297, 298; Stephanos, s.v. Γέλα; cf. Aristophanes, Acharn. 606.
26. Stephanos, s.v. Κορύδαλλα.
27. Strabo, pp. 651, 652.
28. Pliny, XXXI. 20; Seneca, Nat. Quæs. III. 26.
29. Polybios, XXXI. 7.
30. Ib. XXXI. 7; Livy, XXXIII. 18.
31. Polybios, XXII. 27; Livy, XXXVIII. 39.
32. Dio Chrysostom. p. 620.
33. Pomponius Mela, I. 16.
34. Æneas, Poliorc. 18.
35. Pliny, V. 33.
36. Strabo, p. 57.
37. Diodoros, V. 54.
38. Appian, de bel. civ. V. 7.
39. Pliny, V. 36.
40. Livy, XLV. 25.
41. Homer, Iliad, II. 654.
42. Herodotos, VII. 93.
43. Diodoros, XI. 3.
44. Thucydides, II. 9.
45. Ib. VI. 43.
46. K. I. 226.
47. Ib. 231.
48. Ib. 230.
49. Ib. 233.
50. Ib. 235.
51. Ib. 237.
52. Ib. 238.
53. Ib. 239.
54. Ib. 244.
55. Ib. 256.
56. Ib. 262.
57. Harpocration, s. vv. ἀπειπεῖν; &c.
58. Thucydides, VII. 28, VIII. 44.
59. Ib. VIII. 44.
60. Xenophon, Hell. I. 5, 6.
61. Diodoros, XIII. 70.
62. Xenophon, Hell. IV. 8.
63. Diodoros, XVI. 21.

[64] Arrian, Anabasis, II. 20.
[65] Diodoros, XIX. 77.
[66] Ib. XX. 84, 93.
[67] Polybios, V. 89.
[68] Ib. IV. 50, 52, 53.
[69] Ib. XVI. 2.
[70] Livy, XXXI. 22, 46, XXXII. 16, XXXIV. 26.
[71] Livy, XXXVI. 45, XXXVII. 9, 11, 12, 16, 22, 23, 24, 26, 30.
[72] Dio Chrysostom, p. 620.
[73] Polybios, XXVII. 3, 6; Livy, XLII. 45, 56.
[74] Polybios, XXXIII. 11.
[75] Diodoros, XXXVII. 28; Appian, de bel. Mith. 24.
[76] Memnon, Fr. 50.
[77] Cæsar, de bel. civ. III. 5, 27, 106.
[78] Appian, de bel. civ. IV. 66, V. 2.
[79] Suetonius, Claudius, 21; Dio Cassius, LX. 33.
[80] Aristeides, p. 341.
[81] The Parian Marble, Epoch 9.
[82] Pliny, VII. 57.
[83] Cicero, ad Atticum, V. 12, 13.
[84] Diodoros, XX. 82.
[85] Deinarchos, pp. 92, 110; Diodoros, XVI. 21.
[86] Diodoros, XX. 82, 84, 93, 97.
[87] Polybios, XVI. 4, 5.
[88] Ib. XVI. 15.
[89] Livy, XXXVII. 24.
[90] Livy, XXXVII. 30; Appian, de reb. Syria, 27.
[91] Livy, XXXVII; Appian, de reb. Syria, 24.
[92] Diodoros, XXXI. 38.
[93] Appian, de bel. civ. IV. 71; Memnon, Fr. 31.
[94] Ib. de. bel. Mith. 24-26
[95] Memnon, Fr. 50.
[96] Cæsar, de bel. civ. III. 26, 27; Aulus Hirtius, de bel. Alexand. 15, 25.
[97] Appian, de bel. civ. IV. 71, 72.
[98] Diodoros, XX. 85-88
[99] Appian, de bel. Mith. 24, 27.
[100] Ib. de bel. civ. IV. 72.
[101] Lucian, Amores, 8.
[102] Vitruvius, II. 41.
[103] Diodoros, XX. 82.
[104] Ib. XIV. 79.
[105] Aristeides, p. 341.
[106] Strabo, p. 653.
[107] Polyænos, V. 17.
[108] Diodoros, XIX. 58.
[109] Josephus, de bel. Jud. I. 14.
[110] Polybios, XXVI. 7.
[111] Ib. V. 88-90.
[112] Frontinus, I. 7.
[113] Aristeides, p. 355.
[114] Polybios, IV. 56.
[115] N. 343.
[116] Polybios, V. 89.
[117] M. 1852, p. 79.
[118] Dio Chrysostom, p. 621.
[119] F. 1; N. 353; R. H. 23; B. 2525.
[120] Strabo, p. 653.
[121] Aristotle, Politics, V. 3, 5.
[122] B. 2524.
[123] Diodoros, XX. 88.
[124] Polybios, XXX. 5.
[125] F. 1.
[126] Livy, XXXVII. 22, 23.
[127] Diogenianos, Parœmiœ.
[128] Aristeides, p. 346.
[129] Polybios, XVI. 7.
[130] Diodoros, XX. 86.

AT SEA. 61

[131] Livy, XXXIII. 18, XXXVII. 12.
[132] Polyænos, V. 27.
[133] Dio Cassius, XLVII. 33.
[134] Diodoros, XX. 87.
[135] Aristeides, p. 342.
[136] Strabo, p. 654.
[137] Diodoros, XX. 82; Livy, XXXVII. 11.
[138] M. 1852, p. 79.
[139] Suetonius, Cæsar, 4. 74.
[140] Strabo, p. 671.
[141] Xenophon of Ephesos, de amoribus Anthiæ et Abrocomæ, I. 13.
[142] Lycurgos, p. 150.
[143] Demosthenes, pp. 1284, 1285, 1296, 1297.
[144] Diodoros, XX. 81.
[145] Polybios, XXVIII. 2.
[146] Ib. IV. 38.
[147] Aristophanes, Lysist. 944.
[148] Pliny, XIII. 2, XXIV. 1, XXVIII. 71, XXXI. 47, XXXIV. 26, 54; Athenæos, p. 688; Vitruvius, VII. 63, 65.
[149] Polybios, V. 88, 89.
[150] Ib. XXII. 26; Livy, XXXVIII. 38.
[151] Polyænos, IV. 6.
[152] Diodoros, XX. 82, 84.
[153] Lycurgos, p. 149.
[154] Plautus, Mercator, prologue, 11.
[155] Dio Chrysostom, p. 602.
[156] Sextus, Hypotyposes, I. 149.
[157] Festus, s.v.Talenta.
[158] B. 2334.
[159] B. ad. 4380, a.
[160] The Pandects, XIV. II. 9.
[161] Ib. XIV. II. 1.

IV.

ON SHORE.

THE City of Rhodes was built in the closing years of the Peloponnesian War. It is strange that its site was not occupied before. The corn ships passing round the north end of the island on their way from Egypt to Greece must often have anchored where its harbours afterwards were while waiting for the prevailing N.W. winds to fall. The site, however, demanded a large city, for the only hill that could serve as a citadel was more than a mile from the harbours; and perhaps the islanders could not previously have peopled it. Hippodamos of Miletos was the architect: the man to whom Pericles had entrusted the rebuilding of the Peiræus[1]. It is notable that a Deigma – a bazaar of the Oriental type – was found in few Greek cities but the Peiræus and Rhodes. Covering the level ground near the harbours and then rising gradually along the terraces of the Acropolis hill to the vast circle of walls with their lofty towers, the city was compared to the body of a Greek theatre[2]. Thus the people could watch the fleet of Demetrios as it crossed the strait, the men standing on the walls and the women and the old men on the roofs of their houses[3]. But in storms all the rain water rushed down to one place, and in the first century of the city there were three serious floods. The first of these was soon after the city was founded, while there was still much vacant ground; and was the least destructive. More damage was done by the second: and more still by the third, when five hundred lives were lost. This was in 315 B.C. The lower part of the city was inundated till the walls gave way under the pressure and let the water fall into the sea. There were channels under the walls to prevent these floods; but the people had not kept them clear, as they fancied the winter rains were over[4]. A few years later (304 B.C.) Demetrios destroyed all the trees and buildings near the city for material for his camp. The walls by the sea were raised during the siege, and a second line of defence, probably temporary, was built within the walls on the landward side; stones from the outer wall of the theatre and from some of the temples being used for this. When the siege was over, a grove within the city was enclosed with porticos and dedicated to Ptolemy; and the theatre, the walls and the temples were rebuilt with greater splendour than before[5]. A marble theatre was afterwards promised by Eumenes, but was not built[6]. The city was ruined by a great earthquake about 227 B.C., when the Colossos and the greater part of the dockyards and the walls were overthrown[7]. It was soon rebuilt by aid of immense gifts from foreign powers; but it was again shaken by the earthquake of 196 B.C.[8] Some Rhodian monuments to the victims of earthquakes still exist; and also inscriptions recording repairs to older monuments that had been thrown down[9]. The extension of the south end of the Acropolis was earlier than the siege by Mithridates in 88 B.C.; but apparently much later than the rebuilding of the walls after the great earthquake, for the wall there is of very inferior work. The suburbs were levelled by the citizens before this siege[10]. It was the city of this age that called forth Strabo's opinion that "in harbours, in streets, in walls, and in other buildings it so surpasses all other cities that we cannot call any its equal, much less its superior[11]." Two centuries after him, the rhetorician Aristeides talks of the sacred groves in the Acropolis; the symmetric building of the rest of the city, so that it seemed a single house rather than a town; the long, broad streets; and the absence of vacant ground between the walls and the buildings – a thing rare in Greek towns[12]. This city perished in the earthquake of 157 A.D. The sea went back, and returned in a wave; the buildings fell in a shapeless mass of ruin; and then fires broke out that burnt on day and night[13]. The Emperor Antoninus Pius rebuilt the city[14]; and in a few years Aristeides could again call it the fairest of Greek cities[15]. It was probably after this rebuilding that Pausanias reckoned the city walls among the finest he had seen[16].

Six thousand citizens and a thousand aliens bore arms at the great siege of 304 B.C. The aliens that refused to bear arms had been expelled: they were chiefly merchants who had been attracted to the island by its steadfast neutrality in that age of warfare, and not more than one man in six of this class would care to fight. Thus in times of peace the aliens may well have been as numerous as the citizens. In a census taken at Athens a few years earlier 21,000 citizens, 10,000 aliens, and 400,000 slaves were returned. Allowing for women and children, this implies a free population of about 150,000; and assuming that the 400,000 slaves include women and children, the free are to the slaves as three to eight. If this proportion held at Rhodes, 6000 citizens and 6000 aliens would imply 60,000 free persons, and so 160,000 slaves; or 220,000 for the whole population. This was before the city's great prosperity: but most of the islanders must have come into the city for protection during the invasion. The slaves were armed for the siege. Many, no doubt, had gone away with their alien masters, and many would not be trusted: still, if half the able bodied slaves were armed, they added some 16,000 to the 7000 free men for the garrison. The reinforcements were 150 men from Crete and 500 from Egypt: and later on, 1500 more from Egypt. The whole garrison would thus be about 25,000 men. The attacking force was 40,000 men, besides the cavalry, the engineers and the sailors[17].

For the attack Demetrios built the Colossos of siege engines, the Great Helepolis. This was a moveable tower; the base square and the sides sloping inward. Its size is variously given: Plutarch puts it at 99 feet high by 72 broad: Diodoros at 150 feet by 75: Vitruvius at 125 by 60, and gives its weight as 125 tons. It moved on wheels, going very steadily though with much creaking and straining; and was propelled by a body of soldiers underneath. There were portholes for discharging shot at each story of the tower, and huge tridents were carried for breaking away obstacles. On either side of the Helepolis were four shelters to cover the miners and two others with huge battering rams like ships' prows. These shelters also moved on wheels, and were connected by a covered way for the men working them. At the first attack a very massive tower built of squared stone was thrown down and the wall on either side so damaged that the citizens could not get to the battlements. These siege engines were built only of wood and so were covered with basket work and raw hides to resist fire balls and the heavy stone shot. The citizens once knocked off some of this covering with their shot and set fire to the woodwork; but there were water tanks in the upper parts of the engines, and the fire was put out. The Helepolis itself was designed to resist stone shot of 2½ cwt., but no stone shot heavier than ½ cwt. seem to have been used at the siege. In a night attack many were killed because they could not see the stone shot and the pointed shot coming and get out of their way, so the velocity was low. Pointed shot nearly two feet long were used. In this night attack over 1500 pointed shot and 800 fire balls were discharged by the citizens. It is said that a little before the siege a certain Callias of Arados came to Rhodes with a design for a huge crane to stand on the city walls: it would grapple a common helepolis as it came up and lift it over the walls into the city. The Rhodians forthwith made him state architect in place of Diognetos, who then held that office. But the Great Helepolis was too much for the crane. Diognetos would do nothing, till at last he was moved by the prayers of ingenuous maidens and youths escorted by priests. He then diverted the sewage of the city toward the Helepolis, which soon clave to the swamp and could not be moved. After the siege he brought it within the city and dedicated it to the people. It was designed by Epimachos of Athens[18].

Besides the second line of defence erected within the walls during the siege, half-moons were built to cover weak points and a great trench was dug round the first breach made by the Helepolis. Fifteen hundred picked men, however, got through this breach by night, killed the guards at the trench, and occupied a portion of the city near the theatre. But next day they were attacked by the best of the Rhodian troops and the fifteen hundred mercenaries from Egypt, and very few of them escaped. The mines were met by countermines: these the enemy tried to seize by bribing the officer of the guard, a certain Athenagoras, but with very poor success. The citizens rewarded him with a golden chaplet and five talents (£1200) for betraying this attempt. He was not a Rhodian, but of Miletos and in command of the mercenaries from Egypt: and they hoped by this to attach the other mercenaries. They attached the slaves by a decree that all who fought well should be purchased by the state and enrolled as citizens: and the decree was carried out. The citizens themselves were encouraged by a decree that those who fell should be buried at the public cost, their parents and children maintained out of the treasury, their daughters dowered on marriage and their sons on reaching manhood crowned in full armour in the Theatre at the Festival of Dionysos. The rich had readily given their money for the defence, and the workmen their work; some at arms and ammunition, but most at strengthening the walls. Ransoms were arranged with Demetrios at 1000 drachmæ (£40) for a free man and half that sum for a slave[19]. It is said that at the siege of 88 B.C. Mithridates exchanged all his Rhodian prisoners for Leonicos, who had saved his life, thinking it better to endanger his success than prove ungrateful[20]. In that siege there was little fighting by land, and in the siege by Cassius none at all. Mithridates intended to surprise the south end of the Acropolis by night and thence give the signal by a fire for his troops to attempt the city walls with scaling ladders while his ships attacked the harbours. But the citizens discovered his plans and lighted the fire themselves; and his troops finding the walls manned did not deliver the attack[21].

Among the mercenaries sent in from Egypt during the siege of 304 B.C. were Rhodians who had taken service with Ptolemy[22]. Telephos of Ialysos who has carved his name on the leg of one of the colossi at Abu Simbel seems to have come there among the Greek troops in the service of Psametik II. nearly three centuries earlier. A coin with the lion's head of Lindos and the silphion tree of Cyrene on the obverse and the eagle's head of Ialysos on the reverse was probably struck as pay for Rhodian mercenaries in the army of Arcesilaos III. on his restoration at Cyrene in 530 B.C. Seven hundred Rhodians served on the Sicilian Expedition of 415 B.C. as slingers[23]. Early in the retreat of the Ten Thousand in 401 B.C. Xenophon found there were Rhodians among them and formed a body of two hundred slingers. Their leaden bolts carried twice as far as the stones from the Persian slings and further than most arrows; and in the next action Tissaphernes soon retired out of range, for not a Rhodian missed his man. They had obtained the cords and lead from the villages they passed[24]. Some sling bolts lately found in the island are about an inch in length and shaped like filberts, bearing in low relief an arrow head on one side and on the other their owner's name, Bagyptas. In later times the Rhodians kept mainly to the sea. The force with which Pausistratos recovered the Peræa in 197 B.C. comprised Achæans, Gauls, Pisuetæ, Nisuetæ, Tamiani, Arei from Africa and Laodiceni from Asia, but no Rhodians: yet when this same Pausistratos commanded the fleet the best men among the Rhodians eagerly served under him[25]. By the treaty with Hierapytna two Rhodian trieres could be demanded for service off Crete and two hundred heavy armed Cretan soldiers for service in Rhodes. Transport for these was to be provided by the Rhodians and pay from the date of arrival at the rate of nine obols (15*d*.) a day a man and two drachmæ (20*d*.) a day for officers commanding not less than fifty men. Hierapytna was to aid Rhodes in levying mercenaries in

Crete, and Rhodes was to do the like for Hierapytna in Asia Minor[26]. The forts in the Rhodian possessions in Asia Minor were garrisoned with foreign mercenaries[27].

The Rhodian sailors were capable of service on shore. In Cento's descent on Chalcis in 200 B.C. they forced Philip's strongest jail, and liberated his political prisoners. In the war with Nabis five years later they helped to construct the works for the siege of Gytheion and took part in the assault on Sparta[28]. At Ruspina in 46 B.C. Cæsar employed them as light armed troops to act with his cavalry[29]. It is characteristic that when the Ten Thousand were stopped in their retreat by the river Tigris a Rhodian came forward with a plan for crossing it on a pontoon of inflated skins[30]. Polyxenidas, the Rhodian exile who commanded the fleet of Antiochos the Great against his own countrymen, had thirty years earlier commanded Cretan mercenaries in Hyrcania[31]. In 190 B.C. he treated with Pausistratos the Rhodian admiral for his recall from exile in return for the surrender of the king's fleet, apparently compromising himself irrevocably by letters written with his own hand and sealed with his seal, and then surprised Pausistratos in his false security[32]. Memnon the Rhodian, who commanded the Persian fleet against Alexander the Great, had previously commanded against him on land at the battle of the Granicos and at the siege of Halicarnassos, and had alone urged the true policy of Persia when the war began – defensive operations in Asia and an attack on Macedon by sea[33]. He was satrap of the west of Asia Minor, as was his brother Mentor before him. Mentor had held a joint command in Egypt with Bagoas, the chief eunuch of the Persian king, and he had there arranged with some Greek mercenaries serving on the other side that Bagoas should be taken prisoner and then had rescued him from them. He owed his satrapy to the eunuch's gratitude for this escape[34]. A sister of Memnon and Mentor married Artabazos, the satrap of lower Phrygia; and from this marriage sprang Barsine, the mother by Alexander the Great of Heracles[35]. That young prince had no small chance of obtaining the throne of Macedon at the time of his assassination in 311 B.C. Under Memnon's government at Lampsacos it was the custom to give the soldiers their rations on the second day of the month. But by delaying three days one month and five days another till he made up thirty days, he was enabled to save the state the cost of a month's provision for the army. Then he obtained a loan from some wealthy citizens on the security of certain revenue shortly due: but when this revenue was paid he felt bound to apply it to the pressing needs of government, and the citizens had to be content with a promise of interest while their loan remained. Another Rhodian, Aristoteles, when governor of Phocæa, informed the leaders of one of the political parties in that city that the other party had bribed him to put them in power; but, as those whom he addressed were better administrators, he would rather be bribed by them for that purpose: and they bribed him. He then used the same argument to the leaders of the other party; and when he had really obtained a bribe from them, he formed a coalition government. Again, perceiving that many heavy lawsuits were pending, he formed a new court and ordered that all pending suits should be at once brought before it or be barred; and by fining those litigants that did not appear and by taking bribes from both sides at the trials he greatly augmented the revenue. When Antimenes the Rhodian was warden of the highways around Babylon under Alexander the Great, he discovered an obsolete right to a tithe on imports and suddenly revived it when certain high officials and others well able to pay were expected, to the great advantage of the treasury. Then he insured slaves at eight drachmæ (6s. 8d.) a-head per annum for whatever sum their owners chose to name. This brought in a good revenue; and when a slave ran away, he simply ordered the governor of the province to catch the slave or pay the insurance[36]. Another Rhodian placed in office by Alexander was Æschylos, whom he made governor of Alexandria just after its foundation[37]. Long afterwards Phanagoria on the Black Sea was held for Mithridates by Castor the Rhodian, who opportunely betrayed the city and the king's sons to Pompey in 63 B.C. and was rewarded with the title 'Friend of the Romans'[38]. He married a daughter of Deiotaros, the able king of Galatia, and his son and grandson held royal dignity. This son unluckily made political charges against Deiotaros at Rome in 45 B.C., whereupon the king slew Castor[39].

There were probably twelve generals, strategœ, at Rhodes, of whom the strategos ἐκ πάντων was presumably the chief: one of them commanded in the Peræa and another in the parts of the island which lay outside the cities[40]. No other military officers are mentioned. The prytaneis, however, sometimes took command both by sea and by land during the siege of 304 B.C.[41] These prytaneis were at the head of the state. They probably held office for a year. One was president during the first six months and another during the last six. There were probably more than two, but it is not clear how many there were. They presided at assemblies of the citizens in the Theatre. Reports from abroad were addressed to them; and so also the admirals' despatches, for these were preserved in the prytaneion. They received foreign ambassadors in the prytaneion at the state altar. In later times despatches from the Roman Emperor were directed to them[42]. There were probably seven treasurers, tamiæ, and five intendants, episcopœ: the latter with a secretary[43]. There were officers of revenue, poletæ, and guardians of foreigners and slaves, prostatæ; these last acting in committees, for "the prostatæ; those with Charinos" are mentioned: and there were also five overseers, epimeletæ, of the foreigners, with a secretary[44]. There were also guardians of public buildings, astynomæ[45]. Probably all these offices were elective. An admiral, however, dying on active service, could appoint his own successor[46]. At Camiros the demiurgos appears to be the chief magistrate after the founding of the great city[47]; and the same office was probably introduced at Naxos when that island was subjected to Rhodes[48]. At Lindos there were probably three commanders, agemones[49]. A certain Rhodian was commander in the territories – presumably on the mainland – in time of war[50]; and three others were respectively commander at Caunos, commander in Caria and commander in Lycia[51]. This was probably the office of Podilos, of whose oppression envoys came from Iasos to Rhodes to complain[52]. The Rhodians certainly governed their subjects harshly. The islands subjected to them by Antony were soon forfeited through their oppression[53]. The Lycians, when subjected to them in 188 B.C., found they had fared better even under Antiochos: actual violence was now offered to them and their wives and children, and they were contemptuously insulted merely that the Rhodians might shew their mastery[54]. This[55] led to three wars in the next twenty-five years. A century later the tribute was so rigorously exacted that the

Caunians and others begged the Roman Senate that it might be collected by publicans from Rome[56].

Rhodian envoys were constantly at Rome. In their prosperous days they were entertained at a public mansion and escorted thence to the Senate and then to the Capitol to make their offerings. But those that came just after the blunder about the war with Perseus were forbidden to stay in the city and could hardly get lodgings for money at a wretched inn in the suburbs; they put off their white robes and went in mourning to the houses of the leading men to beg their aid with prayers and tears, and in the Senate they bowed to the ground holding twigs of olive toward the Senators[57]. A few years earlier some Rhodian envoys had lost their temper in the Senate and others had declined the customary present of 2000 asses (£5) offered to each envoy[58]. Long afterwards some Rhodian magistrates sent despatches to Tiberius without the clause 'that they would ever pray,' and the Emperor ordered them to Rome to insert the clause[59]. By sending over their admiral, who had always power to conclude alliances, the Rhodians were able to negotiate quietly with Rome for a treaty of alliance after the war with Perseus, when they feared damage to their reputation if it were generally known they had asked for such a treaty without success[60]. Their treaty with Hierapytna was to be sworn to by five men elected by the Commons on behalf of all Rhodians of full age; and the like oath was to be administered by the prytaneis to the envoys from Hierapytna at an Assembly[61]. Envoys from abroad were heard before the Senate as well as before an Assembly of the citizens in the Theatre, and various honours were granted them[62]. Honours granted to Rhodians by foreign states with which they had negotiated a treaty were proclaimed at Rhodes at the Festival of

Helios[63]. Rhodian envoys were also employed abroad in several cases in mediating between belligerents[64]. Similarly a disputed claim to territory was referred by Samos and Priene to the arbitration of Rhodes[65]. After the great earthquake about 227 B.C. envoys were sent to nearly all the Greek states to ask for assistance; and the same course was proposed after the earthquake of 157 A.D. But the immense gifts sent in response were received in a patronizing way, quite as a favour to the givers[66]. Still the Rhodians occasionally made some return for the gifts that were always being sent to them, even from sovereigns as remote as Herod of Judæa[67]. During the siege by Demetrios they captured the ship bringing his royal wardrobe, and sent it to their ally Ptolemy[68]. When the wife of Seleucos was taken by the Gauls and brought to Rhodes to be sold as a slave, they bought her and sent her dressed as a queen to her capital[69]. Four Athenian ships captured by the Macedonians in 201 B.C. were recaptured by the Rhodians and sent back to Athens. Upon this the Rhodians were granted such rights of citizenship at Athens as Athenians then had at Rhodes[70]. Some time afterwards, Glaucon son of Eteocles, apparently the Olympic victor, was consul (proxenos) for Rhodes at Athens[71]. He dedicated a statue in the great city; as did Zeno son of Nahum, who was consul for Rhodes at Arados[72]. Nine Rhodians are named among the consuls for Delphi in the list for 180 B.C. inscribed on the south wall of the enclosure of the great temple of Apollo[73]. Philophron, a Rhodian statesman of the period of the war with Perseus, seems to have been consul for Delphi. The grant was to him and his descendants, and the recompense for their duties to Delphians at Rhodes included priority in consulting the oracle[74].

Beside the Senate in the great city, the Senates of the three ancient cities, or at any rate of Lindos, existed as late as the Roman Empire[75]. There was a secretary to the Senate in the great city, and an undersecretary to the Senate and apparently to the Prytaneis as well: and also a public secretary[76]. At Lindos there was the Commons (ὁ δῦμος) of the Lindopolitæ[77]: and also the Entire Commons (ὁ σύμπας δῦμος) apparently consisting of the Argeiœ, Brasiœ, Bulidæ, Camyndiœ, Cattabiœ, Clasiœ, Ladarmiœ, Nettidæ, Œiatæ, Pagiœ and Pedieis, who were citizens of places in the territory of Lindos, together with the Lindopolitæ, who were citizens of Lindos itself[78]. These were all termed Lindians, but were distinguished as citizens from the People (τὸ πλῆθος) of the Lindians. A Polites was presumably a citizen of the great city. Very little remains of Cicero's account of the constitution about 100 B.C. But it appears that the Senators were not a class: the same men sat as Senators in the Senate House and among the Commons in the Theatre, serving for some months in one place and then for some months in the other; and they were paid for attendance in both places[79]. These changes probably occurred every six months, when the prytaneis changed office. At this period all citizens served as jurymen without regard to their wealth or poverty; and they were proud of the justice thus administered[80]. Alexander the Great had previously recognized the uprightness of the Rhodians by leaving his will in their keeping[81]. Before his days the administration of the democrats had sometimes been so incompetent and corrupt that the wealthy classes had been compelled to put an end to their government in self-defence[82]. It was by means of a party among the citizens, which he afterwards repudiated, and not by foreign troops that

Mausolos upset the democracy[83]. By the treaty between Rhodes and Hierapytna each state was bound to oppose any attempt to upset the democracy established in the other[84]. As late as Domitian's time the clumsy government of the democracy caused serious disturbances[85]. Later still, the Rhodians were still meeting daily for deliberation, though other Greeks seldom met[86]. Even under the Antonines they had energy enough for political disturbances, and it was a saying that they would refuse immortality itself unless assured of eternal democracy[87].

The revenue was large. About 170 B.C. the harbour dues reached a million drachmæ (£40,000) a year. Most of Lycia and Caria was at this time tributary; the cities of Stratoniceia and Caunos alone paying 120 talents (£28,800), though Caunos had been purchased rather more than a century before for only 200 talents (£48,000). Rome replied to the conceit of the Rhodians during the war with Perseus by making Delos a free port; and by 164 B.C. their harbour dues had fallen to 150,000 drachmæ (£6,000)[88]. But Lycia and Caria remained subject, with some intervals, as late as the Roman Empire; and in those days there were many other tributary states[89]. Besides the immense gifts from abroad, large sums used to be presented to the state by private citizens for public purposes and especially for maintaining the poor. An ancient custom, moreover, required the rich to see that the poorer citizens did not want[90]. Fees must have been paid to the state on admission to citizenship, for after the great earthquake about 227 B.C. Hiero and Gelon sent ten talents (£2,400) to increase the number of citizens[91]. Many of the slaves were made citizens after the siege of 304 B.C., and in one case of much later date a slave was emancipated by the City and made Guest of the Senate and Commons[92]. He was of foreign birth. The slaves, or emancipated slaves, whose dedications have been found in numbers near the great city, were mostly natives of Asia Minor. There were slaves belonging to the City, and probably a board of masters to manage them: they seem once to have rebelled[93]. Adoption was very popular. Nearly half the Rhodians named in inscriptions are described as 'son of so-and-so, but by adoption son of so-and-so.' Pliny in one instance has evidently mistaken the Rhodian phrase καθ' υοθεσίαν by adoption for καθ' υπόθεσιν by hypothesis; and has founded a curious story on his blunder[94].

Public life brought many dangers. Cassius and Artemisia killed the leading men on capturing the great city. Hostages were taken by Demetrios after his siege and by the Persians just before Marathon, while the leaders of the Persian party were exiled by their fellow-countrymen. After the war with Perseus the citizens tried to exonerate themselves by executing the leaders of the anti-Roman party. There was civil war in the island soon after the great city was founded. A little earlier the leading aristocrats had been driven into exile by Athens. Doricus, the most famous of these retired to Thurii and there fitted out ships to serve against Athens during the Peloponnesian War. His men were devoted to him: and when Astyochos once raised his staff against him, the act nearly cost the Spartan admiral his life at the hands of the indignant soldiers and sailors[95]. He was taken in 407 B.C. and brought to Athens. The people had already decreed his death: but on seeing a man so famous for his Olympic victories in chains before them, they set him free without even a ransom. Twelve years later he was in the

Peloponnese when news came that Rhodes had again gone over to Athens: and he was put to death at Sparta in blind vengeance for the revolt. When his ancestor Damagetos, the despot of Ialysos, enquired of Apollo at Delphi whence he should choose for himself a wife, the god bade him wed a daughter of the best man among the Greeks, and Aristomenes did not refuse him his daughter's hand. The hero of the Messenian Wars came with his daughter to the island and there ended his days[96].

Ialysos and Camiros were in ruins before the earthquake of 157 A.D., though Ialysian decrees occur down to the time of the Emperor Titus[97]. The chief remains at Camiros are of structures for the supply of water. At the top of the Acropolis a gallery about two feet wide and six high runs under the surface for about 230 yards in a straight line, having on one side three branches of about 27 yards each, one at the centre and one at each end. From these main galleries many others diverge, generally one or two yards in length and none longer than ten yards; and these all end in shafts opening to the surface. It is clear they were for water supply and not for drainage, as the bases of the shafts are always lower than the galleries leading to them. The city was supplied by a conduit hewn straight through the eastern limb of the Acropolis hill to a cistern on the east side; and this was itself fed by another conduit running southward under the hill to a spring. These conduits are about four feet high and two wide. Pliny mentions a Rhodian marble with golden veins[98], but the ruins throughout the island are of stone. The gymnasion in the great city was a magnificent building, full of famous pictures and statues[99]. No less than 75 talents (£18,000) were sent by Hiero and Gelon to supply oil for it after the great earthquake about 227

B.C.[100] Under the Roman Empire the gymnasiarch of the young men in the great city gave his name to the year, but presumably only for purposes of the gymnasion[101]: and a great athlete and officer of the gymnasion at Philadelphia was made citizen and senator of Rhodes[102]. The Rhodian builders invented a type of courtyard that was afterwards adopted in many of the wealthier houses at Rome: it had a colonnade on all the four sides, and that facing the south was carried on higher columns[103]. "They build for eternity, but they eat as though they were to die to-morrow" was an ancient saying against the Rhodians[104]. They judged a man by what he ate. A connoisseur in fish was at once pronounced a gentleman: and a man who was content with meat, a mere shopkeeper[105]. Lynceus of Samnos in an epistle[106] written about 250 B.C., in which he compares the delicacies of Rhodes and of Athens, calls the island admirable in its fish and praises the aphye (? anchovy), the ellops (? sword-fish), the orphos (? sea-perch) and a kind of shark called the alopex, the fox. A popular saying advised a gourmet who could not afford a Rhodian alopex to steal one even if he died for it. Varro and Pliny, however, thought the ellops the greatest delicacy of the island[107]. Then in the matter of milk cakes, Lynceus thought highly of the Rhodian echinos at the second course of a dinner. For dessert he approved the Rhodian escharites, a sweet cake that made drinkers sober and restored to gourmands their appetites. Martial, however, suggests that a Roman gentleman need not break his slave's jaw with a blow: he might give him a Rhodian cake[108]. The peach tree, when introduced from Egypt, proved sterile and tantalized the people by merely flowering[109]. But the wild figs were admired by Lynceus, and also the custom of eating them before dinner instead of after. The figs had a fine flavour and were known in Rome[110]. The dried figs called brigindarides were a local growth in the island, for the ethnic of one of the demes is Brygindarios[111]. Lynceus also commends a grape called hipponios that ripened in July. The Rhodian grape was a well-known species, and must have been largely grown throughout the island[112]. A bituminous earth found there about 100 B.C. proved very useful in killing the insects off the vines[113]. The Rhodian wine was in repute at Athens and at Rome[114], and was widely exported. Some of it was sweetened with boiled must, but most of it was pure: and a delicate flavour was imparted by just the right quantity of sea water[115]. Cato economized by flavouring his home-made wine in this way, and flattered himself that it passed for Rhodian or the kindred Coan[116]. The Rhodians frequently drank theirs mulled with myrrh, cinnamon, mint, etc., with divers beneficial results[117]. There was much drinking and gambling with dice among the Rhodian aristocrats in early times, often for very curious stakes[118]; and cock-fighting was common. Their fighting cocks rivalled those of Tanagra, and became favourites at Rome[119]. A sumptuary law could not be enforced even against shaving[120]. And in many ways the austerity of these Dorians was tempered with Oriental luxury[121]. The Rhodian youths disturbed Diogenes by appearing at the Olympic Games in more costly attire than any of the Greeks[122]: and in later times the Roman satirists did not spare them[123]. On the other hand there is a story of a grave Rhodian rebuking a Roman lictor for fussiness[124].

Wealthy Romans frequented the island. Its sunny climate attracted them[125]. Cæsar, Brutus, Cassius and Cicero, all stayed there to study rhetoric. Pompey halted there in 67 and 62 B.C. on his way between Rome and his commands in the East[126]. Herod of Judæa came there to meet Octavian after Actium[127]. Nero, who had as a boy pleaded the cause of the Rhodians before Claudius, afterwards talked of abdicating the Empire for a life of leisure at Rhodes[128]. Titus visited[129] the island in 68 A.D. before he became Emperor. Tiberius lived there for seven years. He had been struck with the climate and the beauty of the island when touching there on his return from Armenia, and so chose it for his retreat. He was tribune; but he lived as a private gentleman with a moderate house in the great city and a villa outside, and would stroll about the gymnasion without lictor or attendant, mixing with the Greeks on almost equal terms. One day when he was going to visit the sick, some blundering official caused them all to be brought down to one place and arranged in groups according to their complaints for his convenience: and there was not one of them, however humble, to whom he did not apologize. When the term of his office as tribune expired in 2 B.C., Augustus forbade his return to Italy; and he stayed on at Rhodes. He was now in daily fear of assassination. He gave up exercise with horse and arms, exchanging the Roman toga and sandals for the Greek cloak and slippers – probably the peculiar Rhodian shoes[130] – and retired to the country to avoid the visits of the Roman officials touching at the great city. There he devoted himself to the study of astrology, keeping a stalwart slave in attendance to throw untrustworthy astrologers down the cliff to the sea as they left his house. At last an eagle, a bird then rarely seen in the island[131], perched on the gable; and in a few days news came of his recall. When Emperor he once wrote a friendly letter to a Rhodian acquaintance inviting him to Rome. He was absorbed in his enquiries into the murder of Drusus and was torturing everyone for evidence when the guest arrived, and he absently ordered him to be tortured. On finding out the blunder, he had the man killed that he might not go about talking of it[132]. He had been virtually an exile during the last years of his stay in the island; and many Romans must have lived there in like case, for Rhodes was excepted in the decree of 11 A.D. that exiles interdicted from fire and water should live in no island within forty miles of the continent[133].

Amid the general corruption of the Greeks in the IInd century A.D. the Rhodians retained much of the old Doric severity and quiet good sense. They kept gladiators out of the island, just as they kept the public executioner out of the city and held trials for murder outside the walls. The rest of the Greek world could not rival them in wealth or culture. The every-day duties of life were performed with perfect finish, and even the rustics seemed less clumsy than usual in the gymnasion there. At the Theatre they listened in silence and did not applaud till the end. They dined quietly like men who knew how to order a dinner, and cared more for conversation than for drinking. Their dress was simple and strangely moderate in the use of purple. They did not bustle about the streets; and if strangers failed to fall in with their pace and walked about without looking where they were going, they called them to order[134]. It is significant that a word that elsewhere meant a jester, at Rhodes meant a liar[135].

1. Strabo, p. 654.
2. Diodoros, XIX. 45, XX. 83.
3. Ib. XX. 83.
4. Diodoros, XIX. 45.
5. Ib. XX. 83, 85, 87, 93, 100.
6. Ib. XXXI. 36.
7. Polybios, V. 88-90.
8. Justin, XXX. 4.
9. B. C. H. II. 617, V. 331; L. U. 9.
10. Appian, de bel. Mith. 24, 26.
11. Strabo, p. 652.
12. Aristeides, pp. 342, 343.
13. Ib. pp. 345, 349, 351, 353.
14. Pausanias, VIII. 43.
15. Aristeides, p. 396.
16. Pausanias, IV. 31.
17. Diodoros, XX. 82, 84, 88, 98.
18. Diodoros, XX. 91, 95-97; Plutarch, Demetrios, 21; Vitruvius, X. 46-48; Ammianus Marcellinus, XXIII. 4.
19. Diodoros, XX. 84, 93, 94, 97, 98, 100.
20. Valerius Maximus, V. 2, Ext. 2.
21. Appian, de bel. Mith. 26.
22. Diodoros, XX. 88.
23. Thucydides, VI. 43.
24. Xenophon, Anabasis, III. 3, 4.
25. Livy, XXXIII. 18, XXXVII. 12.
26. M. 1852, p. 79.
27. Dio Chrysostom, p. 621.
28. Livy, XXXI. 23, XXXIV. 29, 38.
29. Aulus Hirtius, de bel. Afric. 20.
30. Xenophon, Anabasis, III. 5.
31. Polybios, X. 29.
32. Livy, XXXVII. 10, 11; Appian, de reb. Syria, 24.
33. Arrian, Anabasis, I. 12, 20, 23, II. 1.
34. Diodoros, XVI. 50.
35. Ib. XX. 20, 28.
36. Aristotle, Economics, II. 15, 29, 34.
37. Quintus Curtius, IV. 8.
38. Appian, de bel. Mith. 108, 114.
39. Strabo, pp. 542, 568; Cicero, pro rege Deiotaro, 1, 11.
40. R. I. 275; N. 353; M. I. A. II. 224.
41. Diodoros, XX. 88, 98.
42. Polybios, XV. 23, XVI. 9, 15, XXVII. 6, XXIX. 5; Livy, XLII. 45; R. H. 23.
43. R. I. 275; M. I. A. II. p. 224.
44. N. 343; M. I. A. II. p. 224
45. B. 2524.
46. Polybios, XVI. 9.
47. F. 59; B. C. H. v. p. 337.
48. B. ad. 2416, b.
49. B. C. H. 1885, p. 106.
50. B. 2524.
51. M. I. A. II. p. 224.
52. W. 251.
53. Appian, de bel. civ. V. 7.
54. Livy, XLI. 6.
55. Polybios, XXXI. 7.
56. Cicero, ad Quintum, I. 1.
57. Livy, XLV. 20, 25; Diodoros, XXXI. 5.
58. Livy, XLIV. 15; Appian, de reb. Macedon, 9.
59. Dio Cassius, LVII. 11; Suetonius, Tiberius, 32.
60. Polybios, XXX. 5.
61. M. 1852, p. 79.

[62] Polybios, XV. 23; B. 3656; W. 251.
[63] R. I. 93.
[64] Polybios, V. 63, XXII. 8, XXVIII. 19; B. 3047.
[65] B. 2905.
[66] Polybios, V. 88-90; Aristeides, p. 361.
[67] Josephus, de bel. Jud. I. 21; de ant. Jud. XIV. 14.
[68] Plutarch, Demetrios, 22. Diodoros, XX. 93.
[69] Polyænos, VIII. 61.
[70] Polybios, XVI. 26; Livy, XXXI. 15.
[71] F. 18; Pausanias, VI. 16.
[72] B. 2526.
[73] W. F. 18.
[74] B. C. H. V. p. 403.
[75] R. H. 23.
[76] N. 346; R. I. 275; M. I. A. II. 224.
[77] N. 345; F. 6.
[78] N. 357; R. A. 21, 24; F. 68.
[79] Cicero, de repub. III. 35.
[80] Sallust, de repub. ord. 2.
[81] Diodoros, XX. 81; cf. Pseudo-Calisthenes, III. 33.
[82] Aristotle, Politics, V. 3, 5.
[83] Demosthenes, p. 194.
[84] M. 1852, p. 79.
[85] Plutarch, præcept. ger. reip. 19.
[86] Dio Chrysostom, p. 567.
[87] Aristeides, pp. 384, 385.
[88] Polybios, XXXI. 7.
[89] Dio Chrysostom, p. 620.
[90] Strabo, pp. 652, 653.
[91] Polybios, V. 88.
[92] R. I. 278.
[93] N. 346.
[94] Pliny, XXXVI. 4.
[95] Thucydides, VIII. 84.
[96] Xenophon, Hell. I. 5; Pausanias, IV. 24, VI. 7.
[97] Aristeides, p. 354; R. H. 23.
[98] Pliny, XXXVII, 62.
[99] Strabo, p. 652.
[100] Polybios, V. 88.
[101] R. A. 26.
[102] B. 3426.
[103] Vitruvius, VI. 50.
[104] Plutarch, de cupid. divit. 5.
[105] Ælian, var. hist. I. 28.
[106] Athenæos, pp. 75, 109, 285, 295, 360, 647, 654.
[107] Varro, de re rust. II. 6; Pliny, IX. 79.
[108] Martial, XIV. 68.
[109] Theophrastus, hist. plant. III. 5; Pliny, XV. 13, XVI. 47.
[110] Athenæos, p. 80; Pliny, XV. 19.
[111] Athenæos, p. 652.
[112] Pliny, XIV. 4; Macrobius, Sat. II. 16.
[113] Strabo, p. 316.
[114] Vergil, georg. II. 102; Aulus Gellius, XIII. 5.
[115] Athenæos, pp. 31, 32.
[116] Pliny, XIV. 10, 12; Cato, de re rust. 112.
[117] Athenæos, p. 464.
[118] Ib. p. 444.
[119] Pliny, X. 24; Martial, III. 58, 17; Columella, VIII. 2, 11.
[120] Athenæos, p. 565.
[121] Anacreon, XXXII. 16; Athenæos, pp. 129, 352.
[122] Ælian, var. hist. IX. 34.
[123] Juvenal, VI. 296, VIII. 113; Terence, eunuch. III. 1, 29; Plautus, epid. II. 2, 115.
[124] Plutarch, de cohib. ira. 10.

[125] Horace, Odes, I. 7, 1; Martial, IV. 55, 6, X. 68, 1; Pliny, VII. 31.
[126] Strabo, p. 492; Pliny, VII. 31.
[127] Josephus, de ant. Jud. XV. 6.
[128] Suetonius, Nero, 7, 34.
[129] Tacitus, hist. II. 2.
[130] Pollux, VII. 22.
[131] Pliny, X. 41.
[132] Suetonius, Tiberius, 11-14, 62; Tacitus, annals, I. 4, VI. 20, 21.
[133] Dio Cassius, LVI. 27.
[134] Dio Chrysostom, pp. 620, 632, 650, 651, 679; Aristeides, pp. 353, 360, 373.
[135] Hesychios, s.v. πυλαιαστής.

V.

THE GODS.

HELIOS was the great god of Rhodes. The whole island was sacred to him, as Cythera was sacred to Aphrodite or Delos to Apollo. The people revered him, the grandsire of the heroes Lindos, Ialysos and Camiros, as ancestor of their race[1]. His priest gave the name to the year. The Colossos was in his likeness, and the coins of the great city bore his image. The worship, however, was not so marked in early times: Athene of Lindos had then the greatest honours. But when the great city was founded, some worship must have been needed in which Ialysos and Camiros should have as large a share as Lindos: and it was probably then that Helios took the first place. His temple in the great city is often mentioned; but there is no record of any temple to him in the ancient cities.

The festival of Helios was yearly, in September[2]. A team of four horses was then sacrificed to him by casting them into the sea[3]. Horses were sacrificed to him in many places; but not in teams of four, nor were they cast into the sea. The team was in this case referred to the chariot of the sun: and within the temple was a statue of the god standing in the chariot with its four horses[4]. But every ninth year in Illyricum a team of four horses was devoted to Poseidon Hippies and cast into the sea[5]: and at Lindos Poseidon was worshipped as Hippies[6]. Thus the custom may have arisen from some blending of the worships. The ancient sacrifice to Helios of white or tawny lambs was also offered in the island[7]. In the games at the festival there were races for horses and for chariots, gymnastic contests for men and for boys, and contests in music[8]. The prize was a wreath of white poplar[9]. The contests were severe; for victors there were victorious also at the Pythia, the Isthmia and the Nemea; and great athletes from abroad, like Marcus Aurelius Asclepiades, thought it worth their while to compete[10]. In the great days of Rhodes the neighbouring independent states and the kings of Pergamos sent envoys to the festival[11]: and it was still flourishing centuries afterwards[12].

Athene Lindia was greatly reverenced throughout the island and abroad. Though Diagoras was of Ialysos, it was in her temple at Lindos that Pindar's ode in his praise was dedicated[13]. From over the sea Egyptians, Phœnicians and Greeks sent offerings to her. Even after her eclipse by Helios, the Roman Marcellus on taking Syracuse in 212 B.C. sent gifts to her temple[14]. She was worshipped "with flameless sacrifices." Fire, it would seem, was made ready and the victim was slain on an altar of burnt offering in a grove on the Acropolis, but the fire was not set to the altar[15]. The sacrifice was daily, and the victims were eaten within the temple[16]. A rock-cut inscription on the Acropolis records the planting of a grove of olive trees there in honour of Athene[17]. The ruins shew that the temple consisted of a cella, measuring externally some sixty feet by twenty-five, with two columns in antis in both pronaos and posticum, and probably a portico of four columns at each end. The order cannot be traced, but was presumably Doric. About the middle of the Acropolis are the ruins of another small temple, which was certainly Doric and of the best period of Greek art. This perhaps belonged to Zeus Polieus, guardian of the city, who was commonly worshipped with Athene Lindia[18]. Athene Polias and Zeus Polieus were worshipped together both at Camiros[19] and in the great city[20]: where Athene Ialysia Polias and Zeus Polieus Camires were also worshipped[21].

Zeus was also worshipped in Rhodes as Pæan, the healer[22]; as Endendros, protector of trees[22]; as Eridimios, guardian of the people[22]; at Netteia as Patroios, guardian of the family[23]; at Camiros as Teleios, fulfiller of prayer[24]; and on Mount Atabyros as Atabyrios[25]. Athene was worshipped with Zeus Atabyrios at Acragas, and therefore probably with him on Mount Atabyros[26]. In the ruins of his temple on the top of the mountain the walls of a cella measuring some forty-five feet by thirty-five can be traced, and also the walls of a peribolos about forty yards square; but no columns have been found. On the Acropolis of the great city was another temple of Zeus Atabyrios[27]. In the temple on the mountain were certain bronze kine that bellowed when any evil was to happen[28]. The bronze bull of Phalaris at Acragas bellowed when a man was put inside and a fire lighted beneath. And it is to be feared that when the bronze kine were heard bellowing on Atabyros the priests were offering baked sacrifices to avert the coming evil. Then a man was always sacrificed to Cronos in August. This custom endured after the founding of the great city; but in later times the victim was a criminal already condemned to death. He was led outside the city gates and then, near the temple of Artemis Aristobule, wine was given him to drink and he was slain[29]. Human sacrifices to Cronos were common among the Phœnicians, and Zeus Atabyrios seems closely related to the Canaanite Molech of Mount Tabor. These rites would therefore have been brought to Rhodes by the Phœnician settlers, either directly from their homes or by way of Crete. The custom that no herald should enter the shrine of Ocridion[30] may point to human sacrifices like those of the Athamidæ at Alos. If the eldest of the lineage of Athamas entered the prytaneion there, the people straightway decked him with garlands and offered him to Zeus[31]. Small bronze figures of bulls (Plate IV.) which probably served as offerings to Zeus Atabyrios are sometimes found upon Mount Atabyros.

Zeus and Hera were worshipped together in the deme Pontoreia as Orolytœ, whatever that may be[32]; and Hera was worshipped in the great city as Basileia, the queen[32].

Dionysos was much honoured in the great city. His altar was probably the chief place in the Agora[33]. His temple was the richest in offerings, and was crowded with works by the greatest painters and sculptors[34]. There also the tripods given as prizes at his festival were dedicated[35]. At his festival at Lindos there were contests, processions and sacrifices: and both citizens and foreigners, whether holding land or merely resident, could be called on to supply a choros[36]. Lambs were sacrificed to him in the island[37]. The Pagladia, a Rhodian festival when the vines were trimmed, must have been sacred to him[38]. He was also worshipped in Rhodes as Thyonidas, child of Semele: a phallic rite[38]. In the great city there was also a worship of Dionysos Bacchos; to which belonged the festival of Bacchos, celebrated with greater pomp every third year as the Tricteris[39]. The Roman Trieteris, which was also kept in the island, did not fall at the same time[40].

90 RHODES.

Hermes was worshipped in Rhodes as Epipolæos, protector of traders[41], and as Chthonios, guide of the dead"[42].

Apollo was worshipped at Lindos as Pythios[43], as Olios[43], averter of death, and as Lœmios[44], averter of pestilence; at Camiros as Epimelios[44], guardian of flocks, as Aeigenetes[44], perpetual giver of increase, as Mylas[45], guardian of mills, as Carneios[46], god of corn, and again as Pythios[46]; at Ixia, as Ixios[47]; again as Pythios in the great city[48]; as Erethimios, Erythibios, or Erysibios, averter of mildew, near the modern village of Tholo, where the temple and a marble omphalos forming part of the statue have been found[49]; and as Smintheus, destroyer of mice, both at Lindos and in the great city, for there were sacred enclosures for the festivals at both places[50]: and these festivals differed from the Sminthia elsewhere, for Philodemos or Philomnestos wrote a book concerning the Sminthia in Rhodes[51].

Artemis was worshipped together with Apollo Erethimios[52]; also at Lindos[53] and near the modern hamlet of Artamiti on Mount Atabyros[54] as in Cecœa or simply as Cecœa, whatever that may be; as Aristobule[55], admirable in counsel, near the great city; in the island as Euporia[56], goddess of plenty; and at Lindos as Pergæa[57] apparently of Perge in Pamphylia. And it was a custom in Rhodes to crown the statues of Artemis and of Persephone with asphodel[58], probably as deities of the nether world.

The worship of Poseidon at Ialysos was in the hands of a priesthood of Phœnician origin[59], but nothing further is known of it. On occupying the volcanic island upheaved between Thera and Therasia in 196 B.C. the Rhodians built there a temple to him as Asphaleios, bringer of safety[60]. He was worshipped at Lindos[61] and in the great

THE GODS. 91

city[62] as Hippies, creator of the horse; also as Gilæos[63], apparently of Gela in Sicily, in the great city; as Cyreteios[64], apparently of Cures in Italy, at Camiros; and near the modern village of Yannathi as Phytalmios, giver of life, with sacrifices of mature pigs[65].

Hestia was worshipped with Zeus Teleios at Camiros[66].

References to the worship of Apollo Telchinios at Lindos, of Hera Telchinia at Ialysos and at Camiros, and of the Nymphs Telchiniæ at Ialysos shew only that the statues of the deities in certain temples were held to be the handiwork of the Telchines[67].

At Lindos there was a strange worship of Heracles. While the sacrifice was offered, the priest heaped curses and abuse upon the hero; not, however, at random, but in a fixed sequence handed down from early times[68]. There was nothing like this elsewhere in Greece; and it may have arisen from some outburst of the Egyptian settlers at Lindos against the sacrifice of animals that they held sacred. "Lindians at their sacrifice" or "Rhodians at their sacrifice" became a proverb for bad language in sacred places[69]. The sacrifice was probably of one ox of the plough. Lactantius, however, says that two oxen of the plough were sacrificed yoked together on an altar called Buzygon. If this was so, the rites of Heracles Buthœnes, the beefeater, had been blended with those of the harvest festival Buzygia at which a yoke of oxen was thus sacrificed.

The temple of Asclepios was an important place in the great city[70]. The guild of the Asclepiadæ, however, was extinct at Rhodes in the IInd century A. D., though the guilds at Cos and at Cnidos were still flourishing[71]. The worship probably came from Epidauros in very early times, but the legends about this have perished[72].

The ancient tree worship perhaps survived at Lindos in that of Helen Dentritis[73]: and all running streams were reverenced in the island, as in many parts of Greece, by the worship of the river Acheloos[74].

Among the characters in Rhodian history or legend Halia[75], the bride of Poseidon, was worshipped as an immortal under the name Leucothea and therefore as a sea goddess: while Alectrona[75], Phorbas[75], Althæmenes of Crete[75], Aristomenes of Messene[76], Ocridion[77] and Tlepolemos[78] had the honours of heroes. It is not clear in what part of the island the temple of Tlepolemos stood. Every year there was a solemn assembly there with a procession, a burnt sacrifice of sheep, and contests wherein the prize was a wreath of white poplar. There is extant a curious decree for keeping holy the temple and precinct of Alectrona near Ialysos. "There shall enter in to the precinct no horse, donkey, mule, jennet, or any other beast of burden, nor shall any man drive any of these into it; nor shall any man bring in shoes or anything made of pigskin: whosoever breaketh this law shall purify the temple and precinct and offer sacrifice or else be liable for impiety: but if any man drive in sheep, he shall pay one obol (twopence) for each sheep[79]." To Phorbas the Rhodians sacrificed for good luck before setting out on a long voyage[80]. Mylas, one of the Telchines, was held to be the founder of the sacred rites Mylanteia, presumably some festival of the millers, at Camiros[81]; and a promontory near there was sacred to him[82]. In like manner another promontory was sacred to Pan[83]; and a third to a certain Thoas, of whom nothing is known[84]. There was also in Rhodes a worship of the Macrobiœ, the elderly nymphs[85].

THE GODS. 93

Egyptian gods of course found followers in Rhodes. Sarapis was worshipped in the great City[86] and at Lindos[87]. The temple of Isis in the great city stood near the walls by the sea, and during the siege by Mithridates a spectre of the goddess was seen to hurl down a mass of fire upon his floating siege engines[88]. Thus the Rhodians gained something from the wisdom of the Egyptians: the phantom goddess that came to the Greeks at Salamis gave only good advice. After the siege by Demetrios the Rhodians by leave of the oracle of Zeus Ammon began to worship their ally Ptolemy Soter. They dedicated to him a square grove within the great city, and built on each side of it a portico a furlong in length; and this they called the Ptolemæon[89]. Long afterwards it remained their custom to chant a pæan in his honour[90]. The goddess Pistis, good faith, seems of Roman origin[91].

Although religious zeal was then dying out in Rhodes, the walls and towers of the Acropolis of Lindos were thoroughly restored as late as the time of Hadrian[92].

The panegyreis, the solemn assemblies, of the Lindians were yearly. An inscription found at the temple of Apollo Erethimios mentions "the panegyris after the war" and also a festival called Dipanamia[93]. A festival called Episcaphia was celebrated in the island, presumably when the seed was sown, and at Lindos there was a sacrifice called Telesthia[94].

The festival of the Doric Pentapolis at the Triopian Cape brought over the islanders with their wives and children, and led to much friendliness between the people of the three Rhodian cities and those of Cos and Cnidos. They met at the temple of Apollo and sacrificed together; and then there were races for horses and gymnastic and musical contests. The prizes were bronze tripods, but the winners were expected to dedicate these in the temple. Once a man from Halicarnassos, Agasicles by name, carried off the tripod he had won to his own house and fixed it there with nails. The dispute arising from this ended in the expulsion of Halicarnassos from the league[95].

At the Olympic games Leonidas of Rhodes was the greatest of all runners. He was four times victor in the race itself, and was twelve times crowned as victor in the heats. No family could rival the Diagoridæ of Rhodes. Diagoras himself won the boxing for men in 464 B.C. Of his sons, Acusilaos also won the boxing for men, Damagetos won the pancration, and after him Dorieus the youngest won the pancration in 432, 428 and 424 B.C. Of his grandsons by his daughter Callipateira, Eucles won the boxing for men and Peisirrhodos that for boys. Rhodes did not reap all the glory of these victories, for Dorieus and Peisirrhodos were in exile when they won and entered as men of Thurii. Diagoras was at Olympia with Acusilaos and Damagetos when they won, and the young men carried him on their shoulders through the assembly while all the people cast flowers on him calling him blessed in his sons. Callipateira was the only woman that ever ventured to the Olympic games. After her husband's death she accompanied her son Peisirrhodos thither disguised as his trainer. She was discovered, and there was a law that any woman found there should be cast from a certain rock; but they considered of what family she was and sent her away unharmed. The statues of the Diagoridæ formed a notable group in the Altis at Olympia. Near them was a statue bought with a fine paid by the Rhodians to Olympian Zeus because a wrestler from Rhodes had cheated, and another bought with a bribe offered by a Rhodian in 68 B.C. to the wrestler

Eudelos[96]. Replicas of the statues of the victors would have been set up in their native island. At Lindos there is the base of a statue of Agesistratos who won the wrestling for boys at Olympia: the men of Lindos set it up[97]. Diagoras claimed descent from Heracles in the male line through Damagetos the despot of Ialysos who was moreover of the royal line of Argos, and in the female line through Aristomenes the Messenian hero who had thrice offered the sacrifice of him who had slain a hundred foemen: and he was himself a huge man and 6ft. 5 in. in height[98]. He was also victor four times at the Isthmia, twice at the Nemea and often elsewhere[99]. His son Dorieus besides his three victories at the Olympia, gained eight at the Isthmia and seven at the Nemea; while at the Pythia no one would face him[100]. Another Rhodian was afterwards victor at the Isthmia, the Nemea, the Pythia and several other festivals[101].

The Rhodians were generous to the gods abroad. At Delphi the Lindians set up a statue to Apollo[102]. In a list of plate in the temple of that god at Miletos are entries:- vase, plain, on pedestal; offering of Peisicrates the Rhodian: another, on pedestal six feet high; offering of Sophanes chief envoy and the other envoys from Rhodes[103]. At Odessa a Rhodian was honoured for giving money to pay for the sacrifices[104]. Near Beyrût in Syria a drinking fountain was set up by a man "from afar, from island Rhodes; a desired piece of handiwork, a bronze image of horned Ammon, pouring out for mortals holy running water[105]." When certain Greeks set up a statue of the god Tanos near Memphis in Egypt, where they were probably serving with Agesilaos and Chabrias about 360 B.C., a Rhodian was among those who dedicated the table of libation[106]. Other Rhodians, however, shewed little respect for the deified Pharaohs by scrawling up their own names on the tombs of the kings at Bab el Molûk near Thebes; one of these names was written in 75 B.C.[107] The gods at Rhodes were in their turn largely endowed from abroad. For example, after the great earthquake about 227 B.C. Hiero and Gelon of Sicily sent ten talents (£2,400) for sacrifices, and Ptolemy of Egypt sent stores of corn for sacrifices and games[108]. Sometimes the Rhodians imposed the worship of their own deities on foreign countries. When Naxos was subjected to Rhodes about 40 B.C. the worship of Rhodos was introduced there, and her priest took precedence of all others[109]. And the priests of Hierapytna were bound by the treaty with Rhodes to pray to Helios, to Rhodos, and to the rest of the gods and goddesses and founders and heroes of the city and country of Rhodes[110].

The priests were not a caste; except perhaps in the worship of Poseidon at Ialysos. At Lindos they were to be chosen from the Lindians alone, and probably there was the like rule in the other cities[111]. In late times when some families had died out and others had grown too poor to hold the office, this rule must often have brought several priesthoods to one man or the same priesthood to several members of one family. Thus at Lindos a man was priest of five deities[112], and in the great city a man and his two sons successively held the priesthood of Helios[113]. Most priesthoods were held for a year, but in one case at Lindos a man held the office for thirteen months[114], and in late times it may have been held for life[115]. The priesthood of Helios was at one time obtained by lot[116]. Perhaps a retired priest had some status in a temple, for the public secretary in the great city, who had been priest of Zeus Atabyrios, dedicated to that god on behalf of the masters of the public slaves[117]. At Camiros there was an Archiaristas, or Exieristes, a chief purifier; and presumably other purifiers[118]. At Lindos[119], and in the great city[120], there were Hierothytæ: fifteen of them at Lindos with an Archierothytes. They had a hall there, the Hierothyteion, and maintenance in it was granted by the Lindians just as maintenance in the Prytaneion was granted by other cities[121]. There was also a hall of feasting, the Histiatorion, in the temple of Alectrona near Ialysos[122]. In most places the Hierothytæ were attendants who slew the victims, but in Rhodes they apparently formed a board appointed by the state to manage public worship. There were twelve Hieropœœ at Camiros and six at the temple of Apollo Erethimios: and the office existed at Lindos[123]. The Hieropœœ generally were magistrates who saw that the victims were without blemish: and at Camiros they were to see that no intruders beheld the sacrifice. In one instance a Rhodian was sent as Hieropœos to Lemnos and to the Didymæon near Miletos, presumably to attend sacrifices offered there by his city. At Lindos there was a Hierotamieus, and at Camiros and at the temple of Apollo Erethimios a Tamieus, treasurer of the temple[124]. A man could be Hierotamieus more than once. Dionysios the historian was priest of Helios and a retired priest became public secretary[125]: but the men who held these other offices were of another type; they became admirals, ambassadors or Prytaneis[126]. At Lindos these officers were, like the priests themselves, to be chosen from the Lindians alone. In the great city and at Lindos and Camiros there was the office of Agonothetes, judge in the festal contests[127]; and in the great city the office of Prophetes, interpreter of oracles[128]. At the temple of Apollo Erethimios there were Hierophylaces, guardians of the temple. They probably managed its property, for they had a secretary and an undersecretary[129].

The territories of the three ancient cities were, for religious purposes, divided into districts called Ctœnæ[130]. Those of Camiros extended to the mainland of Asia Minor and to the island of Chalce, the islanders having some sort of home rule. The inhabitants of each district who had the right to share in the sacrifices to Athene at the city in whose territory the district lay were called Ctœnatæ. This right passed by descent: and perhaps also by adoption. Apparently it was sometimes claimed by intruders who were seeking the position of Ctœnatæ, for it was ordered at Lindos that no one should in future share in the sacrifices who had not before, and at Camiros that the Ctœnæ should be registered and the Ctœnatæ admitted to the sacrifices only in the presence of the Hieropœœ. For such registration the Ctœnatæ in each Ctœna elected an officer, the Mastros, the election being held in the most holy temple in the Ctœna. These Mastrœ superintended religious matters in general. Thus at Ialysos they passed a decree for keeping holy a certain temple: and at Lindos they conducted the election of choregœ, they set up statues to men for their piety, and they passed a decree in honour of men who had carried on lawsuits against intruders to the sacrifices[131]. There was a secretary of the Mastrœ both at Lindos and at Camiros[132]. The form of the decrees is "by the Mastrœ and the Lindians," or as the case may be: so the Mastrœ probably acted as a senate in initiating the decrees to be laid before the people[133]. Some of these decrees are made "with the consent of the Epistatæ," who were probably the chief officers in religious matters. There was, however, in the great city an "Epistates of the boys[134]". Certain Epistatæ sent out by the Commons of Lindos apparently to some of the neighbouring islands are mentioned, but these were natives of the islands to which they were sent[135]. At the temple of Apollo Erethimios there were three Epistatæ and also an Episcopos[136]. At Lindos there were again three Epistatæ, and thirty men were elected to aid them in carrying on the lawsuits against intruders[137]. These numbers point to election by the three Doric tribes and their thirty clans.

Other tribes[138] existed in the island, apparently named from the legendary leaders of the peoples that had migrated thither; for example, from Althæmenes. These were divided into clans, Phratriæ, and these again into families, Patræ. It is notable that some family names are found more than once in the same clan and also in more clans than one. These tribes apparently survived as religious societies based on the sacred rites of the family. The guilds, Erancæ, were open to all, women as well as men[139], and the highest offices in them could be held by foreigners and persons born in slavery[140]. These guilds were the Heliasæ and Heliadæ, the Diosatabyriastæ, the Diosxeniastæ, the Athenaistæ, the Panathenaistæ, the Athenaistæ Lindiastæ, the Poseidoniastæ, the guild of Apollo Strategios, the Dionysiastæ, the Hermaistæ, the Paniastæ, the Asclepiastgæ, the Serapiastæ, the Heroeistæ, the Soteriastæ, the Euthalidæ, the Agathodæmonaistæ, the Thiasitæ, the Pyrganidæ, the Nacoreiœ, the Lemniastæ, the Samothraciastæ and the Lapethiastæ[141]. These guilds broke up into groups probably named from their founders: the Diosatabyriastæ of Euphranor; the Dionysiastæ of Chæremon; the Soteriastæ of Lysistratos; the Agathodæmonaistæ of Philon; the Samothraciastæ of Meson. Then these groups, the guilds themselves, or unions of guilds broke up into temporary branches: the Diosatabyriastæ of Euphranor, those with Athenæos of Cnidos; the Athenaistæ Lindiastæ, those with Gaius; the union of the Samothraciastæ and the Lemniastæ, those who went to sea with so-and-so. These unions were of two or three members, and the members might be entire guilds or groups or branches. They were probably temporary or for limited purposes, for the same guild often figures in different unions. When named together entire guilds take precedence of groups or branches. The guilds Lemniastæ, Samothraciastæ, and Lapethiastæ may have been for people from Lemnos, from Samothrace, and from Lapethos in Cypros, respectively: the Union of the Islanders that set up a statue to a certain Rhodian at Delos seems such a society[142]. At the great city there was a union of the young men[143].

The officers of a guild were the Epistates, the president; the Grammateus, the secretary; the Hierotamieus, the treasurer; the Hieroceryx, the herald; and the Logistæ, the auditors. The members were called Eranistæ, and there was an Archeranistes. This office could be held for many years together and was quite distinct from that of Epistates. The festivals, Hiera, were yearly; probably at the Baccheia. There was a meeting, Synodos, the second day after the festival; and another, Syllogos, the month after the synod, and perhaps every month. The Epichyseis, the libations, was another of their ceremonies. Land was held by guilds and by unions of guilds for their festivals and also for the burial of their members. Thus, an eranist gave his guild a piece of land 50 yards by 32 in extent as a burial-ground: another paid 550 drachmæ (£22) costs in a lawsuit to defend the title to the grounds of a union of guilds, 560 to put the grounds

THE GODS.

in order, 100 for buildings on them and another 100 probably for furniture: and an archeranist rebuilt certain walls and monuments after an earthquake at his own cost and paid over to the guild the money collected for the rebuilding. These men were all rewarded, as were others who had enlarged a guild or paid for its sacrifices[144]. In one case an archeranist receives rewards from his fellow eranists, but in all others the rewards are granted by a guild or by a union of guilds. The rewards were the title of Euergetes, the benefactor: a laudatory speech: remission of all dues payable to the society for one or for two years: a wreath of gold, of young olive or of white poplar: a proclamation at the synods of a man's good works and his rewards: the dedication in a temple of a pillar engraved with a decree in a man's honour. With chaplets of gold the degree of the reward could be measured by the size: thus, one is to be made from ten pieces of gold (£8), another of the largest size allowed by law. With chaplets of leaves it was an honour to be crowned first at the synod. The chaplet of gold was most commonly granted 'for virtue.' One decree orders that a man's tomb be crowned with a chaplet of gold every year in Hyacinthos (July-August), and that his good works and rewards be proclaimed at the yearly synods for evermore; and for this it provides a sinking fund, trustees, and a separate account; imposes a fine of 100 drachmæ (£4) on any one failing to carry out any part of these honours or bringing forward a motion to discontinue them; and declares that such motion should be of no effect. The dedication in a temple of a pillar bearing the decree of a guild in a man's honour required the consent of the Senate and Commons of the city in whose territory the guild was established[145].

The end of setting up such engraved pillars was, as one decree puts it, "that it may be manifest to all that may hereafter be born that the Lindians make a memorial of their worthy men to all time." The Mastrœ and Lindians who ordered this decree, which referred to their sacrifices, to be set up in the temple of Athene at Lindos, directed the priest of Athene to pay for the pillar and inscription and the epistatæ to see that the work was done. The Camires directed the three men conducting the registration of the Ctœnæ to contract at the lowest tender for supplying a pillar, inscribing and engraving the Ctœnæ thereon, setting it in the temple of Athene and fixing it there with lead in all security and seemliness; and the treasurer was to pay the cost. The guild of the Euthalidæ directed their treasurer to spend no more than fifty drachmæ (£2) in setting up a pillar engraved with a decree in honour of a member in the temple of Zeus Patroios at Netteia. The mastrœ and Ialysians, when ordering the temple of Alectrona to be kept holy, directed the treasurers to see that three pillars were made and the decree engraved thereon, and that one was set in the temple and the others on roads leading to it. The decree forbad various things to be brought into the temple, and these two last pillars must have served as notice boards. Three copies of a subscription list for the navy were set up in the great city; one in the Theatre, another in the temple of Asclepios, and the third in the Agora near the altar of Dionysos: presumably for greater publicity. The poletæ were to contract for making these pillars and putting them up. The treaty between Rhodes and Hierapytna was to be engraved on two pillars, one for Hierapytna and the other for the temple of Athene in the city of Rhodes. The poletæ were to contract for the

THE GODS. 103

Rhodian copy at a price not exceeding 100 drachmæ (£4), and the treasurers were to pay for it. Foreign states sometimes engraved their decrees in honour of Rhodians on pillars and set them up at Rhodes. Some of the decrees order the stone of the pillars to be Lartos, probably a local name: it is in fact fœtid limestone[146].

The law against sacrilege protected material honours. Thus it was sacrilege to erase a word on an inscribed pillar, to steal a spear or a shield or a horse's bit from a statue, or even to carry off a faded wreath from a tomb: and for sacrilege a man was liable to torture on the wheel or to death. Mere portrait statues were protected by this law if the formula "to the Gods" was added to the inscription on the base[147]. On capturing the great city, Artemisia set up there a bronze group of herself scourging Rhodes and dedicated it to the gods. The citizens held that it was not lawful for them to cast it down: but they removed it from their sight by building a wall round it and roofing it over, and then proclaiming the place holy ground so that none might go therein[148]. Just before the siege of 304 B.C. when there was still hope of peace the citizens set up statues of Antigonos and Demetrios. During the siege the Assembly was urged to cast these down, as it was not seemly that men who besieged the city should be honoured like those who aided it: but the motion was angrily thrown out[149]. And during the siege of 88 B.C. they respected the statue of Mithridates, though they were daily shooting at the king himself[150].

In late times the custom of setting up statues was abused. At Lindos and in the great city statues were set up not only to the Cæsars and their wives[151] and the officials of the province[152] but to nearly every Roman who touched at the island. Indeed, Romans cared more for a statue at Rhodes than at Athens or Byzantion. To meet this demand the Rhodians used up their old statues. The strategos would take off the old inscriptions and put up others till some figures had done duty for Greeks, Romans, Macedonians and Persians. Sometimes the strategos was careless and assigned an old man's statue to a young man, or an athlete's to an invalid, or that of a general on horseback marshalling his troops to some man too lazy to leave his litter. But when a statue was once named after a Roman they hesitated about changing the name, and the Cæsars were always allowed new statues[153]. Portrait statues were often set up by the people themselves or by their relations. Thus a girl's statue was set up by her mother, her sister, her maternal grandfather and grandmother, her maternal uncle, and her mother's second husband[154]. A cheaper honour was to set up a silver mask: this could be done for nine drachmæ (7/6)[155]. At Camiros they engraved the names and honours of commanders on shields of white marble[156]. At Lindos the same group of honours was commonly granted; and women could receive it with a few variations. It consisted of a laudatory speech, a wreath of gold, a bronze statue, the right to wear a wreath and sit in a place of honour at the sacred games or at the solemn assemblies, maintenance in the Hierothyteion, and proclamation of those honours for evermore. A similar group was granted in the great city[157]. Such honours served for international courtesies. Thus the Commons of Ilios crowned the Commons of Rhodes[158]. In 201 B.C. the Athenians sent a wreath of gold to the Rhodians for their valour; and in 167 B.C. the Rhodians sent to the Romans a wreath made from ten thousand pieces of gold (£8,000), or from twenty thousand according to another account; and then set up in the temple of Athene in the great city a statue of the Commons of Rome forty-five feet in height[159]. Hiero and Gelon set up in the great city a group of the Commons of Syracuse crowning the Commons of Rhodes[160]. In some cases a tenth or a first-fruit was spent in setting up a statue[161].

The road leading up to the Acropolis of Camiros on its landward side seems to have been a sacred way bordered with statues, of which fragments have been found. Many of the tombs in the valley below are rock-cut chambers approached by vertical shafts, like the typical Egyptian tombs; and in many cases large jars containing children's bones have been buried in these shafts after the tomb chambers themselves had been filled. Curiously the finest tombs contained coins of the great city, and therefore were in use when Camiros was presumably falling to decay. The finest tomb at Lindos apparently belongs to the IInd century B.C. In front there have been twelve Doric columns about 15 feet high hewn in the rock, four in the centre standing clear and giving access to the tomb chamber, the other eight engaged. Above these have been architrave, frieze and cornice: and upon that four marble altars. Just to the south of the present city of Rhodes are remains of a remarkable monument, hewn out of a sandstone hillock. On a square base of about 90 feet each way it rose vertically to a height of about 20 feet, and above that there was probably a pyramid. Three steps led to the base, and from the highest of these rose twenty-one engaged columns on each side. These are unfluted and their capitals are lost: but they were probably Doric, as they have no bases. Within are two chambers surrounded by various niches. These chambers together occupy only about a quarter of the area of the base, and there may be others entered by some hidden door. The entrance to these is ostentatiously marked by the altered spacing of the columns. The monument is rather Phœnician than Greek in character, but there is nothing to shew its age.

In late times the authorities merely followed public opinion in changing the inscriptions on the statues of the gods so often that it was hard to know one from another, for all the gods were then commonly regarded as a single power and force. Nor did they spend more on sacrifices than on new statues: they put on their garlands and went to the altars, but they made no offering, and then went their way deeming they had sacrificed[162]. There is, however, little trace of other religions. When Tiberius was living in the island there were many Chaldæans there, who gained a livelihood by casting horoscopes and teaching astrology[163]. About this time Diogenes the grammarian disputed only on the seventh day[164]. This points to the Jewish influence, that might be expected in a great commercial city. And the Jewish community in Rhodes was of importance a century before[165]. The Apostle Paul passed Rhodes on the return from his third journey, but apparently did not land[166]. There is a tradition that he afterwards preached at Lindos: probably when he visited Crete and Ephesos in the time of the Pastoral Epistles.

THE GODS. 107

1 Diodoros, V. 56.
2 Scholia to Pindar, Ol. VII. 80.
3 Festus, s.v. October.
4 Pliny, XXXIV. 19.
5 Festus, s.v. Hippius.
6 R. A. 7, 12.
7 R. H. 45.
8 R. H. 23; F. 10, 12, 13; B. 3208, 5913; L. U. 2; L. B. 201.
9 Scholia to Pindar, Ol. VII. 80.
10 F. 12, 13, B. 5913.
11 Appian, de reb. Macedon. 9.
12 Athenæos, p. 561; Xenophon of Ephesos, V. 11.
13 Gorgon, Fr. 3.
14 Plutarch, Marcellus, 30.
15 Pindar, Ol. VII. 48; Diodoros, V. 56.
16 Suidas, s.v. Ῥοδίων χρησμός.
17 L. U. 55; Anthologia Palatina, XV. 11.
18 R. A. 3-8, 10, 14-16, 19, 28; F. 63, 65, 66, 71.
19 B. C. H. V. 337.
20 F. 17.
21 Ib. 71.
22 Hesychios, s. vv. Ἔνδενδρος, Ἐριδίμιος.
23 J. H. S. II. 354
24 N. 353; F. 59.
25 Diodoros, v. 59; Strabo, p. 655.
26 Polybios, IX. 27.
27 Appian, de bel. Mith. 26.
28 Scholia to Pindar, Ol. VII. 8.
29 Porphyry, de abstinentia, II. 54.
30 Plutarch, quæst. græc. 27.
31 Herodotos, VII. 197.
32 F. 71.
33 N. 343.
34 Strabo, p. 652; Lucian, amor. 8.
35 Aristeides, p. 399.
36 R. H. 47.
37 J. H. S. IV. p. 352. N. 343.
38 Hesychios, s. vv. Παγλάδια, Θυωνίδας.
39 B. 2525, b.
40 R. I. 277.
41 Gorgon, Fr. 2.
42 Scholia to Aristophanes, pax, 650.
43 R. I. 272; R. A. 7; F. 65.
44 Macrobius, Sat. I. 17.
45 J. H. S. IV. 351.
46 B. C. H. V. 337.
47 Stephanos, s.v. Ἰξίαι.
48 F. 71.
49 Strabo, p. 613; R. I. 276, 277; R. H. 43, 44.
50 Strabo, p. 605.
51 Athenæos, pp. 74, 445.
52 R. H. 43.
53 R. A. 4, 6, 8, 15; R. I. 272; F. 65, 66, 71.
54 B. C. H. IX. 100.
55 Porphyry, de abstinentia, II. 54.
56 Hesychios, s.v. Εὐπορία.
57 F. 67.
58 Suidas, s.v. Ἀσφόδελος.
59 Diodoros, V. 58.
60 Strabo, p. 57.
61 R. A. 7, 12.
62 F. 71.
63 F. 71.
64 B. C. H. V. 337.
65 Ib. II. 615.
66 F. 59.
67 Diodoros, V. 55.

68 Conon, Nar. 11; Apollodoros, II. 5; Philostratos, imag. II. 24; Lactantius, I. 21.
69 Hesychios, s. vv. Λίνδιοι τὴν θυσίαν, 'Ρόδιοι τὴν θυσίαν.
70 N. 343.
71 Galen, de meth. med. 1.
72 Aristeides, p. 396.
73 Pausanias, III. 19.
74 Scholia to Homer, Il. XXIV. 616.
75 Diodoros, V. 55, 56, 58, 59.
76 Pausanias; IV. 24.
77 Plutarch, quæst. græc. 27.
78 Scholia to Pindar, Ol. VII. 77.
79 N. 349.
80 Polyzelos, Fr. 1.
81 Hesychios, s.v. Μῦλας.
82 Stephanos, s.v. Μυλαντία.
83 Ptolemy, geographia, V. 2.
84 Strabo, p. 655.
85 Hesychios, s.v. Μακρόβιοι.
86 F. 71.
87 R. A. 12.
88 Appian, de bel. Mith. 27.
89 Diodoros, XX. 100.
90 Athenæos, p. 696.
91 A. Z. 1878, p. 163.
92 B. C. H. IX. P. 109.
93 R. A. 21; R. I. 277.
94 Hesychios, s. vv. 'Επισκάφια, Τελεσθία.
95 Dionysios of Halicarnassos, IV. 25; Herodotos, I. 144.
96 Pausanias, V. 6, 21, VI. 7, 13; cf. Aulus Gellius, III. 15.
97 R. A. 25.
98 Scholia to Pindar, Ol. VII. 15.
99 Pindar, Ol. VII. 80-87.

100 Pausanias, VI. 7.
101 F. 14.
102 Pausanias, X. 18.
103 B. 2860.
104 B. ad. 2060, c.
105 B. 4535.
106 B. 4702.
107 B. ad. 4778, b, ad. 4789, a^2, ad. 4807, d.
108 Polybios, V. 88, 89.
109 B. ad. 2416, b.
110 M. 1852, p. 79.
111 N. 357.
112 R. A. 7.
113 F. 16.
114 B. C. H. IX. P. 108.
115 F. 71.
116 B. C. H. IX. P. 96.
117 N. 346.
118 N. 353; B. C. H. V. p. 337.
119 N. 357; F. 61; R. A.9, 16, 17; R. I. 271; B. C. H. IX. p. 112.
120 F. 1.
121 R. A. 1, 21, 22.
122 N. 349.
123 N. 351, 353, 357; R. I. 276; B. C. H. V. 337
124 N. 351; R. A. 17; R. H. 23; R. I. 276.
125 N. 346; Suidas, s.v. Διονύσιος Μουσωνιου.
126 N. 353; R. H. 23; F. 1.
127 R. I. 279; B. C. H. V. 337, IX. 106.
128 B. C. H. IX. p. 96.
129 R. I. 276.
130 N. 351, 357; B. C. H. IV. 138, IX. 114.
131 N. 349, 351, 357; R. A. 26; R. H. 47; R. I. 271.
132 N. 353; R. A. 15; R. H. 47.
133 Hesychios, s.v. μάστροι.

THE GODS. 109

[134] F. 1.
[135] R. A. 9.
[136] R. I. 276.
[137] N. 357.
[138] N. 345, 352; F. 6.
[139] F. 20; B. C. H. IX. 121; L. U. 61.
[140] B. 2525, b; B. C. H. V. p. 331.
[141] B. 2525, b, 2528; N. 353, 358; R. I. 282; F. 1; J. H. S. II. p. 354; Rev. A. 1864, p. 469; B. C. H. IX. p. 122; L. U. 1, 50, 61, 64.
[142] B. ad. 2283, c.
[143] F. 1.
[144] B. 2525, b; N. 358; J. H. S. II. p. 354; B. C. H. IV. p. 138, V. p. 331.
[145] B. 2525, b, 2528; N. 358; R. I. 282; F. 1, 20, 52; J. H. S. II. p. 354; Rev. A. 1864, p. 469; L. U. 50, 61, 64.
[146] N. 343, 349, 351, 357; J. H. S. II. p. 354; M. 1852, p. 79; F. 5.
[147] Dio Chrysostom, pp. 610-612, 614.
[148] Vitruvius, II. 41.
[149] Diodoros, XX. 82, 93.
[150] Cicero, in Verrem, II. 2. 65.
[151] R. A. 20, 28-30; L. U. 54.
[152] F. 7-9.
[153] Dio Chrysostom, pp. 569, 589, 613, 622, 623, 648; cf. R. A. 20.
[154] F. 11.
[155] R. H. 23; B. 1570.
[156] N. 353.
[157] R. A. 1, 21, 22; R. H. 23; F. 4, 68-70; B. C. H. IX. p. 96.
[158] B. 3598.
[159] Polybios, XVI. 26, XXX. 5, XXXI. 16; Livy, XXXI. 15, XLV. 25.
[160] Polybios, V. 88.
[161] R. A. 10, 13; B. C. H. IX. 106.
[162] Dio Chrysostom, pp. 569, 570.
[163] Tacitus, Annales, VI. 20, 21.
[164] Suetonius, Tiberius, 32.
[165] Maccabees, I. XV. 23.
[166] Acts, XXI. 1.

VI.

ART.

THE materials for the history of ancient art in Rhodes fall into two groups. On the one hand are passages from ancient writers and inscriptions referring to the works of art in the island or to the men who made them. Of the works thus noticed there remain only the Laocoon in the Vatican and the group commonly called the Toro Farnese in the Museum at Naples. On the other hand are several thousand antiquities discovered in the island of late years. These all belong to minor arts that were ignored by ancient writers: but they are of interest now in the absence of greater works. The groups are so distinct that they are best treated apart.

Rhodes was an abode of the legendary Telchines; and in historic times certain ancient statues were called after them, Apollo Telchinios at Lindos, Hera and the Nymphs Telchiniæ at Ialysos, and again Hera Telchinia at Camiros[1]. These statues must have been of metal, for the Telchines were the patrons of metal work just as the Cyclopes were the patrons of stone work. The earliest metal statues in Greece were made of wrought plates nailed to a framework of wood; and these were presumably of that class. The Telchines probably reappear in a Rhodian legend as the Heliadæ. Athene granted them to master with cunning hands every art of mortals, and the highways bore their handiwork in the likeness of men and creeping things. Indeed, they chained up their statues by the legs to hinder them from walking abroad[2]. The Homeric legend of the golden handmaidens of Hephæstos and the gold and silver dogs that kept watch over the palace of Alcinoos belongs to this order of thought.

In the temple of Athene at Lindos was a cup made of electron; that is, of mingled gold and silver. Tradition said it was the gift of Helen and had been moulded on her breasts[3]. The notion recalls the electron masks moulded on the faces of the dead heroes at Mycenæ. There was also "a notable bronze caldron, fashioned to the ancient form and bearing an inscription in Phœnician letters." It was accounted the gift of Cadmos[4]. This reference to the legendary founder of the Phœnician priesthood of Poseidon at Ialysos suggests that the caldron was the gift and perhaps the work of the Phœnicians in that city. The earliest statue of Athene Lindia was a post, just as the earliest statue of Hera at Samos was a plank. Tradition ascribed its dedication to Danaos, the legendary founder of the temple[5]. Like other primitive Greek statues, it was draped. There is extant a subscription list for the renovation of Athene's robes at Lindos[6]; and possibly it was for this statue that Amasis of Egypt sent to Athene Lindia a cuirass of fine linen, wherein each thread was spun from as many strands as there were days in the year[7]. There was another statue of Athene Lindia. Cedren, who apparently had seen it, says that it was six feet in height and made of λίθος σμάραγδος: he adds that it was the work of the sculptors Dipœnos and Scyllis and a gift from Sesostris of Egypt to Cleobulos of Lindos[8]. Cleobulos rebuilt the temple early in the VIth century B.C. and doubtless set up a new statue to the goddess[9]. Sesostris had then been dead for seven centuries: but Amasis was alive, and he certainly dedicated two statues in the temple at Lindos[10]. If this statue of Athene was of Egyptian origin, the material must have been one of the green marbles of that country. The notion that the material was glass is hopeless, for the statue survived a conflagration[11]. Dipœnos and Scyllis lived in the days of Cleobulos; but they always worked in white marble, when working in stone. The reference to these pupils of Dædalos was perhaps suggested by the Egyptian stiffness of the figure.

Among the statues of the victors at Olympia was a striking group of Rhodian athletes. Diagoras, standing with his right arm uplifted, towered over the others. On his right was his grandson, the boy Peisirrhodos; and on his left his three sons, Damagetos, then Doricus, and then Acusilaos: the last wearing the boxing-glove on the left hand and raising the right as if in prayer. The statue of Eucles, the other grandson of Diagoras, stood apart. It was the work of Naucydes, a master of the family and of the school of Polycleitos. The pedestal was found in the late excavations, but not the figure. The statue of Diagoras was by Callicles of Megara; and thus could hardly have been set up before that of his grandson Eucles[12]. At Delphi the great group dedicated by the Spartans after their victory at Ægospotamœ (405 B.C.) included statues of two Rhodians who had commanded on their side in the battle, Timarchos and another Diagoras: both the work of Tisandros. There was also at Delphi a statue of Apollo dedicated by the Lindians[13].

The building of the Mausoleion at Halicarnassos soon after 350 B.C. attracted thither several of the great Greek sculptors; and the neighbouring cities began to collect statues. Cnidos had an Aphrodite from Praxiteles, an Athene and a Dionysos from Scopas, and another

Dionysos from Bryaxis: Cos had another Aphrodite from Praxiteles: Patara had a Zeus and an Apollo from Bryaxis: and Rhodes had from Bryaxis colossal statues of five of the gods[14]. This was perhaps an incomplete group of the twelve gods, for no five were worshipped apart at Rhodes. The material would have been white marble, in which Bryaxis commonly worked when not using the precious metals. It is strange that the Rhodians employed Bryaxis rather than Scopas or Praxiteles: a young Rhodian, however, Alcetas by name, outraged two statues by Praxiteles, the Aphrodite of Cnidos and the Eros of Parion[15]. The bronze group of Artemisia branding the Rhodian State like a runaway slave, which she dedicated at Rhodes soon after 351 B.C., may have been by one of the great sculptors then working for her on the Mausoleion[16]. A similar personification occurs in a group of the Commons of Syracuse crowning the Commons of Rhodes, which Hiero and Gelon set up in the Deigma at Rhodes about 220 B.C., and in a statue, set up by certain Lindians, of their "native land, most beauteous Rhodes"[17]. A masterpiece of Lysippos in the temple of Helios in the great city belonged to this period[18]. The subject was "a quadriga with Helios of the Rhodians." Quadrigæ of many kinds are mentioned among his works, but not another Helios. He had for a pupil, however, Chares of Lindos, the master of the Colossos: and it may be that the Helios was by Chares and the quadriga alone by Lysippos. The material must have been bronze, as in all works of that school. Lysippos did not teach Chares by study of the older masters: he merely let his pupil watch him at every part of his work[19]. But he set the example of a huge bronze statue in the open air by his Zeus, sixty feet in height, in the market place at Tarentum.

The Colossos attracted comparatively little notice in ancient times. As a work of art it did not rank among the masterpieces of Greek sculpture; and in size it was rivalled by earlier statues and was afterwards surpassed. It was, indeed, placed in the list of the Seven Wonders: and to this it owed its celebrity in the Middle Ages, when such lists were in repute. But the list may have been of merely local origin: and in fact four of the seven wonders, the Artemision at Ephesos, the Mausoleion at Halicarnassos, the Colossos at Rhodes and the Pharos at Alexandria belong to the same region and period. The Athenians had employed their booty from Marathon in setting up the great bronze statue of Athene Promachos on the Acropolis at Athens: and this no doubt prompted the Rhodians to utilize their trophies of the great siege of the city of Rhodes for a huge bronze figure of their own national god, Helios. Three hundred talents (£72,000) were obtained for building the Colossos by the sale of the siege-train which Demetrios Poliorcetes had abandoned on raising the siege[20] in the spring of 303 B.C. It is, however, said that Ptolemy offered three thousand talents (£72,000) for rebuilding it after the earthquake[21]: but a tenth of that sum seems more probable. Lucian makes the Colossos boast that he cost as much as sixteen golden gods, to say nothing of the art and the finish of the workmanship in spite of the size[22]. This fine finish might be expected from a pupil of Lysippos. There is a very doubtful story that the Rhodians at first intended the figure to be but half its actual height, and that Chares only doubled his charge when they doubled the height, and was driven by his miscalculation to bankruptcy and suicide[23]. The height was probably 105 feet[24]: but it is also given as 90 and as 120 feet. It may be gathered from a somewhat rhetorical account that the figure was in a standing posture; that it was hollow and was steadied by a framework of iron rods resting on pillars of masonry inside; that it was cast in many sections and built up gradually; that the material employed was 500 talents (12½ tons) of bronze and 300 talents (7½ tons) of iron; and that the base was of white marble and overtopped the other statues[25]. This reference to the other statues suggests that the Colossos stood in some public place within the city, such as the Deigma. The Deigma was in the lowest part of the city by the water[26]. There is now a piece of very low ground near the south-west corner of the northern harbour; and perhaps the figure stood here on the site of the church of Saint John of the Colossos. The ludicrous mediæval notion that it stood across the harbour would have been suggested by the two curious towers at the mouth of the southern harbour rather than by an ancient epigram[27]. The Colossos was twelve years in building, and then stood for only fifty-six years. There was a great earthquake about 227 B.C. which threw down the greater part of the city walls and of the dockyards, and the upper part of the figure broke away at the knees and fell. It was still lying on the ground in the time of Strabo and of the elder Pliny; and its subsequent restoration is most improbable. Pliny describes it as marvellous even after its fall: few men could clasp its thumb in their arms: its fingers were larger than most statues: vast caverns yawned in the broken limbs, and within was seen the massive masonry that had supported it[28]. It is said that when the Saracens occupied Rhodes in the VIIth century A.D. they sold the remains of the Colossos to a Jew for old metal, and that he loaded 900 camels with it[29]. The twenty tons of metal would not, however, load more than

90 camels. The only other known work of Chares was a head of colossal size[30].

The rebuilding of the great city after the earthquake of about 227 B.C. was followed by a sudden development of the political power of Rhodes, which culminated in 190 B.C. during the war with Antiochos and then declined equally suddenly after the defeat of Perseus in 168 B.C. All the sculptors of the Rhodian school appear from the style of their signatures to belong to this period of little more than fifty years. Many of them were men of foreign birth who migrated to Rhodes, and whose sons worked there after them. From Salamis – probably the island near Athens – there came Simos, son of Themistocrates[31], and Onasiphron, son of Cleionæos[32]. From Miletos there came Archidamos[33]. From Laodicæa there came Charinos, "to whom the right of residence was granted[34]." From the Rhodian colony of Solœ in Cilicia there came Sosipatros and Zenon[35]; and also Epicharmos, "to whom the right of residence was granted": and with him there worked Epicharmos of Rhodes, son of Epicharmos[36]. From Cydonia in Crete there came Protos[37], and from Eleuthernæ in Crete there came Timocharis[38]. Then there was Pythocritos of Rhodes, son of Timocharis[39]: perhaps the Pythocritos who was famous for his statues of athletes, hunters, warriors and priests[40]. From Lucania there came Botrys, whose signature (ἐχαλκούργησε) marks him as a worker in bronze[41]. From Halicarnassos there came Phyles[42]. He was the sculptor of a statue set up by the Union of the Islanders to a Rhodian at Delos[43]. A single base at Lindos bore statues of a man and of his son, who were both priests of Athene Lindia, the one by Phyles and the other by Mnasitimos and Teleson[44]. There was also Mnasitimos of Rhodes, son of Teleson[45]. A work by this Mnasitimos stood next to a work by Theon of Antioch, "to whom the right of residence was granted," on a long base for the statues of athletes in the great city[46]. There were other works of Theon in the island[47]: and a plinth was found at Alexandria, apparently belonging to the statue of a horse in white marble, with the signatures of Theon and of Demetrios of Rhodes, son of Demetrios[48]. It is not likely that the horse was made at Rhodes and afterwards removed to Alexandria, for this signature of Theon omits the phrase about the right of residence. There was also a Demetrios of Rhodes, son of Heliodoros[49], and probably the father of this Demetrios: and also Plutarchos of Rhodes, son of Heliodoros[50]. The absence of Doric in these signatures suggests that Heliodoros was not a native of Rhodes. Andragoras of Rhodes, son of Aristeidas, worked in the neighbouring island of Astypalæa[51]: and in Rhodes itself there worked a certain Leochares[52], whose signature differs from that of the great Leochares; a certain Peithandros[53]; and Mnasitimos, son of Aristonidas[54]: probably the Aristonidas who is said[55] to have mixed iron with the bronze in his statue of Athamas at Rhodes that a rust might shew through the lustre of the bronze and thus render the shame of the king when he had slain his son in his madness, just as Silanion had mixed silver with the bronze in his statue of Iocaste to render her pallor. The Laocoon was the work of Agesandros, Polydoros and Athanodoros the Rhodians[56]. Several signatures of Athanadoros of Rhodes, son of Agesandros, have been found: and the order in which the names occur suggests that Polydoros was also a son of Agesandros. These signatures are inscribed on a plinth found at Capri; on another found at Antium with a fragment of drapery in white marble from the statue that it carried; on two very small pedestals found at Rome and at Ostia respectively; and on a fragment of a small vase of white marble found at Olympia[57]. The inscription[58] from Lindos recording a decree in honour of Athanodoros, son of Agesandros, does not appear from its style to be later than 168 B.C. And the somewhat later style of the signatures of Athanodoros is not conclusive for their date; for the Greek copyists reproduced the signatures as well as the works of famous sculptors, and the merely decorative size of the pedestals from Rome and Ostia shews that the works of Athanodoros were copied. The only difficulty about the authenticity of the Vatican group is that it is in six blocks, and that Pliny says the Laocoon was made from a single block: but he may well have been deceived in this, for the joints are not easily detected. Pliny adds that the Laocoon was made *de consilii sententia*, probably meaning, by leave of the Senate of Rhodes or of Lindos[59]. Rhodian guilds could not set up a pillar engraved with a decree in any temple without the leave of the Senate and Commons permission may well have been of the place, and a similar needed for a statue[60]. This Athanodoros, son of Agesandros, was perhaps the Athanadoros who was famous for his noble statues of women. The Toro Farnese was the work of two brothers Apollonios and Tauriscos, who came from Tralles in Caria. There were also statues of Hermerotes, figures half Eros and half Hermes, by this same Tauriscos. Philiscos of Rhodes, the sculptor of an Apollo and an Aphrodite, and Alcon, the sculptor of a Heracles in iron that stood at Rhodes, are also mentioned[61]. The bronze statue of the eunuch Combabos by Hermocles of Rhodes that stood at Hierapolis in Syria must have been set up about 300 B.C., if a contemporary portrait[62]. The numerous inscribed pedestals found at Lindos and in the great city show that much sculpture was made in Rhodes after 168 B.C.: but the group of men who signed their works was extinct, and only one of the later pedestals bears a sculptor's signature, that of Euprepes who migrated from the river Lycos – there were rivers of that name in Syria, in Phrygia and in Pamphylia – and became a Rhodian[63].

The style of this Rhodian school is not clearly known. The inscriptions shew that the works of sculpture which existed in Rhodes itself or were executed elsewhere by Rhodians were almost invariably portrait statues. The statue of the Commons of Rome that the Rhodians set up in their temple of Athene to appease the Romans for the blunders of 168 B.C. was forty-five feet in height[64]. Pliny speaks of a hundred colossal statues in the great city, smaller than the Colossos itself but still very notable. He then mentions separately the five colossal statues by Bryaxis, which were probably in marble; and thus suggests that the rest were in bronze[65]. The statues granted in Rhodian decrees were always bronze, and traces of bronze can be found on most of the remaining pedestals. This taste for colossal works and this use of bronze would mark the school of Lysippos. On the other hand the Laocoon and the Toro are in marble, as are the fragments by Athanodoros from Olympia and from Antium and the fragment by Theon and Demetrios: and a statue by Theon that stood near Lindos was also in marble[66]. Thus the Laocoon and the Toro differed from the mass of products of the Rhodian school in material as well as in subject: and consequently are not the typical works of that school. The Laocoon group was probably suggested by the great relief of the Gigantomachia at Pergamos, which was set up early in the IInd century B.C. when Rhodes was more closely connected with Pergamos than with any other foreign power. The notion of the serpents in the Rhodian group seems borrowed from that of the serpent-giants in the Pergamene relief, and the pose of Laocoon himself from that of one of the more human giants: and though the Rhodian group is in the round, it can be viewed only from the front just as if it were a relief. The Toro also has the air of an adaptation. The figures which form a confused crowd in the marble would group themselves distinctly in a painting; and the animals and plants of the background have been carved as they might have been painted, without regard to the personification needed in sculpture. The same subject is represented in several frescoes at Pompeii: and perhaps Tauriscos the painter was the Tauriscos who worked on this marble group.

Pliny mentions Tauriscos as the painter of a Discobolos, a Clytæmnestra, a Paniscos, a Polynices seeking his kingdom, and a Capaneus: Simos, probably the sculptor from Salamis, as the painter of a youth reposing, a fuller's shop, a person celebrating the festival Quinquatria, and a fine Nemesis: and the sculptor Mnasitimos, the son and pupil of Aristonidas, as a painter deserving a passing notice[67]. There is a curious story that Dionysios the grammarian painted his master, the great Aristarchos, and painted Tragedy in his heart, for that he knew by heart all tragedy: but he may have done this at Alexandria before he settled at Rhodes[68]. Philostratos describes a picture of the descent of Plutos upon the Acropolis of Lindos or of the great city: the god was of golden body, winged, and with watchful eyes, in remembrance of the legend that Zeus rained gold upon the Rhodians when they had been the first to sacrifice to the new-born Athene. He also describes a picture in which Heracles was seen feasting at Lindos, while the ploughman Theiodamas looked on with imprecations; and the rugged country near Lindos was in the background. But it is doubtful whether he is describing pictures that he had actually seen, or is merely suggesting good subjects for painting[69]. There was, however, at Lindos a Heracles by Parrhasios, one of that master's most famous works. "Even as he was ofttimes revealed by haunting vision to Parrhasios in sleep, such is he here to behold," were the verses on the panel: and the painter boasted that the hero, when thus revealed, had put himself in an attitude for the picture. A panel by Parrhasios of Meleager, Heracles and Perseus, stood in the great city: it was there thrice struck by lightning but not destroyed. It had perhaps been brought from Lindos, for Parrhasios probably visited the island before the great city was built. A reference to "all his works at Lindos" suggests that he stayed there for some while. It was there that he placed on his pictures the verses beginning, "living daintily, Parrhasios painted this," and one letter was changed and another added so that they read, "living by his paint brush, Parrhasios painted this." Deeming himself the child of Apollo and little lower than the gods he painted, Parrhasios passed his days in wealthy and graceful ease wearing purple raiment and a chaplet of gold and singing in lightness of heart as he worked[70]. In striking contrast to him was Protogenes, who dwelt in poverty in a suburb of the great city and lived wholly on boiled beans, that no luxury of diet might stay him in his painting. He was a native of Caunos on the mainland opposite Rhodes, but had settled in the island. The Rhodians did not, however, appreciate the great man who was among them till Apelles arrived and told everyone that he was buying Protogenes' unsold pictures for fifty talents (£12,000) to sell as works of his own. The story of the contest between these masters is well known. When Apelles landed he went at once to see Protogenes; and failing to find him at home, drew a very fine coloured line across a large panel that was standing on an easel. On returning, Protogenes at once perceived that such a line could be the work of no one but Apelles: and in reply he drew a still finer line upon the first with another colour, and then went out. Apelles called again and with a third colour drew a third line upon the second, making it so fine that there was no space for a fourth. Protogenes then saw that he was beaten, and hurried down to the port to call upon his visitor. The panel was preserved for centuries afterwards with only these lines upon it[71]. The masterpiece of Protogenes, the Ialysos, on which he worked for seven years, so amazed Apelles that his voice deserted him: but after a while he managed to observe that though the work was marvellous in its laborious finish, it missed the grace that made his own works immortal. Nothing is known of the composition but that beside the hero there was a dog, panting and foaming at the mouth. It was reported that Protogenes worked long at the foam without success, and at last threw his sponge at the picture in a rage: this chanced to hit the dog's mouth and thus rendered the foam admirably. It was also reported he gave this picture four coats of paint, so that as one peeled off another would take its place. There is a story that during the siege of 304 B.C. Demetrios found the great city impregnable at every point but one, and to attack there would have been to give up the Ialysos to destruction: he spared the picture and thereby failed to capture the city. Another story is that

Protogenes was still working at the picture, then all but finished, in one of the suburbs that fell into the besiegers' hands; and the citizens, on begging Demetrios to spare the work, were answered that he would rather burn his family portraits than such a masterpiece[72]. But another story is that it was the Satyr on which Protogenes was working during the siege. He went on painting placidly in the midst of the fighting; and when Demetrios asked how he ventured to stay outside the walls, replied that he knew the king was at war with the Rhodians and not with the Arts. After that courtly answer Demetrios set a guard for his protection and often found time to watch him at his work. The satyr stood by a pillar, holding a pair of flutes and resting: whence it was named the Anapauomenos. At first there was a partridge perched on the pillar: but when the picture was placed in a temple, probably in that of Dionysos in the great city, the people overlooked the satyr and stood gaping at the partridge; and to make matters worse the partridge breeders brought tame birds to hear them chirp to the picture. At last by leave of the priests Protogenes painted out the partridge[73]. Two others of the eleven known works of Protogenes were at Rhodes: the Cydippe and the Tlepolemos. Cydippe was the mother of Lindos, Ialysos and Camiros; and Tlepolemos was the leader of the Rhodians against Troy. And the war ships in a picture by him in the Propylæa at Athens were probably suggested by his life in the island. There were also at Rhodes portraits by Apelles of a certain Antæos and of Menander, one of Alexander's generals and afterwards satrap of Caria[74]. These scattered notices of the pictures in the island scarcely suggest the ascendancy of painting there that permitted reference to it as the Rhodian art[75].

Pictures and statues seized at the capture of Syracuse in 212 B.C. formed the gift of Marcellus to the temple of Athene at Lindos[76]: and a gift from the city of Rhodes to Alexander the Great was a robe woven by Helicon, one of the earliest weavers of the peplos at Athens[77].

Vases with reliefs by Mys of Sileni and Erotes stood in the temple of Dionysos in the great city. That master of metal work always followed designs by Parrhasios, and perhaps made these vases in the island when his prompter was there. In the same temple were other vases with reliefs by Acragas of Centaurs and Bacchanals: and in the temple of Athene at Lindos were similar works by Boethos, the famous sculptor of children[78]. And it was at Rhodes that Dionysios the grammarian modelled from the description in Homer the vase of Nestor with its reliefs[79]. The vases called "Rhodians" were devised by a certain Damocrates as an improvement on a Bœotian rendering in metal or in clay of the Scyphos, an ancient type of wooden vase. Lynceus of Samos mentions them in his epistle; and also a type of metal vase called the Hedypotis, which was invented at Rhodes to rival the celebrated Thericleians of Athens in form and surpass them in lightness[80].

In denouncing Verres for carrying off works of art from Greek cities, Cicero instanced the Ialysos of Protogenes at Rhodes as a work that it would be scandalous to carry off[81]. A century later it was in the temple of Peace at Rome: and the panel with the rival lines of Protogenes and Apelles had arrived at Rome in time to be burnt at the fire at Cæsar's House on the Palatine in 53 A.D.[82] The linen cuirass presented by Amasis to Athene of Lindos was then in Rome, where men of distinction were allowed to try it on till at last it came to pieces[83]. In Pliny's time the Laocoon was in the Palace of Titus: the Apollo by Philiscos was in a shrine of Apollo near the Portico of Octavia, and his Aphrodite in a temple of Juno within the same portico: the Toro Farnese and the figures of Hermerotes by Tauriscos, one of the sculptors of the Toro, were in the collection of Asinius Pollio: and the colossal head by Chares was in the Capitol. Lentulus, who dedicated this head, was consul in 57 B.C., and the collection of Asinius Pollio was formed a little later. The "quadriga with Helios of the Rhodians" was at Rome in Nero's time: it unluckily struck the Emperor's fancy, and by his order was covered with a plating of gold, which left its traces on the statue[84]. It is said that after the capture of the great city in 43 B.C. Cassius carried off all the statues except this[85]: but it is not likely that he encumbered himself in this way during a campaign. A century later there were still three thousand statues at Rhodes[86]: and the island suffered less than the rest of Greece from the Roman passion for collecting[87]. The statue of Athene of Lindos was taken to Constantinople, and stood opposite the statue of Zeus of Dodona at the entrance of the Senate House. When that was burnt in the riots of 404 A.D. these statues marvellously escaped the melted lead from the roof and the falling masonry: and Cedren apparently saw this statue of Athene at Constantinople six hundred years afterwards[88].

The antiquities found in the island of late years have been obtained mainly from tombs on the sites of Ialysos and Camiros and of some town near the modern village of Siana and from trenches and shafts on the Acropolis of Camiros. Unlike these places on the western coast, Lindos and the city of Rhodes have survived till now; and

126 RHODES.

their inhabitants seem to have cleared the tombs round them centuries ago.

A group of tombs at Ialysos has yielded works of that early period of Greek art which has been made widely known by the discoveries at Mycenæ. Terra-cotta vases of this period have been found at Hissarlik, at Thera, and at various other places in the islands and on the coasts of Greece, as well as at Mycenæ and at Ialysos. It may be that these were all made at some one place and exported thence: but the various types appear from their prevalence in various districts to be products of those districts; and in that case the vases from Ialysos, which shew the style of this period at its best, would be of Rhodian work. These fine vases are light and graceful in form; and simple patterns of spirals or of network, groups of shells or water-plants, and very often a cuttlefish, are painted in brown upon the light yellow of the clay. Their style seems unfettered by any system of art and inspired simply by nature. With these were found various bronze weapons (Plate III.), swords and spearheads and curved knives, of types found at Mycenæ: a gold ring that resembles the rings from Mycenæ and differs from other Greek rings in the hollowing out of the back of the bezel to fit the finger: and also a gem on which is engraved the subject carved above the gateway at Mycenæ, the two rampant lions and the column between them. This gem is one of those early intaglios in crystal, jasper, sard, carnelian, etc. that are found in most of the Greek islands, and especially in Crete: they are circular in form, with a thickness of about half their diameter in the centre and tapering toward the side, and are pierced from edge to edge for fitting in a ring or a necklace. A small cylinder of Egyptian porcelain bearing figures of the type commonly found on these gems and a scarab with the cartouche of Amenhotep III., a Pharaoh of the XVIIIth Dynasty, were found at Ialysos with these objects of the Mycenæan period. The rock-cut chambers that form this group of tombs open into one another, and all the objects found in them must be of nearly the same date. If the cylinder and scarab were made at Naucratis, they cannot be of earlier date than the accession of Psametik I. in 666 B.C.: and it is pretty clear that they were made at Naucratis, for there have been found there not only a number of porcelain objects with figures in the style that prevails among the early Greek gems, and scarabs with more or less successful copies of the cartouches of various Pharaohs, but also the moulds for making them. It would also appear that the engraved shell of a Tridacna Squamosa that was found at Camiros was made at Naucratis; for these and other shells were found there in different stages of engraving, and the species belongs to the Red Sea and not to the Mediterranean. The subjects engraved on these shells are, however, Assyrian and not Egyptian in character; and engraved cylinders like that from Ialysos were an Assyrian invention. An ivory cylinder of this type with figures of Assyrian deities was also found at Naucratis; and, as Egypt had almost a monopoly of ivory, was presumably made there. It would thus seem that Naucratis produced the ivory statuette of a seated deity in the Assyrian style, of which the statue of Shalmaneser from Ashur is an example, found in this same group of tombs at Ialysos, and an ivory lion in the posture common on Babylonian weights, with an unsuccessful attempt at an inscription in cuneiform character, that was found at Camiros. But many objects of Assyrian or Egyptian character found in Rhodes were clearly not made at Naucratis. Several figures of a seated sphinx wearing the crown of Upper and Lower Egypt, and a standing figure of a deity grasping a lion in the Assyrian fashion, found on the Acropolis of Camiros, a seated figure of the Egyptian ram-headed god Knef, found at Lindos, and many others, are made of the white calcareous stone of Cypros and are in the style of the numerous figures of the same material found in that island. These were clearly the work of the Phœnicians. The strength of Phœnician art, which had no subjects of its own, lay in harmonizing the subjects it borrowed from Assyria and from Egypt: an its success in this may be seen in some little gold plates for stringing on a necklace that were found at Camiros. Some of these bear in relief an Assyrian sphinx above a row of heads wearing Egyptian wigs, and one bears a deity in relief holding in Assyrian fashion in either hand a lion in the round and above this two Egyptian hawks in the round: but the alien subjects have in each case been brought into perfect agreement. Some of these plates, however, bear reliefs of those thoroughly Greek monsters, the Centaurs. Their heads are like those in Egyptian wigs on other plates, and in one case the border of the plate takes the form of an Egyptian gateway with sloping sides: but the centaurs themselves are of the early Greek type with human forelegs, and have no kinship with the beast-footed monsters of the East. Reliefs of centaurs with human forelegs also occur together with the flower and spiral patterns of the Mycenæan period on large terra-cotta jars found at Camiros. These patterns are again moulded in relief on some of the little glass plates found in this same group of tombs at Ialysos, while a sphinx and Assyrian rosettes are moulded on others. These plates are of an opaque white glass tinted with blue, and sometimes bearing traces of gilding; and are pierced with fine holes from edge to edge as if for sewing as ornaments to a garment. Similar glass plates have been found elsewhere, but only with remains of the Mycenæan period. If the Greeks had made these, they would probably have used the Assyrian rosettes, with which they decorated their terra-cotta vases at a later period, to decorate their terra-cotta vases as well as these plates at this period: and if the Phœnicians had made them in their own country, they would hardly have used the Greek flower and spiral patterns. The group of tombs at Ialysos also contained some rude terra-cotta figures of the Mycenæan type: among them a goddess with an almost featureless face and a body like a post with stumps on either side that might be either wings or arms. Similar figures of a somewhat heavier build, but almost as early and as rude as this, were found at Camiros: but in these the heads, which have been moulded apart, are the same Phœnician renderings of heads in Egyptian wigs that occur on the little gold plates. With them were found terra-cotta figures of a closely draped female figure which belong to a class found at Sidon and elsewhere in Phœnicia. Apart from the legends, the existence at Ialysos in historic times of a priesthood of Phœnician origin implies a Phœnician settlement in that district in early times: and these settlers were probably the makers of these abnormal examples of Phœnician art.

Some terra-cotta vases found at Camiros must have been made at Athens about 600 B.C. They are rude and clumsy, but still plainly enough the direct ancestors of the finest Athenian vases. The decoration is brought to bear on a few rectangular spaces, while the rest of the surface is merely painted brown or left to the yellow of the clay: and the favoured spaces are filled with Geometrical patterns in which the lines are generally straight, or with a stiff drawing of an animal surrounded by little angular ornaments. This geometrical decoration was also employed by the islanders themselves, for it occurs on the polygonal masonry of an ancient Greek fort by the church of Aghios Phocas not far from the modern village of Siana. The importation of vases from Athens seems to have been checked for a time by the rise of a local style at Camiros. This style is marked by the use of the lotos for decoration. But this lotos pattern is not derived from nature or from any Egyptian rendering of it, and differs materially from the lotos pattern on the vases from Naucratis: it was rather derived through the Phœnicians from Assyria, and in fact closely resembles the lotos pattern on the pavement of the North Palace at Kouyunjik (Nineveh]). Two shapes prevail: a large jug of fine form that seems to be copied from bronze, and a large flat dish. The clay is of a rich creamy colour; and indeed Camiros probably owed its epithet of "glistening," ἀργινόεις, to the white earth of the district. In the earlier vases of the style the figures are outlined in brown and partly filled in with that colour and partly left to the white of the clay, the details in the brown portion being marked with maroon and in the white portion with brown. The long-horned Cretan goat is often drawn, but the other animals and the angular ornaments seem borrowed from the early Athenian vases. On one dish the Assyrian subject of a deity holding a lion in either hand is adapted to a Gorgon with two swans; and on another the two eyes often seen at the head of Egyptian tablets appear above a combat of Hector and Menelaos over the body of Euphorbos, the names of the heroes being written beside them in early Greek characters. In the later vases of this style the clay is finer and better finished; and the whole figures are filled in with brown, over which maroon is used to pick out some features, while details are marked by fine lines cut through the paint into the clay. The drawings are, however, weaker; and represent mainly foreign or monstrous creatures, leopards and sphinxes and sirens, with Assyrian rosettes in the background. A curious vase found near the modern village of Siana, which shews the later work of this style on the upper part and the earlier work on the lower, is an ancient imitation. It is not made of the white clay of the district, but of a reddish clay painted white at the surface. A peculiar use of white and maroon upon black on a band running round its middle betrays Naucratis as its birth-place. Several phialæ, or libation bowls, bearing the Naucratite lotos pattern in white and maroon on a dull black ground were also found at Camiros. The objects in Egyptian porcelain found at Camiros would also have come from Naucratis; for on the neck of a vase in the form of a dolphin there is inscribed below the glaze "I belong to Pytheas" in Greek characters, and it is not likely that Egyptian porcelain was elsewhere made for Greeks. Some of these porcelain vases are in the form of the aryballos, the common oil jar for Greek athletes, while others are in the form of a helmeted head and in various fanciful shapes. Many of the later terra-cotta vases of the Camiros style are likewise in the forms of birds and animals and of human heads, and especially of the head of a youthful warrior wearing a helmet. And probably the little bronze vase in the form of a helmeted head inscribed "Cœos made me" in very early Greek characters which was found at Olympia was the offering of some man from Rhodes or Naucratis. Most of these porcelain objects are figures of

Egyptian deities and sacred animals and scarabs: but the hieroglyphic inscriptions on these, as on the scarabs found at Naucratis, are generally blundered; and only a few simple cartouches, like those of Ramenkheper and Ramaneb, read truly. A porcelain vase of Egyptian shape engraved with Athor and the Cow resembles those found in the Polledrara tomb at Vulci; and it was perhaps through Rhodes that such products of Naucratis passed on to the lines of Phœnician trade. Some pieces of Etruscan black-ware found at Camiros may have been part of a Phœnician return cargo. The porcelain objects from Camiros were found chiefly upon the Acropolis in various rock-cut trenches and in a deep vertical shaft sunk like a well in the rock and perhaps intended to receive superfluous offerings. The tombs of this period near Camiros have also yielded a number of vases of translucent glass. The body of these is commonly a deep blue; and the decoration, which is always of linear patterns and never of figures, is in white, yellow, green, or maroon. These were presumably the work of Phœnicians; who would, however, have been guided by Greeks in their choice of form, for the Greek amphoriscœ and œnochoœ outnumber the Oriental alabastra. It may be that some Phœnician settlers made them in Rhodes: and certainly they have not been found in such numbers elsewhere. The local style of terra-cotta vases at Camiros seems to have struggled on against a great importation of vases from Athens that began about 500 B.C. Vases have been found there on which the simple painting in brown on the cream-coloured surface has been retained, while their form is that of the Athenian amphoræ with black figures on an orange-coloured body, and their decoration is a rough and bold rendering of that of those amphoræ.

The terra-cotta statuettes found at Camiros form a fairly continuous series extending down to about 400 B.C. They are for the most part of female figures heavily draped; and do not differ from those found on the sites of other Greek cities. With these was found a terra-cotta relief (Plate V.) of a winged maiden rushing away with a youth in her arms. The relief of Eos (or Hemera) carrying off Cephalos which Bathycles carved upon the Throne of Apollo at Amyclæ about 550 B.C. must have been of the same character; and perhaps inspired this relief, which can be of little later date. The group, which has been brightly coloured is in very low relief, and seems from its thinness and the flatness of its back to have decorated some even surface. It was probably made at Melos, where most of the reliefs of this class have been found. Some children's graves contained their terracotta toys, grotesque figures, and dolls with moveable limbs.

Among the earliest of the long series of Athenian vases found in Rhodes is a hydria (Plate VI. A.) in the Chalcidian style. The vases in this style have been termed Chalcidian mainly because the names written on some of them are in the alphabet used in the early inscriptions from Chalcis. But the marked individuality in the writing of this period makes such a test of little value: and in fact this alphabet is used for the names on some Athenian vases, while the Attic alphabet is used on others which are almost in this style. The metallic form of this hydria seems to be derived from the metal vases of the Phœnicians; and the huge lotos flowers growing up in the upper frieze (Plate VI. A, a) and the lotos pattern above and below it must have been borrowed from that people: while the Cretan goats in the lower frieze recall the vases of the Camiros style. In the centre of the upper frieze is

Cebriones, the charioteer of Hector, standing in a chariot with Hector on his right hand and Glaucos, the Lycian chief, on his left. Their names are written beside them, and curiously the initial letter of Glaucos seems hidden behind that hero's hand and the final letter of Cebriones behind a horse's head, although the names were certainly written after the figures were painted. This group may be merely a scene of everyday life to which the painter has sought to give greater interest by naming the figures after these Homeric heroes. But this same group, though without the names, filled a metope in Temple C at Selinos which dates from about 600 B.C.: and as the subjects of the other surviving metopes of that temple belong to the heroic legends, this group must have been already associated with certain heroes. The central figures of the upper frieze having thus been borrowed from some earlier work of painting or sculpture, the remaining figures of that frieze like the animals in the lower frieze merely serve to decorate a vacant space. The subjects on another Athenian vase from Camiros are of some interest. It is of somewhat later date and in the ordinary black-figured style. On one side (Plate VI. B, b) is seen the combat of Heracles with Cycnos which forms the main subject of Hesiod's poem, the Shield of Heracles. Cycnos is supported by his sire, Ares, and Heracles by his patron, Athene; while Zeus, the sire of Heracles, appears between the combatants. But, according to Hesiod, Zeus took no part in the combat, and merely sat in Olympos thundering mightily and raining drops of blood as a sign to his son. And this must be an instance of the early Greek practice of representing the deity who presided over an action as bodily in its midst. Nicosthenes places Athene and Ares with Zeus between Heracles and Cycnos. On the other side (Plate VI. B, a) Heracles is seen attacking Geryon, who is defending his herds. The herdsman Eurytion lies dead between them. Athene supports Heracles, while the figure supporting Geryon may be the deity of his island, Erytheia. In the earliest art Geryon was sometimes a winged monster with three bodies upon one pair of legs: but the type of three men cleaving together was used as early as the 7th century B.C. upon the Chest of Cypselos. It is said that Peisander, the epic poet of Camiros in that century, had equipped Heracles with the club and lion skin in place of the shield and spear or bow and sword of the heroic age: but Heracles here carries a quiver as well as the club and lion skin in his combat with Geryon, and in his combat with Cycnos wears the lion skin and fights with sword and shield. The Athenian vases found in Rhodes are generally much less elaborate than those found in Etruria, and in their careless work recall those found near Athens itself. But two of them are among the finest extant examples of Greek art. One of these is a cylix of the end of the 5th century B.C., on the interior of which there is painted in delicate colours upon a white background Aphrodite riding on a flying swan. The other is perhaps half a century later in date: it is a pelice, and as shapely as a vase of that form can well be. On it is painted the surprise of Thetis by Peleus: most of the figures are seen in the deep red colour of the clay against the black varnish that covers the body of the vase, but Thetis herself and Eros are painted in opaque white, her cloak is a sea-green and his wings are blue, and gilding is used for details in several figures. The drawing breaks the first law of vase painting – that the whole subject should be in one plane – though the defect is cleverly masked by the stronger colouring of the chief figures: and this suggests that it was a direct copy from some great picture. With this vase was found a small gold box (Plate I. A) bearing in relief at one end (Plate I. A, b) Thetis riding on a dolphin across the waves and holding out in her right hand a helmet, part of the armour the Nereids were carrying to Achilles before Troy; and at the other end (Plate I. A, a) a winged Eros leaning against a pillar and with his extended hands forming a noose with two cords for the game called ἱμαντελιγμός by the Greeks. Protogenes had painted his Satyr standing by a pillar; and his picture may have suggested the attitude of this Eros. Figures riding on dolphins were not uncommon, and were to be seen from the 6th century onward on the coins of Tarentum. The somewhat obtrusive rings surrounding these figures seem borrowed together with the form of the box from gold reels for thread (Plate I. B) on which they are appropriate enough.

The earliest Rhodian coins belong to the end of the 7th century B.C. while the earliest coins known belong to the beginning of that century. The three ancient cities coined until the great city was founded, and each kept faithfully to its first types: for Lindos, a lion's head on obverse and a sunk square on reverse: for Ialysos, a winged boar on obverse and an eagle's head in a sunk square on reverse: and for Camiros, a fig leaf on obverse and a double sunk square on reverse. These sunk squares are a relic of the Lydian custom of merely punching pieces of metal, which was the beginning of coinage: but the double sunk square is peculiar to Rhodes and the neighbourhood. The coin with the lion's head of Lindos and the silphion tree of Cyrene on obverse and the eagle's head of Ialysos on reverse must have been struck at Cyrene soon after 530 B.C. as pay for Rhodian mercenaries. There are coins of

Astyra of this period with a vase on each side, a diota on obverse and an œnochoe on reverse. All the above coins are silver. The founding of the great city in 408 B.C. called for a new coinage: and the types then adopted were those of nearly all Rhodian coins down to the Roman Empire, although varying from time to time in detail. On the obverse is the head of Helios seen nearly in full face with long hair thrown carelessly back. On the reverse is the flower of a wild rose with the word ῥόδιον or merely ῥο and very often the name of some eponymos magistrate and an emblem belonging to another magistrate: a very slight sunk square serving to frame the whole. Instead of the head of Helios on the obverse there is in some cases a head of Medusa with serpents in her hair and often winged: this also is nearly in full face. The heads of Zeus, Apollo, Hermes, Dionysos and some uncertain female deities, which sometimes occur on the obverse, and of Poseidon and Sarapis, which sometimes occur on the reverse, are always in profile, as are those of Helios and Medusa on late coins. In rare cases the rose flower is on both sides. A silver coin of Camiros, which can hardly be later than the founding of the great city, bears the rose flower on obverse and a gryphon's head on reverse. Thus the rose flower may have been adopted by the city of Rhodes from Camiros: and at Camiros it may have been developed from a fig leaf, for the outline of this side view of the wild rose flower is not unlike that of the fig leaf on the earlier coins. The emblems on the reverse of the coins of the great city are very various: helmets, strygils, tripods, tridents, ships: dolphins, eagles, rats, butterflies: Athene holding Nike, Artemis with a torch, and so forth. These same emblems with the name of some eponymos magistrate and of one of the months are found stamped on the handles of the Rhodian wine jars in oblong cartouches. Circular stamps like coins, with the head of Helios or the rose flower in the centre and the name of the magistrate and sometimes of the month running round, were also used for these handles, but apparently at a later date. The Rhodian coins of the 3rd century B.C. bear on the obverse a radiated head of Helios, perhaps borrowed from the Colossos, and are without the sunk square on the reverse. This radiation is not found on the earlier coins of the 2nd century: but about the middle of that century the radiation on the obverse and the sunk square on the reverse were both ostentatiously revived, and the full face was exchanged for profile on all the coins but a few gold pieces. Astyra struck copper coins after the founding of the great city, some of them bearing the head of Helios on the obverse while the diota is retained on the reverse, while others have a head of Artemis on obverse and the rose flower on reverse. The silver coins of Megiste with the head of Helios or the head of Artemis on obverse and the rose flower on reverse are distinguished from the Rhodian by the letters με in place of ρο. The group of the infant Heracles strangling the serpents which appears on the obverse of some silver Rhodian coins bearing the rose flower on the reverse appears also on the obverse of silver coins of Ephesos, Samos, Cnidos, and Iasos bearing on the reverse the respective types of those cities. These coins belong to the beginning of the 4th century, and the letters σ υ ν on them may refer to a political alliance between these states after the battle of Cnidos in 394 B.C.: their common type is borrowed from the coinage of Thebes. During the 2nd century B.C. Rhodes and several other states of the Ægean struck coins bearing the types of Alexander the Great: the head of the youthful Heracles on obverse, and Zeus enthroned with eagle and spear on reverse. The name Ἀλεξάνδρου appears on the reverse, and also something to mark the place of coinage: in the Rhodian examples, the rose flower, the letters ῥο or δι as an abbreviation for ῥόδιον, and sometimes the name of some eponymos magistrate. Gold and silver were not coined in the island after the accession of Augustus, but there are copper Rhodian coins of various emperors down to Commodus. The imperial heads on the obverse are generally radiate, but sometimes only laureate. There is sometimes the head of Helios or the head of Dionysos on the reverse; but more often a full length figure, generally of Nike. In some cases there is an imperial head on both sides: for example, Antoninus Pius on the obverse, and on the reverse Marcus Aurelius.

1. Diodoros, V. 55.
2. Pindar, Ol. VII. 50-52, and scholia.
3. Pliny, XXXIII. 23.
4. Diodoros, V. 58.
5. Callimachos, Fr. 105; Diodoros, V. 58.
6. B. C. H. IX. p. 85.
7. Herodotos, II. 182; Pliny, XIX. 2.
8. Cedren, p. 322.
9. Diogenes Laertius, I. 89.
10. Herodotos, II. 182.
11. Zosimos, V. 24.
12. Pausanias, VI. 6, 7: Scholia to Pindar, Ol. VIII. 15; L. B. 86.
13. Pausanias, X. 9, 18.
14. Pliny, XXXIV. 18.
15. Pliny, VII. 39, XXXVI. 4.
16. Vitruvius, II. 41.
17. Polybios, V. 88; R. A. 19.
18. Pliny, XXXIV. 19.
19. Auctor ad Herennium, IV. 6.
20. Pliny, XXXIV. 18.
21. Polybios, V. 89.
22. Lucian, Zeus Trag. 11.
23. Sextus Empiricus, adv. math. VII. 107.
24. Pliny, XXXIV. 18; Strabo, p. 652.
25. Pseudo-Philo of Byzantion, de septem miraculis, 4.
26. Diodoros, XIX. 45.
27. Anthologia Palatina, VI. 171.
28. Pliny, XXXIV 18; Polybios, V. 88; Strabo, p. 652.
29. Cedren, p. 431.
30. Pliny, XXXIV. 18.
31. R. I. 279; L. B. 163.
32. F. 15; L. B. 165.
33. F. 64; L. B. 200.
34. F. 10; L. B. 188, 189.
35. R. A. 2; L. B. 190.
36. R. A. 1; F. 1; L. B. 191, 192.
37. R. A. 8; L. B. 198.
38. R. A. 3; R. H. 37; F. 63; L. B. 170-173.
39. R. A. 4; L. B. 174, 174^a, 175.
40. Pliny, XXXIV. 19.
41. B. C. H. IX. p. 399.
42. R. A. 7; F. 4; L. B. 179, 180.
43. B. ad. 2283, c; L. B. 178.
44. R. A. 6; L. B. 181.
45. R. A. 5; L. B. 182, 183.
46. F. 12, 13; L. B. 184
47. F. 2; L. B. 185, 186.
48. B. ad. 4684, e; L. B. 187.
49. L. B. 193.
50. R. A. 9; F. 11; L. B. 194-196.
51. B. 2488; L. B. 204.
52. L. B. 195, a.
53. R. A. 10; L. B. 199.
54. R. A. 11; L. B. 197.
55. Pliny, XXXIV. 40.
56. Pliny, XXXVI. 4.
57. B. 5870, b, 6133, 6134; L. B. 203, 446, 479, 480, 520.
58. R. A. 21; L. B. 546.
59. Pliny, XXXVI. 4.
60. J. H. S. II. p. 354; B. 2525, b.
61. Pliny, XXXIV. 19, 40; XXXVI. 4.
62. Lucian, de Syria dea, 26.
63. R. H. 36; L. B. 303.
64. Polybios, XXXI. 16.
65. Pliny, XXXIV. 18.
66. L. B. 186.
67. Pliny, XXXV. 40.
68. Scholia to Dionysios, p. 672.
69. Philostratos, imag. II. 24, 27.
70. Pliny, XXXV. 36; Athenæos, pp. 543, 687.
71. Pliny, XXXV. 36.

72 Pliny, VII. 39, XXXV. 36; Plutarch, Demetrios, 22; cf. Aulus Gellius, XV. 31.
73 Pliny, XXXV. 36; Strabo, p. 652.
74 Pliny, XXXV. 36.
75 Pseudo-Anacreon, XV. 3.
76 Plutarch, Marcellus, 30.
77 Plutarch, Alexander, 32.
78 Pliny, XXXIII. 55.
79 Athenæos, p. 489
80 Athenæos, pp. 469, 496, 500.
81 Cicero, in Verrem, IV. 60.
82 Pliny, XXXV. 36.
83 Pliny, XIX. 2.
84 Pliny, XXXIV. 18, 19, XXXVI. 4.
85 Valerius Maximus, I. 5; Dio Cassius, XLVII. 33..
86 Pliny, XXXIV. 17.
87 Dio Chrysostom, pp. 644, 645.
88 Zosimos, V. 24; Cedren, p. 322.

VII.

LEARNING.

THE central position of Rhodes and its policy of neutrality made it a great seat of learning. Thus it was at Athens and at Rhodes that Ptolemy Philadelphos collected books for the library at Alexandria[1]. But the island lay too open to all Greece for any local style to flourish there, and the Rhodians left little mark of their own on any branch of Greek culture but rhetoric.

Homer was born in Rhodes as in most of the Ægean islands[2]. Next after him came Peisander of Camiros, an epic poet of the 7th century. It was said that he stole his great work, the Heracleia, from Pisinos of Lindos: but nothing is known of this Pisinos[3]. The Heracleia was of some interest: for it first selected the twelve famous labours from the many feats ascribed to the hero by local traditions[4]: it first equipped Heracles himself with the familiar club and lion skin in place of the shield and spear or bow and sword of the heroic age[5]: and it first gave the Hydra more heads than one[6]. Years after Peisander was dead the Commons of Camiros set up his statue in bronze and Theocritos wrote his epitaph. A little after him came Cleobulos of Lindos, one of the Seven Wise Men[7]. He was not a legislator like Solon or a natural philosopher like Thales, and merely uttered maxims like the rest. When the wise men went in a body to Delphi and economically dedicated a maxim apiece as the firstfruits of wisdom, his offering was "moderation is best", μέτρον ἄριστον. The maxim of Bias of Priene "the masses are rascals", οἱ πλεῖστοι κακοί, finds an echo in verses of Cleobulos declaring that mankind is mainly clumsiness and chatter. And no doubt the sea-faring populace of Lindos was far below the despot of surpassing beauty and strength who claimed descent from Heracles, the master of the wisdom of Egypt and the second founder of the temple of their patron goddess. It was said that Cleobulos originated the Rhodian custom that children should go round in the autumn singing the Chelidonisma, the song of the swallow, and begging gifts for the bird on its return to the island for the winter. The singing of the Coronisma, the song of the crow, was a similar custom in Rhodes: but the story of its origin has perished, for it was long and Athenæos was too lazy to repeat it. The extant songs are much alike and demand gifts of a basket of figs, a beaker of wine, and other things which are not the common food either of swallows or of crows[8]. The nucleus of the Chelidonisma was perhaps due to Cleobulos, for he wrote songs and epigrams to the extent of some three thousand verses. His epitaph on Midas, sometimes called Homer's, declared that while the forces of nature endured, the bronze maiden upon the tomb would proclaim to the wayfarer that therein rested Midas: whereon Simonides of Ceos took him to task for comparing with such things the endurance of a monument that any man might smash, and ended abruptly "this is the saying of a silly man." Cleobulos perhaps acted on his maxim that men should make companions of their daughters, for his daughter Cleobulina wrote enigmas in hexameters. One other gifted lady is heard of at Rhodes, Myro by name: she was a philosopher, and wrote a book on the sayings of royal ladies, besides novels[9]. Among the kinsmen of Cleobulos was Antheas of Lindos, one of the founders of the Bacchic revelry from which sprang Greek comedy. He was a man of high station and wealthy, and maintained a troop of Bacchanals whose revels he led by day and night: and the comedies and songs that they chanted were his handiwork. He seems to have discovered the art of forming the huge compound words found in later comic poets, but his primitive comedies were probably little more than personal abuse in dialogue[10]. Timocreon of Ialysos, the scurrilous lyric poet, flourished during the Persian wars. He was a man of position: a guest of Themistocles and afterwards of Dareios. He was exiled as a partizan of Persia; but when Themistocles came sailing round the islands in 480 B.C. after Salamis and restored most exiles, he failed to restore the poet to his native Ialysos, being dissuaded therefrom (so run Timocreon's verses) by filthy lucre, to wit, three talents. In the dozen lines that remain of this ode Timocreon charges his former host with treachery, falsehood, murder, oppression, and giving his guests cold meat. But this was nothing to the bitterness of his attack when Themistocles was himself exiled nine years later as a partizan of Persia[11]. He also fell foul of Simonides of Ceos and parodied his verses[12]; but Simonides had the last word in this pretty quarrel, and wrote Timocreon's epitaph: "much I drank, much I ate, much evil I spake of men; now rest I here, Timocreon of Rhodes." The poet figures in a list of unspeakable eaters, and the Great King marvelled at his appetite. Dareios once asked what he would do after the huge dinner he had eaten, and was answered that he would break the heads of countless Persians: and when he had done this, he remained hitting out rhythmically in the air, telling Dareios that those were the blows left over. As an athlete he had conquered in the pentathlon[13]. His works were well known at Athens. Plato refers to a song of his,

Σικελός κομψὸς ἀνήρ,
ποτὶ τὰν ματέρ' ἔφα,

written in the metre called from him the Timocreonticon[14]: and Aristophanes parodies him in a choros in the 'Wasps', and in the 'Acharnians' chooses to find a likeness between Pericles' solemn decree against the men of Megara and Timocreon's drinking song that curses Plutos[15]. Timocreon has been placed, apparently in error, among the poets of the Old Comedy. The great master of that group, Aristophanes himself, has oddly been called a Rhodian of Lindos or of Camiros: and one of the two great masters of the Middle Comedy, Antiphanes, who was probably of Cios, has also been called a Rhodian[16]. Alexis, however, the other great master of the Middle Comedy, wrote a play about a Rhodian woman: as also did Philemon, one of the two great masters of the New Comedy[17]. But Rhodes certainly gave birth to one considerable master of the Middle Comedy in Anaxandrides of Camiros. He brought out sixty-five plays – the first at Athens[18] in 377 B.C. – and of these ten won the first prize. The fragments are meagre: but this is partly explained by the story that in his later years he carried any play of his that failed to win the first prize straight off to the incense market to be torn up. The same deference to public opinion appears in his lines "pleasure lies in finding some new thought to shew the world: men who keep their wisdom to themselves have no judge of what it's worth." To introduce on the stage 'loves and undoings of maidens' was his distinctive work – the Empress Eudocia calls him quite a horrid man – but there is nothing in the fragments to separate him from the other poets of the Middle Comedy. Most of the fragments have been preserved by Athenæos, and consequently deal mainly with food and feeding: perhaps the brightest notion in them being the introduction of the venerable sea god Nereus as the great author of fish dinners. The poet disputed the order of the blessings laid down by Simonides, first health, next beauty, then wealth, on the ground that a handsome man without a dinner was a wretched creature. Some of his plays are noticed by Aristotle, who praises the disreputable Philemon's acting in them[19]. Anaxandrides himself is described as goodly in aspect and tall, with flowing hair, and clad in purple raiment fringed with gold. And there is an odd story of him that once when bringing out a dithyrambic chores at Athens, he dashed in on horseback and declaimed some of the verses himself[20]. Pindar had perhaps set the Rhodian poets an example of splendour in their daily life when he came to the island after the Olympic victory of Diagoras in 464 B.C. chanting with lyre and many-voiced choir of flutes the praise of Rhodos[21]. That grand ode setting forth the great Rhodian legends was engraved in letters of gold upon the temple of Athene at Lindos[22]. The poetess Erinna, the youthful friend of Sappho, is reported on slight authority to have been a Rhodian[23]: and the like report is made of Philetas of Cos, the elegiac poet of the Alexandrine age[24]. In that age Simmias of Rhodes, who was more grammarian than poet[25], devised those epigrams that take the form of some object from the varying lengths of the lines. Of these he wrote the Egg, the Axe, and the Wings[26]: and he made the words respond to the forms; the Egg, for example, beginning "take this fresh egg of an undefiled

LEARNING.   147

nightingale." He also invented two metres called from him the Simmieion and the Simmiacon[27]. A little after him Timosthenes of Rhodes, the admiral of Ptolemy Philadelphos, invented the Pythian melody for the contest for lyres and flutes that was then added to the contest for lyres and voices at the Pythian festival at Delphi. Its theme was the struggle of Apollo with the Python, and it was in five parts: first, the prelude; second, the attack; third, the struggle at its height; fourth, the cries of victory and of defeat; fifth, the dying shrieks of the Python[28]. Apollonios, commonly called the Rhodian, was born in Egypt: and probably at Alexandria itself, though Athenæos claims him for his own birthplace, Naucratis[29]. His youth was spent at Alexandria among the pupils of Callimachos, and in his later years he filled there the great office of President of the Library. But the best forty years of his life were passed at Rhodes, where he received the citizenship: and in his works he preferred to describe himself as the Rhodian. His genius was wasted in the hopeless task of reviving Greek epic. The Argonautica, an affair of some six thousand verses still extant, was produced before he was twenty. The storm of ridicule that it raised drove him from Alexandria to his retirement at Rhodes, where he divided his days between a war of coarse words with Callimachos, who had satirized him as an Ibis[30], and a revision of his poem. In its new form it succeeded as completely as it had failed before: and now faultlessly polished and purged of all vigour it became a standard of Alexandrine taste and had some influence with the Roman poets[31]. He also wrote epics on the founding of several cities, Naucratis, Alexandria, Cnidos, Caunos and Rhodes: but of Canopos he apparently wrote in choliambics, a metre sacred to sarcasm. The remaining fragment of the Founding of Rhodes may refer to the legend of Phorbas. A little before him Antagoras of Rhodes had written an epic, the Thebais. This he recited to the Thebans, but they failed to detect its beauties: and he stopped abruptly, declaring they were rightly named Bœotians (βοιωτοί) for they had the ears of oxen (βοῶν ὦτα)[32]. The poem is lost. One of his epigrams celebrates a bridge erected by Xenocles of Lindos on the road to a temple of Demeter[33]. Antagoras passed most of his life in Macedon as court poet to Antigonos Gonatas: and there is a story that Antigonos, seeing the poet absorbed in cooking a conger eel in camp, asked whether Homer used to cook eels when he wrote Agamemnon's deeds, and was asked in return whether Agamemnon troubled himself about the cooking of eels when he did those deeds. Antagoras would not trust the cooking of his delicacies to a slave or even to his own mother: and for this he is duly commanded by Athenæos, who gives him a place in a select catalogue of epicures[34]. There also lived at Rhodes a certain Idæos, who wrote some three thousand verses on his own account about his native island and then augmented and improved the Homeric poems by setting a line of his own between each two of Homer's; Euodos, an epic poet of Nero's time, a perfect marvel at Latin verse; and Pitholeon, who wrote his poems in a mongrel dialect of Greek and Latin[35]: happily their works have perished.

The many names given to the island, Æthræa, Asteria, Atabyria, Corymbia, Macaria, Oloessa, Ophiusa, Pelagia, Pœessa, Stadia, Telchinis, Trinacria, seem merely poetic[36]. There is no trace of the common use of any of them.

Some ten or twelve Rhodian philosophers are known, Peripatetics and Stoics: none of any great weight as original thinkers, but some of them of importance in formulating or in propagating the doctrines of their school. That some Rhodians were Peripatetics was a mere matter of chance: but Stoicism, the philosophy of the Levant, naturally took deeper root at Rhodes, and a school flourished there for at least a century.

The story goes that a little before Aristotle's death his disciples asked him to name one to succeed him. He evaded their request, but soon after asked for Rhodian and for Lesbian wine. "A sound wine and pleasant", said he tasting the Rhodian: and then tasting the Lesbian, "both thoroughly good, but" (apparently quoting Alexis) "sweeter is the Lesbian." And on his death Theophrastos the Lesbian was preferred to Euderlos the Rhodian as chief of the school[37]. But Eudemos did good work for the school in his copious writings to expound Aristotle's views. Able as he was, he was content to make himself a mere echo of his master[38]. But the voice of the echo was sometimes weaker and less distinct than the original voice. And in the last book of the Eudemian Ethics, which are presumably the work of Eudemos, the disciple falls to a more commonplace sphere than in the previous books in which he was inspired by the Nicomachæan Ethics of the master himself. The original draught of the Metaphysics was lent to Eudemos; but he died while editing it, and the manuscript disappeared. The work as it now stands is mainly a patchwork from Aristotle's other writings, but the excrescence known as ἁ ἔλαττον is said to be the work of Pasicles, a brother of Eudemos and like him a disciple of Aristotle[39]. It may be noted that Mentor the Rhodian was the satrap of western Asia Minor who in 343 B.C. treacherously seized and deposed Aristotle's friend, Hermeias of Atarneus[40]. It is said that Praxiphanes of Rhodes, a Peripatetic and disciple of Theophrastos[41] taught Epicuros[42]: and a little later, Hieronymos of Rhodes, a distinguished Peripatetic, accepted without qualification the doctrine that absence of pain formed the chief good, and consequently was sometimes reckoned a follower of Epicuros[43]. But only one Rhodian, Eucratidas by name, is found among professed Epicureans. The Senate of Brundusium voted a piece of ground for his tomb, but nothing more is known of him[44]. Among the Peripatetics there was no other Rhodian of note till Andronicos, the great editor and chief of the school in the Ist century B.C. Theophrastos had bequeathed his own manuscripts and those of Aristotle that he had to Neleus of Scepsis. After keeping them for a century and a half in a damp cellar, the family of Neleus sold what the worms had left to Apellicon, a collector at Athens. The school gained new life from all these works that had hitherto been out of their reach: but Apellicon was sending out copies full of blunders, for he was a true collector and careless of the contents of books. In 84 B.C. Sulla carried off Apellicon's library to Rome, and there Tyrannion went to work on the manuscripts. Andronicos, who had probably met Tyrannion when that grammarian was studying at Rhodes, obtained copies from him and then brought out a complete edition, rejecting the spurious works and classifying and arranging the rest, which seem previously to have been arranged by chance or at best chronologically. This edition is probably the Aristotle of to-day[45].

There is a very doubtful story that Aristippos of Cyrene, the disciple of Socrates and founder of the Cyrenaic school, taught at Rhodes. He had been shipwrecked off the island; and when he had made some money by his teaching, he lectured his fellow-passengers, who had lost everything, on the advantage of carrying goods that could swim ashore with them[46]. Melanthios of Rhodes, a finished writer, appears among the Academics[47]: and Antonios of Rhodes, who accompanied Porphyry from Greece to Rome in 263 A.D. on his first visit to Plotinos, was perhaps a Neo-Platonist[48].

The Rhodian Stoics all belong to the period of transition between the formulation of the Stoic doctrine by philosophers at Athens and its acceptance by generals and statesmen at Rome. Perhaps the ablest of them and certainly the most successful was Panætios. Coming of a stock famed at Rhodes for generals and athletes and himself a thorough man of the world[49], he saw how to adapt the primitive Stoicism to its new sphere. He abandoned the traditional pedantry in speech and narrowness in study; and Plato and Aristotle were always in his mouth. Instead of going about denying that pain was an evil, he was content with casual speculations on its nature. He softened down the rigid Stoic standard of virtue to meet the needs of trade, as in the well-known opinion that a merchant coming to Rhodes with a cargo of corn in time of scarcity was not morally bound to disclose the fact that other corn ships were coming up from Egypt before selling at famine prices[50]. He represented popular religion as a purely political institution; and went somewhat further than most Stoics cared to follow in wholly denying the immortality of the soul and casting grave doubts on augury[51]. It may be noted that Pythagoras of Rhodes, who draws a touching picture of how terribly the less energetic gods must be bored by constant attendance at the sacrifices in their honour, was presumably a Stoic[52]. The friendship of the younger Scipio Africanus gave Panætios the opportunity of influencing Roman society. He was that general's sole companion on the embassy to the East in 143 B.C.; and afterwards lived for years as an honoured guest at his house, which was then the meeting place of the ablest men at Rome. There he would dispute with them while Polybios looked on, and through them he made Stoicism the fashionable philosophy of Rome[53]. The systematic treatment of the Stoics, which was applied by Stilo, Scævola, Tubero, and others to Roman philology and jurisprudence, must have been derived from him. And he apparently introduced the vastly important notion of the *Jus Gentium*, which mainly made Roman law a great system: and the development of that law from his time down to its great age under the Stoic Antonines was mainly at the hands of Stoics. In philosophy Cicero based his *de Officiis* on a treatise by Panætios on the same subject, and seems indebted to him for the material for some other works[54]. Among the Rhodian disciples of Panætios were Hecato, a copious writer on philosophy and a man of some weight with the Roman Stoics[55], a certain Plato[56] and Stratocles[57]: but he was succeeded in the school at Rhodes by Poseidonios of Apamea[58]. Though a Syrian by birth, Poseidonios was thoroughly identified with Rhodes: he filled the high office of prytanis[59], and was ambassador to Rome in 86 B.C., when he came in contact with Marius[60], and apparently again in his old age in 51 B.C. just before the Civil War[61]. He suffered much from gout[62], but the physical strength that gained for him the name of "the athlete" enabled him to bear his sufferings in the true spirit of his sect: and Pompey, who visited him at Rhodes[63] in 67 and again in 62 B.C., often told how the philosopher had discoursed to him from his sick bed on the theme that nothing was good save what was honourable, pausing at the paroxysms of his attack to declare that pain was not an evil[64]. Cicero studied under him and remained his intimate friend and correspondent[65]. Among his Rhodian disciples were his daughter's son Jason, who succeeded him in the school[66], and probably Leonides[67]. But it was less as a philosopher that Poseidonios was celebrated than as a traveller and historian and the best informed man of his day[68].

Rhodes was of some importance in ancient geography as the point of intersection of the primary meridian of Eratosthenes (about 250 B.C.) with his primary parallel of latitude. The one passed through Merowé, Assouan, Alexandria, Rhodes and Constantinople; and the other through the Straits of Gibraltar and of Messina, Cape Matapan, Rhodes and Alexandretta Bay[69]: both of them somewhat wavy lines when traced on a modern map. This primary parallel had already been used by Dicæarchos some fifty years earlier[70]. The measurement of the circumpolar circumference of the earth by Poseidonios was made upon this meridian on the arc between Alexandria and Rhodes. Eratosthenes had already made observations with the gnomon at both ends of this arc to determine its length[71], but had apparently deduced his result from his own calculation of the circumpolar circumference which was based on a false estimate of the arc between Alexandria and Assouan: and he put the arc at 375 geographical miles instead of 330. The sailors put it at 500; and this estimate was used by Poseidonios in obtaining his result of 24,000 geographical miles for the circumference, an error of observation of the star Canopos cancelling to some extent the error of measurement[72]. His result is also given[73] as 18,000 geographical miles, which would be obtained by putting the arc at 375 instead of 500 without correcting the error of observation. One result is as much above the true value as the other is below it, but his method was sound. The length of the parallel through Rhodes, which is really rather over 17,000 geographical miles, was estimated by Eratosthenes at 20,000 and by Poseidonios at 14,000. Curiously both of them considered sailing round this parallel westward to India; Poseidonios, who knew of the upheaval of an island in the Lipari group in his own lifetime, conjecturing that as the great island of Atlantis was not then to be found, it might have subsided in some volcanic change[74]. Mount Atabyros in Rhodes was among the mountains whose vertical height was calculated by Dicæarchos, apparently the earliest student of this problem, his result was fourteen stades; just double the true height[75]. Geminos uses several observations made at Rhodes, and perhaps resided there[76]. A certain Bacorus of Rhodes is named as a geographer[77]. And a catalogue of notable geographers includes two Rhodians who were otherwise famous: Timosthenes, the inventor of the Pythian melody, and Eudoxos, the historian. As admiral to Ptolemy Philadelphos, Timosthenes was able to explore the western Mediterranean when it was as yet little known to the Greeks; and he wrote technical works on Islands, on Distances –afterwards edited by Eratosthenes – and on Harbours[78]. The tides were never thoroughly understood by the Greeks, who saw nothing but the almost tideless Mediterranean, till Poseidonios made his observations on the Atlantic coast at Cadiz. He then stated accurately the dependence of the daily tides on the moon's position and of the spring and neap tides on the relative position of moon and sun[79]. He also made a sphere to shew the movements of sun and moon and planets; and Cicero considered how it would impress the barbarians in Britain[80].

Little is left of the many histories written by Rhodians. Thus, some remarks on a remedy for the liver alone remain from Cleitophon's history of India[81]. Poseidonios wrote the most ponderous of these histories; and in this he embodied the notes made during his wide travels. Each writer who quotes it finds it a quarry for facts on his own subject. Athenæos can quote him on the frugality of the Romans and the luxury of the Syrians and of the Parthian kings; on the sacrificial feasts of Etruria and the surfeiting of Alexandria; and on barbarian feasts, at which the Celts would alternately listen to their bards and fight, and the Carmani would pledge their friendships in cups of each other's blood[82]. Strabo can quote him on the Parthian constitution, the invasions of the Chersonese, and the sacking of Tolosa[83]. Plutarch can quote him for details about Fabius Maximus, Marcellus, Marius and Brutus[84]. Josephus, however, finds fault with him for errors in describing the interior of the temple at Jerusalem[85]. From the tin mines of Britain and the naphtha wells of Babylon to the turnips and carrots of Dalmatia, nothing comes amiss to him: and here and there is a touch of the man himself; how he laughed at the monkeys in Libya, and how he accustomed himself after a time to the Gauls' habit of adorning their front doors with the heads of their enemies[86]. The histories of India and of Galatia by Cleitophon[87], the history of Ætolia by Diocles[88], the local histories by Dionysios the priest of Helios[89], the history of the kingdom of Egypt by Evagoras of Lindos[90], the histories by Eudoxos[91], and the history of Crete by Sosicrates[92], appear from their scanty fragments to have been equally comprehensive. Antipater[93], Dionysios the grammarian[94], Epimenides[95], Ergeias[96], Eucrates[97], Jason the Stoic[98], Polyzelos[99] and Zeno[100] wrote on the history of Rhodes itself, some of them setting rather wide bounds to their subject: while others wrote on its customs, as Theognis[101] and Gorgon[102] on the sacrifices, Agnocles on the Coronistæ[103], and Philodemos or Philomnestos on the Sminthia[104]. Zeno was less known for his chronicle of Rhodes than for his history, of his own times. His contemporary Antisthenes wrote a like work. They were not professional writers, and had taken up philosophical history as becoming work for statesmen: but Polybios, while reckoning them the leading authorities on the events of that time charges them with caring more for rounding their periods than for looking up their facts. He shows how Zeno contradicts himself in his account of the battle of Panion in 198 B.C. and blunders over the topography of the Peloponnesos in relating the campaign against Nabis three years later, and he points out the folly of both Zeno and Antisthenes in calling the Rhodian defeat off Lade in 201 B.C. a victory, when the admiral's despatch was still extant in the Prytaneion at Rhodes to confute them. It is notable that Polybios, who had been on friendly terms with Zeno, makes these criticisms purely in self-defence to secure a hearing for his own work[105]. This Zeno seems to be the Rhodian historian cited as an authority in the reference by Samos and Priene of a disputed claim to territory to the arbitration of Rhodes[106]. Callixenos, Socrates and Empylos also wrote on events of their own day. The well-known description of Ptolemy Philopator's state vessels, the great sea-going ship and the Nile boat, and of Ptolemy Philadelphos' pavilion and procession come from Callixenos[107]. He is very precise; noting, for example, in the procession a car 30 feet long and 24 feet broad, drawn by 300 men, and thereon a wine press 36 feet by 221: but he clearly thinks no more of the 100 marble statues by the first masters than of the gilded thunderbolt 60 feet long, and ends with an estimate of the value of the plate. With the same tendency to inventory Socrates relates the festivals of Antony and of Cleopatra in his book on the Civil War[108]. Empylos' book on the Slaying of Cæsar, written by a dependent of Brutus and entitled Brutus, must have been a mere party pamphlet[109]. Castor[110], the author of one of the lists of powers holding the Thalassocratia, confined himself to fixing the dates of events. His general chronography came down to 56 B.C., his chronography of Rome ending five years earlier[111].

There are a few stray facts about various branches of learning. Aristeas of Rhodes invented one of the remedies called Acharistos, thankless; for the patient was so quickly cured that he did not know in what danger he had been, and was not duly grateful to his physician[112]. And Cleomenes of Lindos discovered strange and drastic remedies for horses[113]. On the other hand Chrysippos of Rhodes was the physician who aided Queen Arsinoe in her attempt to poison Ptolemy Philadelphos[114]. Timachidas of Rhodes was the author of a huge epic poem entitled Dinners, and Parmenon of Rhodes wrote the School of Cookery[115]. Pythion and Epigenes the Rhodians were notable writers on agriculture[116]. Theodotas or Theodoros, the Rhodian general who won for Antiochos Soter his victory over the Gauls by an ambuscade of elephants[117], treated of the tactics of his own day in his Commentaries[118]; while Stratocles the Stoic a Rhodian statesman and man of letters[119] wrote on Military Tactics in Homer[120]. The Rhodians Attalos[121], Aristoteles[122], and Timarchos or Timachidas[123] are named as commentators; and Aristocles the orator and Aristeas as grammarians[124]. The famous grammarian Dionysios surnamed Thrax was a native of Alexandria, but migrated to Rhodes about 100 B.C. and thenceforth called himself a Rhodian. He had himself been a disciple of the great Aristarchos, and among his own disciples was Tyrannion, who was perhaps a Lindian on the mother's side[125]. Of his many works there remains only part of his grammar, the ancestor of all grammars. His definition of the subject is wide, leading up through "the offhand rendering of phrases and narratives" to "the criticism of poems": but unfortunately it is only the most elementary part that survives[126]. When Tiberius was at Rhodes, a grammarian named Diogenes was disputing there every seventh day. The future emperor, who regularly attended learned disputes and sometimes took part in them, called on Diogenes, but was received with a message that he might come on the seventh day. And when the grammarian afterwards presented himself at Rome to salute the emperor, he was told that he might come in the seventh year[127]. Abron, another Rhodian grammarian, was established at Rome in the days of Augustus[128].

The Rhodian orators, in the opinion of some Romans, formed a third school of oratory beside the Athenian and the Asiatic. But this school, if there was such, had nothing apart from those two great schools, and was at most eclectic. Thus Cicero derives both the Asiatic and the Rhodian styles from the Athenian; and distinguishes them only in this, that the Asiatic had lost the terse and chaste style of Athens more than the Rhodian[129]. And Quintilian considers the Rhodian style a mere compound of the style of Asia with the style of Athens, or rather with the style of Æschines[130]. That orator had settled for a while at Rhodes after his retirement from Athens in 330 B.C. and had apparently given systematic instruction in rhetoric there. It was there that he recited to the citizens his speech against Ctesiphon, and then that of Demosthenes on the Crown, adding when they applauded both "had ye but heard the man himself", or as others report "had ye but heard the beast itself bellowing out its own words". And the founding of the ῥοδιακὸν διδασκαλεῖον, which was apparently for the teaching of rhetoric, was attributed to him[131]. On the other hand Dionysios calls the Rhodian orators Artamenes, Aristocles, Philagrios and Apollonios followers of Hypereides; saying, however, that they missed his grace and power in their imitation, and proved deficient in finish[132]. But though Rhodian oratory is thus derived from the Athenian of the 4th century, there is little trace of its eminence before the 1st century B.C. In the 3rd century Hieronymos the Peripatetic wrote on rhetoric[133], and it is said that Apollonios Rhodios taught rhetoric[134], but the poet has probably been confused with the later orators named Apollonios. The speech which the Rhodian envoy Astyimedes addressed to the Roman Senate in 167 B.C. just after the war with Perseus seems to have been a piece of exaggerated declamation, unsuited to the time and the place: and when he published it, it was universally condemned by the Greeks then at Rome. His successful speech to the Senate three years later was apparently confined to facts and figures[135]. The Rhodian style of the 1st century seems to have been formed by two disciples of the graceful and epigrammatic orators Hierocles and Menecles of Alabanda, who were then at the head of the Asiatic school[136]. Apollonios surnamed Malacos had migrated from Alabanda to Rhodes before

120 B.C., when Scævola heard him, and found that he smiled at philosophy and spoke with less gravity than wit[137]. The more famous Apollonios surnamed Molon came from Alabanda to Rhodes a generation later. He was at Rome as Rhodian envoy in 88 and in 81 B.C., and was the first foreigner who addressed the Senate without an interpreter[138]. Cicero made his acquaintance in Rome; and in 78 B.C., after hearing the orators of Athens and of Asia, came on to Rhodes to study under him. He calls him a consummate advocate and excellent writer as well as a skilful teacher; and admits that his own style was then shorn of some of its youthful redundancy[139]. Cæsar also came to Rhodes to study under Apollonios either just before or just after the impeachment of Dolabella in 79 B.C.[140]. It is stated that Pompey heard the rhetorician Hermagoras at Rhodes in 62 B.C. But Hermagoras of Temnos was then dead, and the younger Hermagoras was not yet born. And a preceding statement that during this visit to the island Pompey heard all the sophists and presented them each with a talent (£240) does not make the tale more credible[141]. Brutus and Cassius both studied rhetoric in the island[142]. And when Cassius afterwards threatened Rhodes, Archelaos, in whose didasjake²om he had studied, was sent to plead with him for the city and made a lengthy speech with tears and all fitting gestures but without result[143]. When the city was taken, the citizens with strange want of tact greeted Cassius as lord and king, and were answered that he was no lord and king – he killed lords and kings[144]. Theodoros of Gadara, who called himself a Rhodian, instructed Tiberius in rhetoric at Rhodes, and perhaps previously at Rome when the emperor was a boy[145]. And when he founded the sect of orators opposed to that of Apollodoros of Pergamos, the

teacher of Augustus, Tiberius declared himself a Theodorean[146]. Empylos the writer was also a rhetorician[147]. Castor the chronographer was a rhetorician and a writer on rhetoric[148]. Evagoras the historian[149] and a certain Athenodoros[150] also wrote on rhetoric. And even Poseidonios was once carried away by the prevalent rhetoric and revelled in hyperbole[151]. Tacitus records an opinion that by the advocacy of some of the Rhodian orators anyone could gain anything[152]. But the cause of Rhodes was often served by foreign speakers. In the first Athenian Empire Antiphon spoke for the Lindians in the matter of their tribute[153]. When Artemisia occupied Rhodes, Demosthenes delivered his speech in favour of the Independence of the Rhodians[154]. A statement[155], however, that Hypereides delivered 170 speeches (λόγους ρό) hardly justifies allusions to his Rhodian Orations. Cato saved Rhodes by his speech in the Senate after the war with Perseus[156], and a few years later the treaty of alliance between Rome and Rhodes was obtained by the arguments of Tiberius Gracchus[157]. When Claudius restored the independence of Rhodes, it was in response to a speech delivered in Greek on their behalf by Nero, who was then a boy of fifteen[158]. Among the rhetoricians of the Roman Empire, Dio Chrysostom delivered a wearisome oration to the Rhodians about 100 A.D. on their stinginess in renaming statues and in other matters[159]; and Aristeides inflicted on them two still more wearisome orations[160], the first on the earthquake of 157 A.D. and the other on their political factions. The oration on the earthquake was perhaps intended more for Antoninus Pius than for the Rhodians themselves, and may have weighed with the emperor in his decision to rebuild their city.

The Doric dialect of Rhodes was very marked. Thus it was said that when the Rhodians who founded Gagæ landed in Lycia, the Lycians asked them what they wanted and were answered in broad Doric, γᾶ, γᾶ, Land, land; whereon they called the new city γάγαι[161]. And when a certain Zeno was discoursing somewhat affectedly before Tiberius, the emperor asked what vile dialect he might be speaking. Zeno replied that it was Doric; and Tiberius at once banished him to Cinaria, thinking the man was sneering at him for his retreat at Rhodes[162]. A century after Tiberius there was hardly a name to be found in the island that was not Doric[163]: and the inscriptions with few exceptions maintained there Doric to the last. Strabo[164] noted that the Rhodians said ἐρυθίβιος for ἐρυσίβιος, but the inscriptions[165] read ἐρεθίμιος. The converse change of β and μ occurs on a Rhodian inscription[166] in περιβολιβῶσαι for περιμολυβδῶσαι. Athenæos[167] remarked that in Rhodes βράβυλα was used for κοκκύμηλα as in Sicily, and λατάγη for κότταβος as in Sicily and in Thessaly. And many expressions peculiar to the island have been preserved by Hesychios. These must once have been numerous, for a certain Moschos thought it worth his while to write a book on the Explanation of Rhodian Phrases[168].

LEARNING. 163

1 Athenæos, p. 3.
2 Suidas, s. v. "Ομηρος.
3 Clement of Alexandria, strom. VI. 2.
4 Theocritos; Ep. 20.
5 Strabo, p. 688.
6 Pausanias, II. 37.
7 Plato, Protagoras, p. 343; Pausanias, X. 24; Diogenes Laertius, I. 89-93.
8 Athenæos, pp. 359, 360.
9 Suidas, s. v. Μυρώ.
10 Athenæos, p. 445.
11 Timocreon, Frs. I. 3; Plutarch, Themistocles, 21, 22.
12 Timocreon, Fr. 10.
13 Athenæos, p. 416; Ælian, var. hist. I. 27.
14 Timocreon, Fr. 6; Plato, Gorgias, p. 493; Servius, VII. 1.
15 Timocreon, Frs. 7, 8; Aristophanes, vesp. 1063, acharn. 532.
16 Suidas, s. vv. Τιμοκρέων, 'Αριστοφάνης, 'Αντιφάνης.
17 Athenæos, pp. 395, 645.
18 The Parian Marble, epoch. 70.
19 Aristotle, Nicom. Ethics, VII. 10; Rhetoric, III. 10-12.
20 Athenæos, pp. 222, 295, 374, 694; Suidas and Eudocia, s. v. 'Αναξανδρίδης.
21 Pindar, Ol. VII. 11-14.
22 Gorgon, Fr. 3.
23 Eustathios, ad Homerum, p. 327.
24 Scholia to Theocritos, VII. 40.
25 Strabo, p. 655.
26 Anthologia Palatina, XV. 22, 24, 27.
27 Hephæstion, pp. 38, 60.
28 Strabo, p. 421.
29 Athenæos, p. 283.
30 Suidas, s. v. Καλλίμαχος, cf. Anthologia Palatina, XI. 275.
31 Suidas, s. v. 'Απολλώνιος, Φιτῶ Απομμοξιι.
32 Maximus Confessor, loc. com. 15.
33 Anthologia Palatina, IX. 147.
34 Athenæos, p. 340; Vitæ arati; Pausanias, I. 2.
35 Suidas, s. vv. 'Ιδαῖος, Εὔοδος, Horace, satires, I. 10, 20.
36 Strabo, p. 653; Pliny, V. 36; Ammianus Marcellinus, XVII. 7.
37 Aulus Gellius, XIII. 5.
38 Simplicius, physica, pp. 29, 201, 279.
39 Asclepios of Tralles, in Brandis, scholia to Aristotle, pp. 519, 520.
40 Strabo, p. 610; Diodoros, XVI. 52.
41 Strabo, p. 655; Proclos, in Timæum, p. 5.
42 Diogenes Laertius, X. 13.
43 Cicero, de fin. II. 3, 6, IV. 18, V. 5; acad. Prior. II. 42; disp. Tusc. II. 6.
44 B. 5783.
45 Strabo, p. 608; Plutarch, Sulla, 26; Porphyry, Plotinus, 24.
46 Vitruvius, VI. proem. I.
47 Diogenes Laertius, II. 64; Cicero, acad. prior. II. 6.
48 Porphyry, Plotinos, 4.
49 Strabo, p. 655.

50 Cicero, de fin. IV. 9; de off. II. 10, III. 12.
51 Cicero, de div. I. 3; disp. Tusc. I. 32.
52 Eusebios, præpar. evang. V. 8.
53 Cicero, acad. prior. II. 2; disp. Tusc. I. 33; de re pub. I. 21; ad Att. IX. 12.
54 Cicero, de off. III. 2.
55 Ib. III. 15.
56 Diogenes Laertius, III. 109.
57 Index Herculanensis, XVII. 8.
58 Suidas, s. v. Ποσειδώνιος.
59 Strabo, p. 316.
60 Plutarch, Marius, 45.
61 Suidas, s. v. Ποσειδώνιος.
62 Cicero, Hortensius, Fr. 18.
63 Strabo, p. 492; Pliny, VII. 31.
64 Cicero, disp. Tusc. II. 25.
65 Cicero, de nat. deor. I. 3, 44; ad Att. II. 1.
66 Suidas, s. v. Ἰάσων.
67 Strabo, p. 655.
68 Ib. p. 753; Galen, p. 460.
69 Strabo, pp. 67, 70, 114.
70 Dicæarchos, Fr. 55.
71 Strabo, p. 125.
72 Cleomedes, cycl. theor. I. 10.
73 Strabo, p. 95.
74 Strabo, pp. 65, 65, 102, 277.
75 Dicæarchos, Fr. 58.
76 Geminos, 1, 2, 4, 5, 14.
77 Avienus, ora maritima, 42.
78 Marcianus Heracleotes, p. 63; Strabo, p. 421.
79 Strabo, pp. 173, 174.
80 Cicero, de nat. deor. II. 34.
81 Cleitophon, Fr. 1.
82 Athenæos, pp. 45, 152-4, 246, 273-5, 527, 549, 550, 662.
83 Strabo, pp. 188, 309, 515.
84 Plutarch, Fab. Max. 19; Marcell. 1, 9, 19, 20, 30; Mar. 1; Brut. 1.
85 Josephus, in Aponem, II. 7, 8.
86 Athenæos, p. 369; Strabo, pp. 147, 197, 743, 827.
87 Cleitophon, Frs. 1, 3.
88 Diocles, Fr. 6.
89 Suidas, s.v. Διονύσιος Μουσωνίου.
90 Suidas, s.v. Εὐαγόρας.
91 Eudoxos, Frs. 1, 2.
92 Sosicrates, Frs. 1-9.
93 Antipater, Fr. 1.
94 Dionysios Thrax, Fr. 1.
95 Diogenes Laertius, I. 115.
96 Ergeias, Fr. 1.
97 Eucrates, Fr. 1.
98 Suidas, s.v. Ἰάσων.
99 Polyzelos, Frs. 1-4.
100 Zeno, Frs. 1, 2.
101 Theognis, Fr. 1, 2.
102 Gorgon, Fr. 1.
103 Athenæos, p. 360.
104 Philemnestos, Frs. 1, 2.
105 Polybios, XVI. 14-20.
106 B. 2905.
107 Callixenos, Frs. 1, 2; Athenæos, pp. 196-206.
108 Socrates, Fr. 1.
109 Plutarch, Brutus, 2.
110 Suidas, s.v. Κάστωρ.
111 Eusebios, Chron. I. 41, 48.
112 Nicolaus Myrepsus, de antidot. 9.
113 Hierocles, hippiatrica, I. 23, 27, 30.
114 Scholia to Theocritos, XVII. 128.
115 Athenæos, pp. 5, 308.

LEARNING. 165

[116] Varro, de re rust. I. 1.
[117] Lucian, Zeuxis, 10.
[118] Theodoros, Fr. 1.
[119] Strabo, p. 655.
[120] Ælian, tact. 1.
[121] Hipparchos, ad Phænom. I. 1, &c.
[122] Proclos, in Timæum, p. 27.
[123] Athenæos, pp. 501, 677, 678; Suidas, s.v. Ἀργάς.
[124] Strabo, p. 655. Varro, de ling. Lat. X. 4.
[125] Strabo, p. 655. Suidas, s.vv. Ἀλεξανδρεύς, Τυραννίων.
[126] Dionysios, gram. 1.
[127] Suetonius, Tiberius, 11, 32.
[128] Suidas, s.v. Ἄβρων.
[129] Cicero, Brutus, 13.
[130] Quintilian, XII. 10.
[131] Cicero, de orat. III. 56; Plutarch, Æschines, 9-11; Quintilian, XI. 3; Pliny, epist. II. 3; Philostratos, Æschines, 2, 5; Scholia to Æschines, de fals. leg. 1.
[132] Dionysios of Halicarnassos, Deinarchos, 8.
[133] Ib. Isocrates, 13.
[134] Vita Apollonii.
[135] Polybios, XXX. 4, XXXI. 7.
[136] Cicero, Brutus, 95; Strabo, pp. 655, 661.
[137] Cicero, de oratore, I. 17, 28.
[138] Valerius, Maximus, II. 2.
[139] Cicero, Brutus, 89-91; Quintilian, XII. 6.
[140] Plutarch, Cæsar, 3; Suetonius, Cæsar, 4.
[141] Plutarch, Pompey, 42.
[142] Aurelius Victor, Brutus.
[143] Appian, de bel. civ. IV. 67-70.
[144] Plutarch, Brutus, 30.
[145] Quintilian, III. 1; Suetonius, Tiberius, 57.
[146] Seneca, suas. 3.
[147] Quintilian, X. 6.
[148] Suidas, s.v. Κἄστωρ.
[149] Ib. s.v. Εὐαγορας.
[150] Quintilian, II. 17.
[151] Strabo, p. 147.
[152] Tacitus, de orat. 40.
[153] Harpocration, s.vv. ἀπειπεῖν, &c.
[154] Demosthenes, pp. 190-201.
[155] Scholia to Æschines, de fals. leg. 18.
[156] Aulus Gellius, VI. 3.
[157] Polybios, XXXI. 7.
[158] Suetonius, Nero, 7.
[159] Dio Chrysostom, XXXI.
[160] Aristeides, XLIII. XLIV.
[161] Etymologicum Magnum, s.v. Γάγαι.
[162] Suetonius, Tiberius, 56.
[163] Aristeides, p. 401.
[164] Strabo, p. 613.
[165] R. I. 276, 277; R. H. 43, 44.
[166] N. 351.
[167] Athenæos, pp. 49, 666.
[168] Ib. p. 485.

VIII.

LEGENDS.

MOST of the Rhodian legends that survive are imbedded in a narrative in which the latest events occur about a thousand years before our era and the date of the earliest can be measured only by generations of the gods[1]. The Rhodian historians whom Diodoros follows, apparently collected the isolated legends that clung round worships and customs and ancient names, and then employed the scheme of the chronographers to piece them together. This scheme, however, is always worthless and often inverts the true order of the legends, for those of the earlier gods belong to a later order of thought than those of the Olympians: and consequently this narrative may be neglected.

The earliest historical inhabitants of Rhodes were Dorians whose parent state was Argos: and they occupied the three cities, Lindos, Ialysos and Camiros.

Several of the legends accord with these facts. Thus in the Catalogue of the Ships:- Tlepolemos brought from Rhodes nine ships of lordly Rhodians who dwelt beneath his sway in threefold division, Lindos and Ialysos and glistening Camiros. Astyocheia, a maiden of Ephyra, bore him to Heracles. And when he was come to man's estate he slew the brother of his sire's mother, the warrior Licymnios. Then he built ships and gathered together much people: and he fled away over the sea, for the other sons of Heracles and their sons threatened him. In grievous wanderings he came to Rhodes, and there his followers made a threefold habitation in their tribes[2]. – Pindar no doubt gives the local version of the legend that he must often have heard at the courts of the Rhodian despots in Sicily. – It was Tlepolemos the son of Heracles that peopled Rhodes. His father's sire was Zeus, his mother's Amyntor, and she Astydameia. Alcmene's bastard brother, Licymnios, he slew at Tiryns, smiting him in headstrong wrath. Then he went to the god and asked his bidding: and Apollo enjoined on him a voyage across the open sea from Lerna's headland to a sea-girt realm where the gods' great king had once bedewed a city with golden clouds[3]. – In this version Tlepolemos comes from Argolis at the bidding of the Dorian god, Apollo: and the tomb of his victim, Licymnios, was pointed out at Argos[4]. But in the Catalogue it is not said whence he comes, nor are his followers there called Dorians. Strabo notes the omission, and argues that the emigrants were Æolians and Bœotians rather than Dorians, as Heracles and Licymnios dwelt at Thebes: and that even if Tlepolemos did start from Argos or Tiryns, his followers would not on that account be Dorians, for it was before the return of the Heracleidæ[5]. But Strabo is merely trying the legend by the standard of the chronographers, and his argument may be left. The same train of thought no doubt produced the statement that Rhodes was peopled by Lacedæmonians who departed out of Peloponnesos on the return of the Heracleidæ[6]. There was perhaps a Thessalian element among the emigrants. Pindar calls the mother of Tlepolemos Astydameia, a daughter of the king of Thessaly: and Hesiod agrees with him[7]. In the Catalogue she is called Astyocheia and comes from Ephyra in

168   RHODES.

Thesprotis, whence the Thessalians migrated to Thessaly: and the Heraclids Pheidippos and Antiphos, who brought the ships from Cos and afterwards settled at Ephyra, are called sons of Thessalos. These leaders from Rhodes and Cos were the only Heraclids who fought before Ilion. Cnidos and Halicarnassos, which were united in the earliest times with Cos and the Rhodian cities in the Doric Hexapolis, were not held by the Greeks at the date of the Catalogue: and the slaying of Tlepolemos before Ilion by Sarpedon, king of Lycia, suggests some repulse of the Dorian islanders from the mainland of Asia Minor[8]. There were, however, legends[9] in which Tlepolemos led the Rhodian colonies to the district of Sybaris and to the Balearic Islands after the return from Ilion. But his death in the war is assumed in the Rhodian legend of Helen. – When Menelaos was dead Helen fled to Rhodes, and came to Polyxo who had been her friend. This Polyxo was by birth of Argos, and had wedded with Tlepolemos there and had shared his flight: and now she ruled the island as his son's guardian. She took vengeance on her guest for the death of Tlepolemos: her handmaidens garbed themselves as the Furies, and they seized Helen while bathing and hanged her to a tree. Wherefore the Rhodians have a temple of Helen of the Tree[10]. – Some survival of the ancient tree worship was probably the nucleus of this legend. It is not clear whether the threefold division mentioned in the Catalogue merely refers to the three Doric tribes, or implies the founding of the three cities by Tlepolemos. Pindar regards them as already founded. Strabo agrees in this, but also mentions a report that Tlepolemos founded them and named them from three of the daughters of Danaos. Diodoros when giving the legends of the Heracleidæ says that Tlepolemos divided the island into three parts and founded the three cities, but in giving the Rhodian legends he says they were already founded, and that the division was an equal allotment of the land among the people[11]. All the legends agree that Tlepolemos was king of the whole island. There is this legend of another Heraclid migration to Rhodes: it seems formed from that of Tlepolemos and that of Althæmenes of Crete. – Althærnenes, a grandson of Temenos the king of Argos, was at variance with his brethren and departed out of Peloponnesos taking with him a body of Dorians and certain of the Pelasgi. An oracle bade him betake himself to Zeus and Helios and ask from them a land to dwell in. Now Crete is the isle of Zeus, and Rhodes is the isle of Helios. Wherefore he sailed first to Crete and left there those of his followers who desired to make that their home: and then he sailed on to Rhodes with the greater part of the Dorians[12]. – It was also reported that some of the Dorians who founded Megara, left the new city and went with him to Crete and Rhodes[13]. Aristeides tells the Rhodians they had Heracleidæ and Asclepiadæ for founders and kings[14]. The legends of the Rhodian Asclepiadæ have perished: but they probably pointed to a migration from Epidauros, for Cos was very closely allied with Epidauros in the worship of Asclepios. Mention is also made of Dorians who departed out of Peloponnesos because of a grievous famine, and made their abode in Rhodes[15]. There is this legend of the national hero of the Dorians. – Heracles came to Lindos, and there he asked from a husbandman food for his son Hyllos who journeyed with him. But the man gave him no food, and treated him despitefully. Whereat Heracles was wroth and slew one of the oxen of the plough wherewith the man was ploughing: he feasted thereon with his son in contentment while the man cursed him from afar. Therefore with curses the Lindians sacrifice to Heracles[16]. – It appears from other versions that the husbandman was named Theiodamas[17], and that Heracles had landed at Thermydron[18]. Probably some Egyptian antipathy to the sacrifice of oxen formed the nucleus of this legend; and then the name Thermydron suggested Heracles, who was patron of hot springs. The version in which Heracles slays both the oxen of Theiodamas apparently confuses these Lindian sacrifices with those of the harvest festival Buzygia[19].

Another group of legends deals with immigrations of Greeks who were not Dorians. – Hæmon departed from Thebes because he had slain a kinsman while hunting, and came to Athens: but he departed again thence with his followers and made his habitation in Rhodes with the men of Argos[20]. – Macareus, the founder of Lesbos, sent out his son Leucippos with much people: and they were welcomed by the Rhodians and shared the land with them. The followers of Macareus were of manifold races, but chiefly Ionian[21]. – The Rhodian land brought forth huge snakes, and many of the people perished by them. Wherefore the Rhodians sent to Delos to enquire of the god concerning the staying of the plague: and Apollo bade them send for Phorbas and his followers and give them a share in the island. This Phorbas was son of Lapithos and was wandering in Thessaly in search of a land to dwell in. And when he was come to Rhodes he slew the snakes and freed the country from the terror: and thenceforth he dwelt in the island[22]. – There is another version of this. – Rhodes was invaded by a multitude of serpents, and among them was a dragon of huge size who slew very many of the people. Then Phorbas, the son of Triopas by a daughter of Myrmidon, was driven to the island in a storm: and he slew the dragon and all the serpents[23]. – This killing of the dragon is very curious, for the legend recurs in the island in the time of the Knights concerning the slaying of the dragon by Deodato de Gozon[24]. The mediæval dragon seems to have been a crocodile. Another Rhodian legend refers to Phorbas. – When Triopas was dead some of his followers returned to Thessaly, but many went with Phorbas to Ialysos or with his brother Periergos to the district of Camiros. Then Periergos cursed Phorbas, and Phorbas and his sister Parthenia were shipwrecked. Howbeit they came safe to shore at Schedia near Ialysos. And there met them one, Thamneus, who took them to his home, sending his slave beforehand to prepare food. But when they came there, nothing was made ready; and he prepared all things himself. Wherefore free men minister at the sacrifice of Phorbas, and no slave may draw nigh[25]. – Phorbas is here called the son of Lapithos or the grandson of Myrmidon, both of them Thessalians, and comes from Thessaly: but he is also called the son of Triopas, the legendary ancestor of the kings of Argos, just as the Argive Tlepolemos is called the son of the Thessalian Astydameia. Settlements in the island of Thessalian and other Greeks who were not Dorian no doubt formed the groundwork of these legends: but such settlers left no other trace, and had been absorbed before historic times by the Dorians.

In another group of legends the heroes are Egyptian or Phœnician. – Danaos fled out of Egypt with his fifty daughters and came to Lindos where he was welcomed by the people of the country. He founded there the temple of Athene and dedicated the statue of the goddess: and after a season he departed thence to Argos. But three of his daughters died while they tarried at Lindos, and afterward Tlepolemos called the three cities of Rhodes by their names[26]. – In another version the temple is founded by the daughters of Danaos[27]. The number of these daughters is explained by the legend that the ship in which they came to Lindos was named the Pentecontoros, the vessel of fifty oars: and this was the first ship that came from Egypt to Greece[28]. In historic times the trade between Egypt and Greece passed through Lindos, and these legends suggest that this was so in the earliest times. It was perhaps by Egyptian sympathies and by commercial wealth that Lindos was at one period isolated among the Rhodian cities. The Thessalians in one legend of Phorbas settle only at Ialysos and Camiros: and the Rhodian legends of the Phœnicians deal with settlements on the western coast, but hardly mention Lindos. – Cadmos, son of Agenor the king of Phœnicia, was sent forth by his sire in quest of his sister Europa. As he sailed there arose a great storm, and he vowed a temple to Poseidon if he were saved. He reached Rhodes: and he founded in the island a temple of that god and left there certain of the Phœnicians to care for it. These joined the men of Ialysos and dwelt with them as fellow citizens: and from them the priests receive the priesthood by descent. And Cadmos also made offerings to Athene of Lindos[29]. – It was declared by an oracle that Althæmenes, son of Catreus the king of Crete, should slay his sire. To escape this abomination Althæmenes fled from Crete, and many of the people went with him. And he came to Camiros and dwelt there honoured by the people of the country: and upon Mount Atabyros he founded the temple of Zeus Atabyrios on a lofty crag whence Crete may be seen. Then Catreus sailed to Rhodes to bring his son back to reign in Crete. But it was night when he landed with some of his men, and the islanders attacked them as pirates: and in the fray Althæmenes hurled his spear and unwittingly slew his sire[30]. – In another version Althæmenes names his settlement Cretenia: and he is accompanied by his sister Apemosyne, just as Phorbas is accompanied by Parthenia, and he slays her also by mishap[31]. Cretenia may here be merely Camiros under another name: it lay below Mount Atabyros[32]. Patriotic genealogists managed to shew that Althæmenes, Cadmos and Danaos were all Argive by descent. – Io was priestess of Hera at Argos. She was changed to a cow and wandered through many lands till she came to Egypt: there Zeus made her once more a woman, and she bore him a son Epaphos. His son Agenor departed to Phœnicia and ruled that land: and there he begot Cadmos and Europa. Zeus in the likeness of a bull carried Europa to Crete, where she bore him a son Minos. His son Catreus was the father of Althæmenes. Danaos was of the lineage of Epaphos in Egypt. – The pedigree suggests that the curses of the Lindians at the sacrifice of oxen and the veneration of the bronze kine on Mount Atabyros were survivals of Totemism. But in spite of the genealogists there probably were true Phœnician settlements in Rhodes. Apart from the legend of Cadmos, the caste of priests at Ialysos in historic times implied such a settlement in that district in earlier times. Then, although Althæmenes comes from Crete, his ancestors have migrated thither from Phœnicia, and the temple that he found in Rhodes is off a Phœnician god: and that legend would be based on some migration of Phœnicians from settlements in Crete to Camiros or Cretenia. And the three privileged cities in Rhodes recall the customary Phœnician unions of three cities. There is also a confused story of the occupation of Ialysos and Camiros by a force of Phœnicians under a certain Phalas in the days of the Trojan war[33]: and the following curious legend of the final expulsion of the Phœnicians. – Phalanthos the Phœnician and his people had an exceeding strong city called Achæa in the district of Ialysos and wanted not for food: wherefore they cared little when Iphiclos the Greek lay siege to them. Moreover they knew from an oracle that they should possess the land till there were white crows and fish swam in the wine jars; and they were confident this would never be. But Iphiclos heard of this response. Forthwith he waylaid a Phœnician, Larcas by name, who went to draw water, and made covenants with him; and then he caught fish and threw them into the water jar, and bade the man pour water therefrom into the jar whence wine was drawn for Phalanthos: and this the man did. Then he caught crows and chalked them, and let them go. And when Phalanthos saw the white crows, he went to the wine jar, and there he found the fish. – According to another version the response was known only to a certain Phacas and to his daughter Dorcia. She loved Iphiclos and was treating with him through her nurse concerning marriage. It was she who persuaded the water carrier to take fish, and she chalked the crows herself[34]. – And Phalanthos seeing the land was no more his, sent heralds to Iphiclos asking that he and his people might be suffered to depart. Iphiclos granted this, and swore an oath that he would give them ships; he sore also that they might take away whatsoever they should carry in the belly. Then Phalanthos slew victims and taking the entrails from out the bellies would carry off gold and silver therein. Whereon Iphiclos took out the rudders and oars and sails from the ships and left only the hulks for the Phoenicians to depart in: and they were at a loss. And they buried much of their treasure, marking the places that they might some day come to dig it up, but much of it they left to Iphiclos. In this wise the Phœnicians departed out of Rhodes, and the Greeks ruled the island[35].

The remaining legends are of another order. – The Telchines were sons of Thalassa. Aided by Capheira the daughter of Oceanos they reared Poseidon, for Rhea delivered the child into their charge. And when Poseidon came to man's estate he loved Halia the sister of the Telchines, and she bore him children, six sons and a daughter: and the daughter was called Rhodos, and the island had its name from her. Then Aphrodite drew nigh the island as she passed from Cythera to Cypros, but she was driven from its shores by the sons of Poseidon in their overweening pride. Wherefore in her wrath she sent madness upon them so that they wronged their mother and did many evil things to the people. And Poseidon buried his sons beneath the earth because of the deed they had wrought, and they were accounted dæmons of the eastern lands. But Halia cast herself into the sea, and the people worshipped her as an immortal under the name Leucothea. Afterward the Telchines, foreseeing the deluge that was to come, departed out of the island and were scattered abroad[36]. – In other versions Rhodos is daughter of Oceanos and of Aphrodite or Amphitrite[37]. This is the legend of a sea-faring race: the sons of the sea and the daughter of the ocean rear Poseidon, the lord of the waters: their sister is Halia, the salt wave: and Aphrodite, the goddess born of the sea foam would visit them. But the legend has been pressed too far on this side: and while an epic poet has pictured the Telchines gathering themselves out of the void abyss of the sea[38], a prosaic archbishop has handed down the report that they were amphibious and had webs between their fingers after the manner of geese[39]. – The Telchines were the first to work iron and bronze: they made the trident for Poseidon and the sickle for Cronos; and they were the first to fashion images of the gods. They discovered certain of the arts and gave to mankind other things advantageous to life. But they were wizards and sorcerers. The charges against them are for the most part general: rain and cloud, hail and snow obeyed their will: they changed their own shapes: and so forth. There is but one specific charge: they sprinkled sulphur in the water of the Styx with intent to destroy animals and plants; and did in fact by watering the fields therewith make barren the soil of fruitful Rhodes[40]. Still, their evil repute clung to them; and objectionable things, such as violent deaths and eclipses and bookworms, came to be called Telchines[41]. Crete was their first home, and they were closely related to the Curetes and the Dactyls of Mount Ida: they migrated thence to Cypros and afterwards to Rhodes[42]. Of the two Telchines whose names are clearly Rhodian, Atabyrios is connected with Mount Atabyros and Mylas with Cape Mylantia[43]. Both these places were near Camiros or Cretenia, the home of the settlers from Crete in the legend of Althæmenes. Another report, however, brings the Telchines from Peloponnesos[44]. – The chronographers placed in the age of the Telchines certain giants who dwelt in the eastward parts of the island: also a people called the Gnetes or the Ignetes: and Spartæos, Cronios and Cytos, whom the nymph Himalia bore to Zeus[45]. The legends of these are lost. The discovery in the island of bones far larger than those of living men may have given rise to that of the giants[46]. – Rhodos was beloved by Helios, and she bore him seven sons, Ochimos, Cercaphos, Macar, Actis, Tenages, Triopas and Candalos; and also a daughter, Electryone or Alectrona, who died young: these were the Heliadæ. Tenages was the goodliest of them all, and certain of his brethren made away with him out of envy. Their plot was afterward found out; and Macar fled to Lesbos, Candalos to Cos, Actis to Egypt and Triopas to Caria, where he dwelt on the cape named from him Triopion. But Ochimos and Cercaphos remained in Rhodes, for they were innocent of the plot: and they dwelt in the district of Ialysos, and there founded the city of Achæa. Ochimos the elder of these was king; and he took to wife one of the nymphs of the country, Hegetoria by name, who bore him a daughter at first called Cydippe but afterward Cyrbia. Cercaphos took her to wife; and when his brother died, he reigned in his stead. And when he died also, his three sons, Lindos, Ialysos and Camiros, ruled the island. In their days a great flood laid waste the city of Cyrbe: wherefore they divided the land between them, and each built a city called after his own name[47]. – In this legend Macar flees to Lesbos and Triopas to Caria, while in others Macareus is father of Leucippos and Triopas of Phorbas, both of whom lead migrations from those places to the island. Then Actis flees to Egypt, whence comes Danaos in another legend; just as in others Danaos and Cadmos go from Rhodes to Argos and Thebes, whence in others again Tlepolemos and Hæmon come to Rhodes. And Electryone is here the sister of the Heliadæ, while in the legend of Tlepolemos Electryon is the father of Licymnios. – Ochimos had betrothed Cydippe to a certain Ocridion. But Cercaphos in his desire for the maid persuaded the herald (for it was a custom to summon the brides by heralds) to lead her to him. And he fled away with her, and returned not again till Ochimos was aged. Wherefore at Rhodes no herald may enter the shrine of Ocridion[48]. — There is another legend of the Heliadæ that served to explain an anomaly in Rhodian sacrifices. — When by the wielding of Hephæstos' axe Athene was loosed from her sire's brain, Helios bade his sons be first to build an altar in very substance to the new-born goddess and gladden with sacrifice the hearts of Zeus and of his daughter. Albeit they had germ of glowing flame, they kindled not the fire: and with flameless sacrifices they made ready a grove in their acropolis. Zeus rained gold on them from tawny clouds, and Athene granted them with cunning hands to master every art of mortals[49]. — This rain of gold was afterwards personified as the descent of Plutos upon the acropolis[50]. Another version is more explicit. — When Athene was born, Helios proclaimed to the Heliadæ that the goddess would abide with those who first made sacrifice to her. And this same proclamation was made to the dwellers in Attica. The Heliadæ in their haste forgot to bring fire, and straightway set the victims on the altar; while Cecrops the king of Attica tarried for fire and was behind them in slaying the victims: and this custom endures in the sacrifices to Athene in Rhodes. And the Heliadæ surpassed all men in learning and most of all in astronomy: and they discovered many things concerning seamanship and the ordering of the hours[51]. — The legend of the Heliadæ may be a purely Rhodian version of that of the Telchines, which occurs in several parts of Greece. Those of the Telchines who settle in Crete after their dispersion from Rhodes become the Curetes: the Curetes are very closely related to the Corybantes: and the Corybantes, in a legend that was current at Præsos in Crete, are sons of Helios[52]. Hierapytna in Crete which Corybas founded was also called Cyrbe and Camiros[53]. This suggests that Cyrbe where the Heliadæ dwelt in Rhodes was Camiros under another name, and Camiros is connected with the Telchines through Atabyrios and Mylas. Achæa, the city of the Heliadæ, was in the district of Ialysos, and the temple of Alectrona was there[54]: and the Telchines are also called Ialysian[55]. But both Telchines and Heliadæ very curiously resemble the Phœnicians. In the legend of Phalanthos the Phœnicians are established at Achæa, in that of Cadmos they settle at Ialysos, in that of Phalas they occupy both Ialysos and Camiros, and in that of Althæmenes they come from Crete to Camiros or Cretenia at the foot of Mount Atabyros and found the temple of Zeus Atabyrios on its summit. The group of three cities founded by the Heliadæ is of a Phœnician type, and the charges of sorcery against the Telchines are such as simple rustics might make against the civilized Phœnicians in the cities. The Heliadæ are endowed with wealth and excellence in handicraft and the Telchines are mighty workers of metal: while the Phœnicians were the rich traders who supplied the early Greeks with all the more costly objects of daily use and especially with metal work. And the Telchines are a race in union with the sea gods and the Heliadæ are skilled in seamanship: while the Phœnicians were the great navigators of antiquity.

The historical basis for all these legends of the peopling of Rhodes was perhaps this. – Three cities were founded in the island among a population presumably Carian by Phœnicians coming from Phœnicia itself and from settlements in Crete. Before these Phœnicians were firmly established at Lindos they were expelled from that city by the Greeks: and some generations later the Greeks expelled them first from Camiros and then from Ialysos. The Greeks migrated to the island from various districts and at various times: the main body coming from Peloponnesos and the chief of the minor bodies from Thessaly. But these minor bodies were in time absorbed by the ascendant body of Dorians, and the Carians were expelled: and a homogeneous Greek population was thus formed.

There was this legend of the island itself. – When Zeus and the immortals meted out the earth, Rhodes was not yet manifest amid the sea waves: the isle lay hidden in briny depths. And Helios was away from Olympos, and they left him without portion of land. When he spake thereof, Zeus would cast the lots again: but this he suffered not, for he beheld within the surging sea that land arising from below to be a dwelling place for men and flocks. Straightway he bade Lachesis proclaim the gods' great oath and join with Zeus in granting him that isle, when it was born into the upper air, to be his realm[56]. – According to the chronographers the Telchines dwelt in the island long before it rose from the sea. To evade this difficulty some writers supposed a deluge after the days of the Telchines, while others rationalized the legend thus: the myth is that Helios loved Rhodos and drove away the water that was above, but the fact is that there was continuous pouring rain which made the lower parts of the island very swampy and muddy till the Sun dried up the damp[57]. But Rhodes certainly rose from the sea. The great limestone mass of Mount Atabyros and the lesser limestone hills, Akramytis, Elias, Archangelo and Lindos, must once have formed a group of islands: and as these were gradually elevated, the lower hills were being formed round them by volcanic action. These facts were no doubt beyond the Rhodians of the mythopœic age: but the elevated beds of sea shells at the base of the hills would readily have suggested the legend.

1. Diodoros, V. 55-59.
2. Homer, Iliad, II. 653-670.
3. Pindar, Ol. VII. 23-34.
4. Pausanias, II. 22.
5. Strabo, p. 653.
6. Dexippos, Fr. 3.
7. Hesiod, Fr. 90.
8. Homer, Iliad, V. 657-659.
9. Aristotle, p. 840; Strabo, p. 654; Silius Italicus, III. 364.
10. Pausanias, III. 19.
11. Diodoros, IV. 58, V. 59.
12. Conon, narrat. 47.
13. Strabo, p. 653.
14. Aristeides, p. 396.
15. Hesychios, s.v. Λιμοδωριεῖς.
16. Conon, narrat. 11.
17. Philostratos, imag. II. 24.
18. Apollodoros, II. 5.
19. Lactantius, I. 21.
20. Menecrates of Nysa, Fr. 1.
21. Diodoros, V. 81.
22. Ib. V. 58.
23. Polyzelos, Fr. 1.
24. [see Cecil Torr, *Rhodes in Modern Times*, 2003, p. 109 ff.]
25. Dieuchidas, Fr. 7.
26. Diodoros, V. 58; Strabo, p. 654.
27. Herodotos, II. 182.
28. The Parian Marble, Epoch. 9.
29. Diodoros, V. 58.
30. Diodoros, V. 59.
31. Apollodoros, III. 2.
32. Stephanos, s.v. Κρητηνία.
33. Dictys Cretensis, de bel. Troj. IV. 4.
34. Polyzelos, Fr. 2.
35. Ergeias, Fr. 1.
36. Diodoros, V. 55, 56.
37. Pindar, Ol. VII. 14, and Scholia.
38. Nonnos, Dionysiaca, XIV. 37.
39. Eustathios of Thessalonica, ad Homerum, p. 772.
40. Diodoros, V. 55; Strabo, p. 654; Nonnos, Dionysiaca, XIV. 47; Callimachos, Hymn. In Delum. 32.
41. Stesichoros, Fr. 93; Anthologia Palatina, XI. 321.
42. Strabo, p. 654.
43. Stephanos, s.vv. Ἀτάβυρον, Μυλαντία.
44. Syncellos, p. 149.
45. Diodoros, V. 55; Stephanos, s.v. Γνὺς; Hesychios, s.v. Ἴγνητες.
46. Phlegon, Fr. 45.
47. Diodoros, V. 56, 57; Pindar, Ol. VII. 72-76.
48. Plutarch, quæst. græc. 27.
49. Pindar, Ol. VII. 36-51.
50. Philostratos, imag. II. 27.
51. Diodoros, V. 56, 57.
52. Strabo, p. 472.
53. Stephanos, s.v. Ἱεραπύτνα.
54. N. 349.
55. Ovid, metamorph. VII. 365.
56. Pindar, Ol. VII. 55-68.
57. Diodoros, V. 56.

INDEX.

Academics, 151
Acanias (harbour), 2
Achæa, 4, 21, 30, 68, 174, 177, 179
Acheloos, 92
Acragas, 37, 38, 88, 124
Administrators, Rhodian, 70
Admirals, etc., 9, 13, 46, 71, 97
Adoption, 77, 98
Æschines, 158
Agrigentum, 38
Alcibiades, 10
Alectrona, 3, 92, 97, 102, 177, 179
Alexander the Great, 14, 44, 58, 69, 70, 71, 75, 123, 124, 138
Alexandria, 15, 17, 32, 40, 49, 56, 71, 114, 117, 120, 142, 147, 153, 155, 158
Althæmenes, 92, 99, 169, 172, 173, 176, 179
Amasis, 111, 124
Ambassadors, 21, 72, 97
Antirrhodos, 40
Antiochos of Syria, 19 ff., 41, 45, 54, 56, 69, 72, 116, 157
Antoninus Pius, 58, 64 139, 161
Apelles, 121-124

Apollo, 5, 40, 74, 78, 86, 90, 91, 93, 95, 97, 99, 110, 112, 113, 118, 121, 125, 133, 137, 147, 167, 170
Argos, 7, 40, 95, 166, 168-171, 173, 177
Aristeides, Ælius, 64, 161
Aristomenes of Messene, 78, 92, 95
Aristophanes, 145,
Aristotle, 146, 149-151
Artemis, 88, 90, 137, 138
Artemisia, 13, 14, 51, 77, 103, 113, 161
Asclepiadæ, 91, 169
Asclepios, 2, 91, 102, 169
Assyrian art, 127 ff.
Astyra, 4, 137, 138
Atabyros, Mount, 5, 38, 88-90, 154, 172, 173, 176, 179, 180
Athene, 1, 4, 44, 88, 98, 102, 105, 110, 112, 114, 119, 121, 134, 135, 137, 171, 178
Athene Lindia, 3, 86-88, 102, 111, 112, 116, 124, 125, 146, 172
Athenian art, 128 ff.
Athens and Rhodes, 8-16, 18, 20, 42, 43, 55, 74, 161

Black Sea, 17, 39, 45, 56, 71
Brutus, 32, 80, 155, 157, 160
Bryaxis, 113, 119
Building, 79
Bulls, 38, 88, 89, 173
Byzantion, 12-14, 17-19, 22, 44, 45, 56, 57, 104

Cadmos, 111, 172, 173, 177, 179
Cæsar, 32, 45, 49, 54, 55, 69, 80, 103, 104, 124, 157, 160
Cakes, 79
Camarina, 37, 38
Camiros, 4 ff., 40, 42, 72 ff., 110, 123 ff., 142, 145, 166, 171 ff.
Caria, 2, 14, 20, 21, 25, 29-31, 41, 72, 76, 118, 123, 177
Cassius, 32, 33, 45, 49, 51, 54, 67, 77, 80, 125, 160
Cato, 29, 80, 161
Caunos, 11, 30, 31, 41, 72, 76, 121, 147
Chæroneia, battle of, 55
Chalce, 5, 9, 42, 98
Chares, 113, 114, 116, 125
Chelidonisma, 143
Chersonese, Rhodian, 41
Chios, battle of, 20, 45, 47, 54
Christianity, 106
Cicero, 75, 80, 124, 152, 153, 154, 158, 160
Circumnavigation, 154
Cleobulos, 8, 111, 112, 142-144
Cnidos, 7, 9, 11, 16, 39, 40, 57, 91, 93, 100, 112, 113, 138, 147, 168

Coins, 4, 11, 56, 57, 86, 105, 136-139
Colonies, Rhodian, 36 ff.
Colossos, 63, 65, 86, 113 ff., 138
Colossal statues at Rhodes, 113 ff.
Comedy, 144-146
Confederacies of Delos, 8, 10, 12, 43
Constantinople, 125, 153
Consuls, 19, 74
Corn, 11, 28, 52, 55, 56, 62, 90, 96, 151
Coronisma, 143
Cos, 8, 12, 20, 37, 41, 42, 44, 48, 57, 91, 93, 113, 146, 168, 169, 177
Crete and Rhodes, 7, 16, 18, 30, 37, 45, 52, 65, 68, 69, 89, 92, 106, 116, 126, 155, 169, 172, 173, 176, 178, 179, *see* Hierapytna.
Cretenia, 5, 173, 176, 179
Cronios, 176
Cronos, 88, 176
Ctœnæ, 98, 102
Cyrbe, 5, 177, 179
Cyrene, 68, 136, 150
Cytos, 176

Damagetos, 8, 78, 94, 95, 112
Danaos, 46, 111, 168, 171-173, 177
Dareios, 8, 144, 145
Deigma (bazaar), 2, 62, 113, 115
Delos, 30, 76, 86, 100, 116, 170, *see* Confederacies.

Delphi, 74, 78, 95, 112, 142, 147
Deme, 89
Demetrios Poliorcetes, 15, 16, 18, 31, 33, 47, 49, 51, 54, 62, 63, 65, 67, 74, 77, 93, 103, 114, 117,119, 122, 123
Democracy, 8 ff., 53, 76
Demosthenes, 55, 159, 161
Despots, 8, 167
Diagoras, 87, 94, 95, 112, 146
Diagoridæ, 94
Diogenes, 80, 106, 158
Dionysos, 2, 67, 89, 102, 112, 113, 123, 124, 137, 139
Dockyard, 19, 51, 52
Dorians of Rhodes, 7, 37, 42, 80, 166, 167, 169, 170, 171, 180
Doric dialect, 62
Dorieus, 9, 10, 94, 95
Dragons, 170, 171

Earthquakes, 16, 44, 51, 52, 56, 63, 64, 74, 76, 78, 96, 101, 114-116, 161
Egypt and Rhodes, 2, 9 ff., 40 ff., 79, 87, 91, 96, 105, 111, 112; Rhodians in, 32, 45, 46; gods of, 93, 95; art of, 126 ff.
Epaminondas, 12
Ephesos, 23-25, 106, 114, 138; league with, 11, 57
Epics, 142, 147
Epicureans, 150
Erethimios, 5, 90, 93, 97, 99, *see* Apollo.
Ethnics, 5, 43

Exports, 17, 44, 56

Farnese Bull, 110, 118, 125
Festivals, 27, 67, 73, 86 ff., 90 ff., 100, 157
Fighting cocks, 80
Figs, 79, 80, 143
Fire balls, 59, 65, 66
Fire ships, 50
Fish, 79, 126, 146
Fleet, 42 ff., 53
Floods, 62, 63, 175, 180

Gagæ, 41, 162
Gambling, 80
Gela, 8, 37-40, 42, 91
Gems, 126, 127
General average, 58
Generals, etc., 71 ff.
Geographers, 154 ff.
Giants, 120, 176, 177
Gifts, state, 16, 17, 44, 63, 74, 76, 87, 143
Glass ornaments, 128, 129, 132
Gnetes, 176
Gods, foreign, 95
Gold ornaments, 101, 04, 121, 125, 126, 128, 129, 136
Government, 10, 11, 27, 70, 75, 76
Gracchus, 30, 161
Grammarians, 106, 120, 124, 146, 150, 156, 158
Grapes, 80
Guilds, 91, 99, 100-102, 118
Gymnasion, 78, 79, 81, 82

Hæmon, 170, 177

INDEX.

Halicarnassos, 7, 12, 13, 40, 51, 57, 69, 94, 112, 114, 116, 168
Hannibal, 24, 45
Harbours of the city of Rhodes, 1 ff., 10, 15, 42, 49, 51, 62, 64
Helen, 92, 111, 168
Helepolis, 16, 65, 66
Heliadæ, 99, 110, 177, 178-179
Helios, 27, 56, 74, 86, 87, 96, 97, 113, 114, 125, 137-139, 155, 169, 177-180
Hera, 89, 91, 110, 111, 173
Heracleidæ, 167-169
Heracles, 70, 91, 95, 118, 121, 134, 135, 138, 139, 142, 143, 166, 167, 169, 170
Hermes, 90, 118, 137
Herod of Judæa, 51, 74, 81
Hestia, 91
Hexapolis, 7, 40, 168
Hierapytna, 84, 69, 96, 179; Rhodian treaty with, 52, 68, 73, 76, 102
Hierothyteion at Lindos, 97, 104
Hippodamos of Miletos, 62
Historians, 155 ff., 166
Honours, 15, 25, 73, 86, 92, 101, 103, 104
Human sacrifices, 88, 89
Hypereides, 159, 161

Ialysos, 3 ff., 40, 42, 67, 68, 78, 86 ff., 122 ff., 136, 144, 166, 171 ff.
Iasos, 72, 138; league with, 11, 57

Ignetes, 176
Inessa (city) 39; 5 (fountain)
Inscribed stelæ, 102-104
Isis, 2, 93
Islands subject to Rhodes, 41, 42
Ixia or Ixiæ, 4, 90

Jettison (maritime law), 58
Jews, 106
Jus Gentium, 152

Lade, battle of, 20, 47, 156
Laocoon, 110, 117-120, 125
Law, Rhodian naval, 58
Leucippos, 170, 177
Lindopolitæ, 75
Lindos, ruins at, 3-5, 10, 95, 105, 111, 116, 118, 119, 121, 124, 125, 128; territory of, 5, 75; colonies of, 38, 40, 42
Lipara, 39
Luxury, 80, 121, 155
Lycia, 23 ff., 40, 72, 76, 162, 168
Lysander, 10, 44
Lysippos, 113, 114, 119

Macareus, 170, 177
Macedonian Wars, 14 ff.
Mastrœ, 98, 102
Mausolos, 12, 13, 76
Megiste (Castelorizo), 25, 41, 138
Memnon, 69, 70, 148
Mentor, 69, 70, 149
Mercenaries, 21, 54, 66-69, 136
Meridian of Rhodes, 153

INDEX.

Mithridates, 2, 17, 31-33, 45, 48, 50-52, 63, 67, 71, 93, 102
Monotheism, 106
Music, 87, 93, 146
Mycenæ, 111, 116
Mylas, 90, 92, 176, 179
Myndos, battles at, 31, 33, 48, 59

Nabis of Sparta, 22, 45, 69, 156
Naples, 37, 110
Naucratis, 39, 56, 130-132, 147
Naval law, 58
Nero, 81, 125, 148, 161
Netteia, 4, 5, 88, 102
Nymphs, 91, 92, 110, 176, 177

Ocridion, 89, 92, 177, 178
Oligarchy, 8-13
Olympia, 94, 95, 112, 118, 119, 131, 166

Painting at Rhodes, 120 ff.
Parallel of Rhodes, 153, 154
Parrhasios, 121, 124
Paul the Apostle, 106
Pausistratos, 21, 23, 52, 54, 68, 69
Peisirrhodos, 94, 112
Peloponnesian War, 8, 43, 62, 77
Pentapolis, 7, 93
Pentecontoros, 46, 56, 172
Peræa, Rhodian, 22, 27, 41, 68, 71

Pergamos and Rhodes, 17, 19, 20, 24, 25, 26, 45, 87, 119, 120, 160
Peripatetics, 148-150, 159
Perseus of Macedon, 26-30, 45, 52, 73 ff., 116, 121, 159, 161
Persia and Rhodes, 7, 8, 12-14, 23, 57, 68, 69, 77, 104
Phalanthos, 174, 179
Phalaris, 38, 88
Phalas, 174, 179
Pharos, 18, 40; of Alexandria, 114
Phaselis, 24, 40-42
Philip II, of Macedon, 14
Philip V, of Macedon, 18-22, 33, 69
Philippi, battle of, 33
Philosophers, 148 ff., 151
Phœnician art, 106, 111, 128 ff.
Phœnicians in Rhodes, 7, 55, 87 ff., 132, 171 ff.
Polyxenidas, 23-25, 69
Pompey, 32, 40, 45, 55, 71, 80, 152, 160
Porcelain, Egyptian, 126, 127, 131, 132
Poseidon, 54, 86, 90, 92, 96, 99, 111, 137, 152-155, 161, 172, 175, 176
Poseidonios, 152-155, 161
Praxiteles, 112, 113
Priests, etc., 96 ff.
Protogenes, 121-124, 136
Prytaneis, 71, 73, 75, 97
Ptolemy Soter, 14 ff., 93
Pydna, battle of, 28

Ramming at sea, 47-49
Ransoms, 54, 67, 77
Revenue, 15, 16, 70-72, 76
Rhetoric, 2, 45, 64, 80, 115, 142, 159-161
Rhodes (city), ruins of, 1 ff. 105, 106; account of, 62 ff.; population of, 64, 65; sieges of 16, 18, 20, 31, 44, 47, 49, 50, 54, 63 ff., 93, 103, 114, 122, 123
Rhodes (island), position and size, 1 ff.; names for, 148; legend of, 180
Rhodes (nymph), 96, 146, 175, 177, 180
Romans at Rhodes, 80, 81, 103, 104
Rome and Rhodes, 16, 18 ff., 56-58, 73, 124, 125

Sacrilege, 103
Sailors, 15, 53-55, 69
Sambuca, 50
Samos league with, 11, 57
Sarapis, 93, 137
Schedia (harbour), 3, 171
Sculpture, Rhodian school of, 111 ff.
Seamanship, 48, 53
Shells, engraved, 126, 127
Ship-building, 51, 52
Ships of war, 42 ff., 166
Shot, 49, 50, 65, 66
Siana, 4, 125, 130, 131
Sicilian Expedition, 8, 38, 43, 68
Sicily, 17, 28, 37, 39, 40, 46, 56, 91, 96, 162, 167

Simonides of Cos, 143, 144, 146
Slaves, 19, 26, 56, 64-67, 71 ff., 97, 99, 113, 148, 171
Slingers, 68
Snakes, 170
Social War, 12, 13, 44, 46
Solœ, 25, 40, 42, 55, 116
Sparta and Rhodes, 8 ff., 77, 78
Spartæos, 176

Tactics, naval, 46 ff.
Telchines, 91, 92, 110, 175 ff.
Thalassocratia, 36, 41, 51, 157
Theatre in the city of Rhodes, 2, 3, 62 ff., 82, 102
Thebes and Rhodes, 12, 138, 167, 170, 177
Themistocles, 8, 144
Θεοῖς on statues, 103, 104
Theophiliscos, 19
Theophrastos 149, 150
Thera, island upheaved near, 41, 90
Thermydron (harbour) 4, 170
Thessalians in Rhodes, 167 ff.
Tiberius, 30, 73, 81, 106, 158, 160-162
Tlepolemos, 37, 92, 123, 166 ff., 177
Tombs, 3, 4, 33, 105, 125-129, 132
Toro Farnese, 110, 118, 125
Totemism, 173
Trade, 15, 17, 18, 22, 30, 36, 46, 55, 56, 58, 90, 132, 151, 172, 179
Tree worship, 92, 168
Tribes, 99, 167, 168

Trierarchs, 53
Triopian Cape, 7, 93
Tyre, 14, 44

Vases, metal, 124; terra-cotta, 126 ff.
Vines, 80, 89

Wine, 52, 56, 80, 88, 143, 149, 157
Wine-jars, 56, 132, 137, 138, 174

Xerxes, 8, 42, 43

Zeus, 89, 91 ff., 102, 113, 120, 125, 134, 137, 139, 167 ff., 180; Atabyrios, 1, 2, 88, 89, 96, 172, 179 ; Polieus, 3, 38, 88

Bibliography and Sources

Cecil Torr: A select bibliography (by date of publication)

Rhodes in Ancient Times (Cambridge, 1883)
Rhodes under the Byzantines (Cambridge, 1886)
Rhodes in Modern Times (Cambridge, 1887)
Ancient Ships (Cambridge, 1894)
Memphis and Mycenæ, an Examination of Egyptian Chronology (Cambridge, 1896)
On the Interpretation of Greek Music (London, 1896)
On Portraits of Christ in the British Museum (London, 1898)
Small Talk at Wreyland (3 volumes, Cambridge, 1918-1923)
Hannibal Crosses the Alps (Cambridge, 1924)
Small Talk at Wreyland (with an introduction by Jack Simmons. Bath, 1970)

Archive material from the Devon Studies Centre (the Devon Record Office, the Westcountry Studies Library, Castle Street, Exeter EX4 3PQ)

Diaries of journeys to Europe, 1867-75 ([s.l.] : [s.n.], [1880] - 176p; 17cm.)(Record no: 44906, s940/LUS/TOR)
Notes on Wreyland: being a reprint of a portion of the introduction to the ... volume of Wreyland documents by Cecil Torr (79p; 23cm., Lustleigh: At the Post Office, 1910) (Record no: 5718, sB/LUS/0001/TOR)
Wreyland documents / edited with introduction ... by Cecil Torr (c, 199p, plates: ill; 23cm.) (For private circulation only. Cambridge, 1910) (Record no: 17614, s347.02/LUS/TOR)

Photographs of Yonder Wreyland etc. / by Cecil Torr (Photograph album, 1916. - 1 vol: of ill; 14 x 20cm.) (Record no: 57922, s728/LUS/TOR)
Small Talk at Wreyland (proofs - [1921?]. - 1vol: ill, port; 25cm., (incomplete) for series 2 & 3 and set of ill.) (Record no: 47151, sB/LUS/1850/TOR)
An Address to the Moretonhampstead Literary Society (16, [5]p; 24cm., Cambridge, 1923.) (Record no: 31362, s806.2/MOR/TOR)
Miscellaneous papers, maps and illustrations relating to Wreyland and Lustleigh (Undated manuscript - 2 vols: ill, maps; 31cm.) (Record no: 11973, sxB/LUS/0001/TOR)

Other archives and source material

Obituary, *The Times* (20 December 1928): 'Mr Cecil Torr (1857- 1928)'
Archives at Harrow School; Trinity College, Cambridge; Lincoln's Inn, London; Inner Temple Archives, London

On Cecil Torr and Wreyland

Crowdy, Joe, *The Book of Lustleigh* (Tiverton, 2001)
Markham, Violet, *Friendship's Harvest* (London, 1956)

Rhodes ("Ancient" Times: History, Art and Archaeology)

Braudel, F., *The Mediterranean in the Ancient World* (Harmondsworth, 1998)
Brilliant, R., *My Laocoön* (California, 2000)
Clayton, P.A., Price, M.J. (eds.), *The Seven Wonders of the Ancient World* (London/New York, 1988)
Hammond, N. G. L., *A History of Greece to 322 BC* (Oxford, 1986)
Hoepfner, W., *Der Koloss von Rhodos und die Bauten des Helios* (Mainz am Rhein, 2003)
Konstantinopoulos, K., *Rhodes Museum I, The Archaeological Museum* (Athens, 1977)

Konstantinopoulos, K., *Philerimos, Ialysos, Kamiros* (Athens, 1971)
Levi, P., *Atlas of the Greek World* (Oxford, 1984)
MacKendrick, P., *The Greek Stones Speak* (New York, 1981)
Paradissis, A., *Fortresses and Castles of Greece, Vol. 3 (the Greek Islands)*(Athens, 1975)
Stoneman, R., *Land of Lost Gods* (London, 1987)

Rhodes ("Modern" Times: History and Archaeology)

Atiya, A.S., *The Crusade in the Later Middle Ages* (London, 1938)
Bodnar, E., *Cyriac of Ancona, Later Travels* (Cambridge Massachusetts, 2003)
Braudel, F., *The Mediterranean* (London, 1992)
D'avenant, William, *The Siege of Rhodes* (1673)(ed. Tupper, J. W., London, 1909)
Knolles, Richard, *A General History of the Turks* (London, 1603)
Luttrell, A.T., *The Hospitallers in Cyprus, Rhodes, Greece and the West, 1291-1440* (London, 1978)
Luttrell, A.T., *The Hospitallers of Rhodes and their Mediterranean World* (Aldershot, 1992)
Luttrell, A.T., *The Hospitaller State on Rhodes and its Western Provinces, 1306-1462* (Aldershot, 1999)
Runciman, S., *A History of the Crusades* (Cambridge, 1951)

Rhodes (Contemporary reading)

Barber, R., *Rhodes and the Dodecanese, Blue Guide* (A & C Black, London, 1997)
Dicks, Brian, *Rhodes* (David & Charles, Newton Abbot, 1974)
Dubin, Marc, *Rough Guide to the Dodecanese and East Aegean* (4th edition, Penguin Books, 2005)
Durrell, Lawrence, *Reflections on a Marine Venus* (Faber & Faber, London, 1953)
Kasseris, N., *Rodos, Nymph of the Sun* (Rodos Image, Rhodes, 1997)

Kasseris, N., *The Dodecanese* (Rodos Image, Rhodes, 1992)
Kasseris, N., *Rhodes Today* (Rodos Image, Rhodes, 2004)
Pavlides, V., *Rhodes 1306 – 1522, a Story* (Rodos Image, Rhodes, 1999)

Greece, and Greek natural history

Baumann, Hellmut (trans. Stearn and Stearn), *Greek Wild Flowers* (London, 1993)
Durrell, L., *The Greek Islands* (Faber & Faber, London, 1978)
Graves, R., *Greek Myths* (London, 1955)
Polunin, O., *Flowers of Greece and the Balkans* (Oxford University Press, 1987)
Rackham O. and Moody, J., *The Making of the Cretan Landscape* (Manchester, 1996)
Sfikas, G., *Wild Flowers of Greece* (Athens, 1976)

Torr's Sources

"*Many years ago I looked through the works of about 200 Greek and Latin authors, in search of information about ancient ships. Of course, I had read the best of them before; but I should never have read the others except for information. I felt I could not speak with much authority on ships or anything else unless I knew the evidence from end to end.*" (Cecil Torr, *An Address to the Moretonhampstead Literary Society*)

For those with time and access to the material, Torr's source-lists for his monographs are a researcher's delight.

Major first-hand sources, accounts, and works of reference used by Torr throughout:

Of the hundreds of writers referred to by Torr, there are a few he consults throughout for 'contemporary' perspectives on Rhodes and the island's influence on the classical world. Scholarly editions of the original texts, with translations, are to be found in the *Loeb Classical Library Series* published by Harvard University Press. (Volume 8 in the

Loeb edition of Strabo gives a place-name index, making an invaluable Gazetteer for the many unfamiliar sites and cities mentioned by Torr in his text.)

Diodoros Siculus (c. 80-20 BC), the Greek historian from Sicily wrote 40 extremely valuable books of history entitled *Library of History*, concentrating on mythological background, within two major periods – to the death of Alexander (323 BC) and to 54 BC. In particular, see his Chapters IV, V, XI, XIII, XIV, XV, XVI, XVIII, XIX, XX, XXVII, XXIX, XXX, XXI, XXXVII, XIX.

Livy (Titus Livius), the great Roman historian (c. 64 BC – 17 AD) from Padua wrote a history of Rome and the Empire in 142 books: book 37 reveals the scope of Rhodian maritime influence. In particular, see Livy Chapters IV, XXVII, XXVIII, XXXI, XXXII, XXXIII, XXXIV, XXXVI, XXXVII, XXXVIII, XL, XLI, XLII, XLIV, XLV.

Pliny the Elder (23-79 AD) in his fascinating *Natural History* (37 books) details the artists who brought fame to Rhodes in the centuries before Christ. Book XXXIV gives an overview of bronzes, Book XXXV covers artists and painting, and Book XXXVI details sculptors in marble and stone.

"But calling for admiration before all others was the colossal statue of the Sun at Rhodes made by Chares of Lindus, the pupil of Lysippus...This statue was 105 ft. high; and, 66 years after its erection, was overthrown by an earthquake, but even lying on the ground it is a marvel. Few people can make their arms meet round the thumb of the figure, and the fingers are larger than most statues; and where the limbs have been broken off enormous cavities yawn, while inside are seen great masses of rock, with the weight of which the artist steadied it when he erected it. It is recorded that it took twelve years to complete and cost 300 talents, money realized from the engines of war belonging to King Demetrius, which he had abandoned when he got tired of the protracted siege of Rhodes. There are a hundred other colossal statues in the same city, which though smaller than this one would have each brought fame to any place where it might have stood alone; and besides these there were five colossal statues of gods, made by Bryaxis. ..." Pliny the Elder, XXXIV.xviii.41-43 (translated by H. Rackham[1])

Polybios (fl. c. 208 BC), of Megalopolis in the Peloponnese, was another early historian of Rome and, like Livy, is of particular interest in terms of Rhodian maritime power between 264-146 BC. In particular, see his Chapters IV, V, IX, X, XIII, XV, XVI, XVII, XVIII, XXI, XXII, XXIII, XXIV, XXV, XXVI, XXVII, XXVIII, XXIX, XXX, XXXI, XXXIII, XLV.

Strabo (c. 64 BC – c. 25 AD) was an Asiatic Greek from Amasia in Pontus who lived in Nysa and Rome. He travelled extensively, as far north as the Black Sea and as far south as Ethiopia. He has left us one of the most complete geographies of the contemporary 'world'. Of his 17 Books the most interesting section on Rhodes is to be found in Book 14, Section 2, Paragraphs 5-15. The 12 pages of the Loeb edition give a fascinating picture of the island's historical, mythological and cultural features.

Historians, commentators, authorities, and other references cited by Torr:

Ælian
Æneas
Æschines
Æschylos
Ammianus
Anacreon
Antipater
Appian
Apollodoros
Aristeides
Aristophanes
Aristotle
Arrian
Athenæos
Aulus Gellius
Aulus Hirtius
Aurelius Victor, Brutus
Avienus

Callixenos
Callimachos
Cato
Cedren
Cicero
Cleitophon
Clement of Alexandria
Cleomedes
Columella
Conon

Deinarchos
Demosthenes
Dexippos
Dicæarchos
Dictys Cretensis
Dieuchidas
Diodoros
Diogenes

---

[1] Reprinted by kind permission of the publishers and the Trustees of the Loeb Classical Library. Harvard University Press, Copyright © 1959.

Dio Cassius
Diocles
Diogenianos
Dionysios of Halicarnassos
Dionysios Thrax

Epiphanios
Ergeias
Eucrates
Eudoxos
Eusebios
Eustathios of Thessalonica
Eutropius

Festus
Florus
Frontinus
Galen
Geminos
Gorgon

Harpocration
Hephæstion
Herodotos
Gesiod
Hesychios
Hierocles
Hipparchos
Homer
Horace

Isocrates

Josephus
Justin
Juvenal

Lactantius
Livy
Lucian
Lycurgos

Maccabees
Macrobius
Marcianus Heracleotes
Martial
Memnon
Menecrates of Nysa

(Nicolaus) Myrepsus
Nonnos

Pausanias
Philemnestos

Philostratos
Phlegon
Pindar
Plato
Plautus
Pliny
Plotinus
Plutarch
Plutarch
Pollux
Polyænos
Polybios,
Polyzelos
Pomponius
Porphyry
Ptolemy

Quintilian
Quintus Curtius

Sallust
Seneca
Servius

Sextus
Silius
Simplicius
Socrates
Sosicrates
Stephanos
Stesichoros
Strabo
Suetonius
Syncellos

Tacitus
Terence
Theocritos
Theodoros
Theognis
Theophrastus
Thucydides
Timocreon

Valerius Maximus
Varro
Vergil
Vibius Sequester
Vitruvius

Xenophon
Xenophon of Ephesos

Zeno
Zosimos

Sidetrack 1

Digging Rhodes: an archaeological guide to 19th-century exploration

The years in Greece from 1000 BC to the birth of Christ are commonly classified within these periods: Protogeometric (1100-900), Geometric Early (900-700), Middle (850-775) and Late (775-700), Orientalizing Period (700-625), Archaic (600-480), Early Classical Period (480-450), High Classical (450-370), Late Classical (4th century), and Hellenistic (323-30).

That the modern discipline of archaeology should have developed, foremost if not first, in Greece and the Levant is not a surprise. Well-educated classicists and topographers poured over the eastern Mediterranean as the dynamics of the Ottoman Empire began to shift. European diplomats were posted to Athens, Salonika, Istanbul, Smyrna, Crete, North Africa...in the service of their governments. Most of these distinguished men (very rarely women) travelled with their pocket editions of the ancient historians and writers, and kept their eyes open for antiquities that would add prestige to their benefactors, newly founded museums, or themselves. The militaries and navies wanted up-to-date maps and intelligence, and their ablest topographers delighted in 'squeezing' classical inscriptions and identifying lost towns and monuments while they scrambled over mountains and charted the thousands of miles of coastline.

After independence, the Greek Archaeological Society, under Government supervision, was established in 1837 to control excavations and antiquities. In gratitude for the assistance of foreign powers in the struggle for liberation, various European (and then the American) 'Schools' of archaeology were invited to open in Athens, coinciding with the foundation of major departments of archaeology in European universities. These schools quickly became important centres of research and study, undertaking substantial excavations all over Greece and providing welcome additional resources (The French School, 1846; The German School, 1874; The American School, 1882; The British School, 1885). Excavation and recording techniques developed quickly over the last decades of the 19th century, with a concentration on 'material culture' and the significance of all discoveries, not just the spectacular; nevertheless, the uncovering of the major sites roused the greatest interest. Before this period the emphasis was on a 'classicist' approach, working more with texts and inscriptions. The great finds were 'works of art', sculpture and ceramics, but by the end of the century the serious research focused on the exploration of continuously inhabited settlements, and providing archaeological evidence for datable sequences of civilizations.

During Torr's researches, of course, in 1885, the island of Rhodes was not Greek but a relatively quiet corner of the Turkish Empire, and had been so for almost 400 years. (A good-natured debate between Torr and a Rhodian over the last time the island actually was indeed Greek would have been interesting to eavesdrop upon.) Apart from the Colossos, and perhaps the Lindean acropolis, Rhodes' 'classical' past did not attract scholars and antiquarians in the way the fabled sites on the coast opposite did. The Rhodian remains of the golden centuries either side of the death of Alexander had long since been looted, or buried by floods and earthquakes, or reused by the Byzantines and Hospitallers a thousand years later.

Torr's intention in *Rhodes in Ancient Times* was that visitors should look back, beyond the modern and the medieval, and picture the 'great city' as it steadily developed its leading trading and mercantile position by negotiating with the far larger powers that lay at the ends of the winds that filled the sails of her fleets.

An early 'archaeologist' interested in early Rhodes was the delightful and enquiring Cyriac of Ancona, who typified the Renaissance spirit as he travelled the Levant copying inscriptions and sketching monuments. Torr does not mention him in his footnotes, but the Italian visited the island when it was in the hands of the Knights and acquired several Rhodian coins as he visited the islands. He was evidently keen to trace the three original city-states, and wrote in a letter (12 August, 1445) to a friend, a priest in the service of the Order, "... I recall having searched out the monuments of the island of Rhodes several times, and had entered into my Asian journal the ruins of the cities of Kamiros, Lindos, and Ialyssos, wonderful structures left behind for us and our age..."

Few equalled his enthusiasm for the past until the publication in 1678 of Spon and Wheler's antiquarian researches, arguably the most valuable contribution to early archaeological studies.

But, as with all other major areas of Greece and the eastern Mediterranean, it was in the 19th century that 'modern' archaeology began on Rhodes and on the mainland opposite. In his Preface, Torr calls the roll of the most celebrated among the pioneer archaeologists of the region.

In 1837, Sir William J. Hamilton (whose father was involved in bringing the Rosetta Stone to London) first records an inscription found on Rhodes. Some 350 were known by Torr's time and had been published. Hamilton (1805-1867) published his findings in *Researches in Asia Minor, Pontus and Armenia* (1842). The published inscriptions were available to Torr from the pages of various archaeological journals. Large numbers of statuettes, vases, coins, gems had also been found, chiefly in the excavations on the sites of Ialysos and Kamiros. The finest were by then on show in London, Paris and Berlin. A few years after Torr's histories were published, it was Danish excavators at Lindos who made the most significant finds. In 1904 a marble was found, now known as the Temple Chronicle. The stone records gifts made to Lindian Athene from the great and the good, and the not so good, of the times. The celebrities included Phalaris, Tyrant of Sicily, Amasis of Egypt, Artaphernes of Persia, Alexander, Philip V of Macedon, Pyrrhus of Epirus, Hiero, Tyrant of Syracuse, and Ptolomy I.

If there was little or nothing remaining of the wonderful Colossus in Rhodes when the English scholar (Sir) Charles Newton was on the island in 1853 (as a consular official), he did make a monumental discovery in 1857 with his excavations of the Mausoleum at Halicarnassus on the Asia

Minor coast. Newton (1816-1894) was to have a long and illustrious career. He joined the British Museum in 1840 and undertook extensive work in the Levant. He became Keeper at the Museum and was involved in the setting up of the Society for the Promotion of Hellenic Studies (1879) and the British School at Athens (1885).

Of his stunning finds at Halicarnassus, the fragments of Scopas' frieze, now exhibited in London, are without parallel. His many published works include his *Travels and Discoveries in the Levant* (1865); Torr considers him to have provided, "...the first accurate accounts of the ancient remains and inscriptions in Rhodes."

Between Hamilton and Newton, the Turkish island of Rhodes welcomed the greatest antiquary of Greece, Ludwig Ross. Ross was a courtier to the young King Otto and appointed Ross (1806-59) to supervise and initiate what was to become the Greek Archaeological Service. As a result Ross travelled widely in the Aegean, including some Turkish provinces, and his books feature still in modern bibliographies: his island accounts being particularly valued (*Reisen auf die griechischen Inseln des ägäischen Meeres* of 1845 and 1852).

Perhaps the most collectible of illustrated works on Rhodes, however, are the volumes (plates, 1828; text, 1830) of Rottiers' *Description des monuments de Rhodes*. The beautiful engravings (almost all of medieval sites) are the ones most widely seen reproduced in the tourist shops of the Old Town today. Of the contemporary maps, Torr recommended *The Admiralty Charts of Rhodes Island* and *The Mediterranean Archipelago* (south sheet) as "...admirable maps of the island itself and of its neighbourhood".

Between 1869 and 1974, the Englishman John Turtle Wood was at Ephesos. His eventful excavations resulted in seven large column drums – one inscribed to Croesus himself – being shipped back to London, where 20 dray horses were required to transport them to the British Museum.

The great discoveries on Rhodes itself were made by a Frenchman and an Italian, and most modern archaeologists in their summaries of Rhodian contexts begin with the couple's discoveries at Kamiros and Ialysos. August

Salzmann (1824-1872) was a photographer and explorer, and Alfred Biliotti (1833-1915) a career diplomat.

It was during a posting as a (British) consular official on Rhodes that Biliotti persuaded Salzmann to help him explore the overgrown region of Kambiros on the north-west coast of the island in 1858. They quickly discovered tombs and material that convinced them that this was the famous site of Kamiros, one of the three early Rhodian city-states. The finds from the tombs, superb jewellery and ceramics, are in various museums, including the British Museum.

With the discovery of Kamiros – and Lindos never lost its name or fame – Biliotti then dug (from 1868) at the site of present-day Trianda, below Filerimos; he was searching for Ialysos, the third of the famous Rhodian city-states. His luck was to hold, and he began to uncover what was to prove both a Minoan and a Mycenaean 'settlement' and trading base. (Excavations continue there today, over a hundred years after Biliotti.) Again, many of the richest finds are in the British Museum, including some given via John Ruskin, and they formed the first substantial group of Greek Bronze Age objects acquired by the museum.

Torr has left no record of why he chose Rhodes as his main field of study in the 1880s, other than noting in a travel journal an interest in the Rhodo-Cretan colonies on Sicily, but the stir caused in London at the time by Biliotti's finds from Kamiros and Ialysos may well have excited him. Salzmann's *Nécropole de Camiros*, containing some 60 chromolithographs of objects found in the excavations between 1858 and 1865, appeared in 1875: the text was never published owing to his early death at the age of 48. In 1881, Biliotti (with Cottret) published *L'Ile de Rhodes*. Torr comments that "... the chapters on the topography and ruins are creditable". Biliotti also published, at Rhodes, three accounts of his researches (*Report on the Excavations at Ialysos from February to April 16, 1870; Rhodes 14th June 1870; Rhodes 14th May 1871*)

Biliotti was knighted by the British for his services to the *Corps*. His travels took him to Rhodes (as Vice Consul) from 1856 to 1873, Trebizond and Sivas from 1873 to 1885, Crete from 1885 to 1899, and he retired as Consul General of Salonica in 1903. He returned to the island of his most significant (amateur) archaeological discoveries, giving his address as "The Island of Rhodes, Turkey". He died on 1st February 1915; Rhodian winters can be as unkind as anywhere else's.

Two names not on Torr's list, however, are those of Theodore and Mabel Bent. This extraordinary couple, and Torr would certainly have known of them, made their reputations in Greece and Turkey as explorers and archaeologists, before adventuring as far south as modern-day Zimbabwe. The pair spent only eleven days on Rhodes – on their way to dig clandestinely on Kalymnos – and did not excavate. But they met Alfred Biliotti. Mabel Bent writes in her 'Chronicle' of Thursday, February 12th 1885: 'Here we have been 5 days in Rhodes, having very bad weather in this favoured isle, "where there is rarely a day without sunshine".

'We are at a clean little inn in the separate village called Neo Maràs, the Christian quarter, quite close to the sandy and windmilly point Kum Burnù at the north of the isle. It is quite a little walk to the town where no one but Jew or Turk may remain after sun set.

'On Monday we had been to call on the Pasha, Khamel Bey, with Mr. Calvert and Mr. Biliotti. He was not at home but his plump 18-year old son Khem Bey was there. I went to see the Harem...

'We... took several walks and also on Tuesday went to Phileremo at the top of a mountain, about 12 miles.

'The view from the top of the hill is lovely – the coast of Caria and several islands. It was formerly the acropolis of Old Ialysos...'

Now, as then, and 3000 years ago, it is a beautiful place to be. Torr used to dream of it... "In dreams I have imagined myself in Rhodes, walking up the hill at Ialysos..." (Wreyland II, p.48). And Torr was not one to share his dreams with us readily.

Sidetrack 2

Rhodes, the Olympic Games and Athletic Fame

With the Athenian Olympic Games (2004) a not too distant memory, it is timely to pick up on Torr's references to the sporting prowess of Rhodes in classical times (Chapter V). Of all the famous Olympian athletes, the Dorian family of the Eratidai, Herakleidai of the family of Tlepolemos, was the most famous. Pindar's celebrated ode (Olympian VII) on the family of Diagoras, praises the glories of the island and was engraved in golden letters in the temple of Athene at Lindos. Torr adds that in 464 BC Pindar came to the island after the Olympic victory of Diagoras "chanting with lyre and many-voiced choir of flutes the praise of Rhodos". What follows is a free adaptation.

Pindar, 7th Olympian Ode, 464 BC

For Diagoras of Rhodes,
Winner in the Boxing

Just as when, easy with wine, the too generous host lifts his cup at the feast he is giving for his son-in-law to be, and, fully aware he is flaunting his wealth while bringing prestige to his family, makes himself the envy of his friends at the prospect of the happy event to come...

I do the same, by sending out these honeyed words, the gift of the Muses, the sweet fruit of my heart, making this special offering to those champions of the Pythian and Olympic Games. Blessed is he of good report. Grace favours a man, and tunes up for him the lyre, and a chorus of flutes.

And so, to the sound of lyre and pipe I come sailing, with Diagoras the Boxer, to sing an Ode for sea-girt Rhodes, child of Aphrodite and bride of Helios; an Ode to the praise of a mighty and hard-fighting man, who, by the waters of Alpheos and at Kastalia, has won himself many laurels. I glory him, and his father too, the just Demegetos, for his great boxing skills: they who dwell with their Argive families on the isle of three cities, within sight of the vast lands of Asia Minor.

Indeed, let me tell my story about the Eratidai family from the very beginning; from the time of Tlepolemos and Herakles: way back on their father's side they claim Zeus as progenitor, and Amyntor is related from their mother, Astydameia.

Now, sadly, men are not strangers to misfortune – and one of life's great challenges is to decide what do for the best, and avoid folly. But we all make mistakes, even the very founder of this country, Rhodes. Likymnios, in Tiryns - with a hard olive staff - one day struck Alkmene's bastard brother, as he left Midea's chamber, and slew him as his anger blazed. Even the wisest of men will let his heart rule his head.

Likymnios then went to the Oracle for advice, and he of the golden hair, from his incense-sweet shrine, told him to set sail from Lerna for a land of sea-ringed meadows, where sometimes Zeus showers golden snow on the city of Lindos.

Long before the Argives arrived on Rhodes (around the time Athena sprang from her father's brow – freed by a blow from Hephaistos' beautiful bronze axe – and she filled the air with a great cry and Heaven trembled, and Mother Earth too), Hyperion, the god who lights men's way, told his sons on the island to be sure to build for Aphrodite an altar in the sight of all, and placing on it a holy offering, praise the Father and his Daughter with her resounding spear.

Now Reverence, the offspring of Forethought, may well put courage and joy of battle into the hearts of men, but they are still able to fall victim to forgetfulness. And the sons of Hyperion, even though their torches were lit, forgot to light the sacred flame and made their rites without the holy fire in the grove on the hillside of the citadel. And from this act of omission the special Rhodian fire-less rites began.

Later, Zeus floated a yellow cloud into the sky for the sons of Hyperion and golden snow fell upon the land; and Glaukopis herself saw to it that they excelled all others in every form of skill and art, and by this they had power over many living things. This in turn brought them great glory: those blessed with knowledge know that right living, is true living.

Now, ancient legends say that when Zeus and the other gods divided the earth among themselves, the island of Rhodes had not yet surfaced, but lay submerged in the salty depths. By chance, Helios at the time was elsewhere and no one drew a lot for him; and so the god was left without a realm of his own. Aggrieved, he asked Zeus to draw the lots again, but the Father replied only that he knew of a beautiful island floating beneath the sea, ready to surface; a fertile land that would provide food for many and sustain great herds and flocks. Immediately Zeus commanded Lachesis, the Fate with the golden diadem, to stretch out her hands, and witness his oath, promising the son of Kronos that the isle newly rising in the light of heaven should be Helios' alone.

And no sooner had he spoken than the deed was done. Up floated the island from the depths, and the god who brings us all the bright rays of day had mastery of it: he who is lord of the fire-breathing stallions. And by his union with the beautiful Rhodes Helios produced seven sons, wisest of the men of old; and from them came Kameiros, Ialysos and Lindos: and they each controlled many cities, dividing into three the land of their fathers, and giving their names to the three regions.

A happy outcome, then, for the sad fate ordained for Tlepolemos, leader of the Tirynthians long ago, at the beginning, fit for a god, with provision of sacrificial sheep and honours won at the games...

Indeed, Diagoras twice won crowns at the Olympic games, four at the famous Isthmian event, and twice at Nemea and rocky Athens. At Argos he won the bronze shield, and was lauded for his prowess in Arcadia, Thebes, Boeotia, Pellene and Aegina, where he won six times; the stone monument at Megara also boasts his name.

We pray to you, O Father Zeus, on the mountain-ridges of Ataviros, to hear this customary hymn for an Olympic champion, and glorify the man who has been so courageous with his fists: let him be honoured by citizens and foreigners alike; for he walks that straight path that won't tolerate dishonour, true to himself and his conscience and his noble lineage: offend a descendant of great Kallianax at your peril!

Surely the whole city of Lindos may now celebrate the achievements of the Eratidai family and be merry, while the many breezes rush their own separate ways over the seas...

Even today the names of athletes, ancient and modern, are remembered in the names of shops, squares and streets of Rhodes. A pleasant walk up to the ancient Acropolis leads to the old stadium which is still used for athletic events. Until recently there was a DANE Line ferry, named after the boxer Diagoras, which sailed between Rhodes and Pireas.

Sidetrack 3

Cecil Torr and Rhodes

Torr does not seem to have recorded his motives for choosing the island of Rhodes (then Turkish) for his first published academic monograph; he visits Rome (1876, at 19) before he visits Athens (1880, at 23). In 1881 he was in the waters of what we now know as the northern Dodecanese, and en route for an extensive tour of the Holy Land (1882); he could well have steamed through the short 18km straits between Rhodes and Marmaris, glimpsing the island to starboard, or even touching there. His travel journals do not reveal as much, but there are clues in both his works on the island and the historian confirms a sojourn there in several references in *Small Talk at Wreyland* (II, p.48), but without, sadly, telling us the actual dates (as he so often did on other journeys): "I have been to see the remains of two of the Seven [Wonders], the Pyramids at Memphis and the Temple of Diana at Ephesos and the sites on which two others stood, the Zeus at Olympia and the Colossos at Rhodes..."

In London in the 1880s there was a deal of interest raised in archaeological circles over the recent finds from Kamiros and Ialysos, and a collection of wonderful Bronze Age artefacts had recently been acquired by the British Museum. These may well have added to Torr's fascination for the island.

There is something 'magnetic' about Rhodes, in any event, and Torr would have encountered the island's influence – to a greater or lesser extent, depending on his current historical interests – early on in his studies of the history of the eastern Mediterranean.

Geographically, Rhodes is the largest island in the group known as the Dodecanese. Kos is the next largest in this group of fourteen, not twelve, major islands, and at least 40 islets. Patmos to the north and Kastellorizo to the southeast are 300km apart. Rhodes (approximately 1,400sq km) lies close to the south western coast of Asia Minor, between latitudes 35° 20´ and 37° 30´ N and longitudes 26° 15´ and 28° 40´ E. Lawrence Durrell's "some great sea-animal asleep in the water" slumbers – in roundish kilometres – 450 from Athens, 725 from Istanbul, 400 from Izmir, 440 from Limassol, 625 from Beirut, and 575 from Alexandria.

The first clue Torr provides of his interest in Rhodes is in *Small Talk* (III, p.29): "At first I only thought of writing about the Rhodian colonies in Sicily, but the subject led me on to Rhodes itself, and then to the adventures of the Knights..."

Torr seems, then, to have pulled back from a tight focus on Rhodian colonies on Sicily, which he visited in 1883 when he was 26, to a wide-angle coverage of some 3,000 years of Rhodian history. Two years after his visit to the Rhodian/Cretan colony of Gela on Sicily, *Rhodes in Ancient Times* was published.

This was followed in 1886 by a shorter study of Byzantine Rhodes and it was this essay that he expanded into *Rhodes in Modern Times*, first published in 1887. "Modern" for Torr meant Rhodes after the Romans, and this completion of the island's history (to 1522) takes up the story from the fall of Rome, through the Byzantine era, to the Knights of St John and the start of Ottoman rule.

Accordingly, readers may be interested in the young classicist's Preface to his *Rhodes in Modern Times* (1887):

THE ancient history of Rhodes closes with the Second Century of our Era. Its history thenceforward has not yet been seriously attempted, except that from 1309 to 1522 it is incidentally treated in works on the Knights Hospitallers.

The great historian of the Knights is Bosio, *Istoria del sacro militare ordine Gerosolimitano*, 1594-1602. He has directly or indirectly furnished the later historians with nearly all their facts: and he is seldom responsible for their fictions, which they have generally obtained from Vertot, *Histoire des chevaliers hospitaliers*, 1726. But Bosio did not use his materials accurately or critically or impartially; and he had not access to much that is now at hand. In fact, anything approaching an authentic history of the Knights has yet to be written.

The works dealing with the modern history of Rhodes are mainly compounded from histories of the Knights and from books of travel: and these books of travel are chiefly by archæologists who despised mediæval castles or churches, unless ancient sculptures or inscriptions had been built into the walls. Coronelli and Parisotti, *Isola di Rodi*, 1688, took their facts from Bosio. Rottiers, *Description des monuments de Rhodes*, 1828-1830, obtained his drawings from one Greek and his facts from another; and neither Greek was trustworthy. It seems necessary to point out once more that the monuments and epitaphs of the Grand Masters of Rhodes given by Villeneuve-Bargemont, *Monuments des Grands Maîtres*, 1829, are purely fictitious. Guérin, *Ile de Rhodes*, 1856, gives an account of a six weeks' tour in the island two years before, with some unimportant remarks on its history. Berg, *Die Insel Rhodus*, 1862, was a painter; and his illustrations and his text are alike picturesque and inaccurate. Biliotti and Cottret, *L'Ile de Rhodes*, 1881, are deeply indebted to Vertot and Guérin: but the book is of bibliographic value as the first printed in the island.

The scope of the present volume is this. The period of Byzantine rule ending in 1309 is treated fully. The period of Turkish rule beginning in 1523 is not touched. For the intervening period the affairs of Rhodes are distinguished from the affairs of the Knights: for their history while at Rhodes involves that of all Europe, and is moreover unintelligible apart from their earlier history while at Jerusalem and their later history while at Malta. The distinction is artificial, but necessary. And the affairs of Rhodes themselves are not treated fully, an immense mass of minor detail being neglected. Thus this volume is not in any sense exhaustive or final. Its justification is, first, that it is accurate so far as it goes, every statement resting on a critical comparison of the primary authorities: and secondly, that it goes further than any previous work on the subject, information being derived from new sources.

CECIL TORR.

19, OLD BUILDINGS,
LINCOLN'S INN.

Sidetrack 4

Rhodes – an island chronology to March 7, 1948

The 6-page table that follows is a selected chronology of key dates from Rhodes' long and dynamic story. The objective is to illustrate contemporaneous events in the fields of political relations, the arts, literature and learning.

A brief account of 'modern' dates, until the union of the Dodecanese with Greece in 1948, is appended.

Torr's spellings have been retained and the majority of dates are those quoted by him in his text; supplementary dates from other sources have been added. Readers should bear in mind the variety of calendars employed by early commentators at different times: more than a few dates are, of course, debateable.

Era	Events	The Arts	Literature and Learning
Prehistory	Neolithic and Early Bronze Age activity at Archangelos and elsewhere on Rhodes. The island is only 12 km from the Asia Minor coast 1500. Minoan 'colony' at Ialysos 1400. Mycenaeans and Minoans on Rhodes until decline of Minoan influence 1100. Dorians on Rhodes, end of Mycenaean influence	2000-1000. Bronze Age objects of Minoan, Mycenaean, Egyptian, Phoenician origins are on show in the museums. Ialysos provides Minoan statuettes. A bulls' head rhyton from near Lindos is unique. There is volcanic ash from Thera in the archaeologists' trenches	
1000-500 BC	900. In the lists of powers holding the 'Thalassocratia', the sovereignty of the seas, Rhodes stands sometimes 4th and sometimes 5th. 9th c. Growth of three city-states of Lindos, Kamiros, Ialysos 884. Olympic games founded 800. Phoenician/Syrian artefacts point to further development of trade routes 720. Rhodian colony of Rosas (Spain) founded with Emporium 700. The Dorian confederacy of city-states. Rhodes a key member 688. Rhodian colonies of Gela (Sicily) and Phaselis founded with Cretans 630. Thera founds colony of Cyrene (Libya). This is a boost to Rhodes' trade 609. Rhodian colony of Apollonia Pontica on the Black Sea founded with Miletus and Phocaea	7th c. The earliest Rhodian coins 600. 'Some terra-cotta vases found at Kamiros must have been made at Athens. They are rude and clumsy, but still plainly enough the direct ancestors of the finest Athenian vases.' [The British Museum has finds from graves in the area. Torr sees them]	7th c. Peisander of Kamiros, the epic poet. 'It was said that he stole his great work, the 'Heracleia', from Pisinos of Lindos: but nothing is known of this Pisinos' 7th c. The poetess Erinna, the youthful friend of Sappho, is reported on slight authority to have been a Rhodian
500-0 BC	546. The Greek cities on the mainland opposite Rhodes taken by Cyros 500. There is a Rhodian 'treasury' at the site of the Nemean Games	6th c. early. Cleobulos rebuilds the Lindian temple 530. Coin with the lion's head of Lindos and the silphion tree of Cyrene, struck at Cyrene as pay for Rhodian mercenaries	6th c. Cleobulos of Lindos, one of the 'Seven Wise Men'
Persian Wars	5th c. Gradual decline in influence of the three city-states of Lindos, Kamiros, Ialysos 490. Rhodian fleet captured by Persian ships before Battle of Marathon 480. Rhodian seamen in the fleet of Xerxes on its way to Salamis. Battle of Salamis. Battle of Thermopylae 479. Final defeat of the Persians at Battle of Platea and sea victory off Mycale		480. Timocreon of Ialysos, the scurrilous lyric poet, flourished during the Persian wars. He satirises Themistocles for not restoring him to Rhodes. Simonides writes his epitaph: 'much I drank, much I ate, much evil I spake of men; now rest I here, Timocreon of Rhodes'
Peloponnesian Wars	476. The city-states of Rhodes join the Athenian League 431. Peloponnesian War breaks out. Most of the Aegean islands (inc. Rhodes) fall to Athens 415. Athens forces Rhodians to fight against Gela, their own colonists 412. Dorieus comes to Cnidos with twelve ships and puts pressure on the Rhodians. Rhodes allies herself to Sparta, not Athens, at this stage of the Peloponnesian Wars. 408. **Foundation of new city of Rhodes**. The city could accommodate 80,000-100,000. Hippodamus of Miletus issupposed to have plotted the grid. Final decline of Kamiros and Ialysos, but Lindos retains her status, thanks to the famous temple 407. Alcibiades ravages the island 406. Lysander crosses via Rhodes to Ephesus. Negotiations with Cyrus, son of Darius 404. Sea battle and Spartan victory at Aegospotamoe. Peloponnesian War ends and Rhodes remains in the power of Sparta 401. Early in the retreat of the 'Ten Thousand'. Xenophon notes there were Rhodians among them, forming a body of two hundred slingers 395. Rhodians revolt and drive off Spartan fleet of 120 in the	464. **Victory of Diagoras, the greatest Rhodian athlete, at the Olympic Games** 408. The founding of the 'great city' in 408 BC called for new coinage: and the types then adopted were those of nearly all Rhodian coins down to the Roman times; on the obverse is the head of Helios, on the reverse the iconic flower of Rhodes. Many of today's sites in the Old Town date from this time. The 'Street of Knights' is on an original thoroughfare down to the sea. The Palace of the Grandmasters is built over a famous temple of Helios 407. The famous Rhodian Olympic champion, Doricus, taken in chains to Athens, but he is immediately released because of his sporting prowess 405. At Delphi, Tisandros of Rhodes sets up statues of Rhodian commanders at Battle of Aegospotamoe	464. Pindar Olympic Ode 7, for Rhodes and Diagoras 'And thus to the sound of lyre and pipe I come sailing, with Diagoras the Boxer, to sing an Ode for sea-girt Rhodes, child of Aphrodite and bride of Helios; an Ode to the praises of a mighty and hard-fighting man, who, by the waters of Alpheos and at Kastalia, has won himself many laurels. I glory him, and his father too, the just Demegetos, for his great boxing skills: they who dwell with their Argive clan on the isle of three cities, within sight of the vast lands of Asia Minor...'

History of Rhodes

	394. Conon utterly defeated the Spartans off Cnidos, and frees the Rhodian democracy
	378. New Athenian Confederacy formed. The Rhodian democrats at once join Athens
	363. Rhodes, Byzantium and Chios are strongest naval powers among Athenian allies. When Epaminondas of Thebes seeks to raise a navy, the Rhodians readily assent to his plans
	357. The Rhodian "Social War". Rhodes, Byzantium, Chios, Kos, and Mausolus of Caria split from Athens in favour of Macedonians. Mausolus used the influence acquired through his support during the war to establish an oligarchy at Rhodes
	355. Athens refuses to raise Rhodes in revolt from Persia
	346. Artemisia, the daughter of Mausolus invades Rhodes. A Rhodian fleet had set off to attack her but she captured the ships and, pretending to be the successful Rhodian vessels returning, takes the city. She is eventually driven off
Rise of Macedonia	341. Rhodes and Chios join Athens against Philip II of Macedon
	340. Idrieus, Artemisia's successor, temporarily seizes Rhodes. On the first advance east by the Macedonians, Rhodes joins Athens and other Greek cities in forcing Philip to raise the siege of Byzantium
	338. At Battle of Chaeronea, Philip effectively gains control of Greece
	394. Distinctive coins with the letters s u m on them may refer to a political alliance after the battle at Cnidos
	392. Fire at temple of Athena at Lindos
	350. The building of the Mausoleum at Halicarnassos
	351. Artemisia dedicates a bronze group at Rhodes, no doubt the work of one of the great sculptors then working for her on the Mausoleum
	377. The master of the 'Middle Comedy' Anaxandrides of Kamiros produces a play in Athens
	343. Mentor the Rhodian, treacherously seized and deposed Aristotle's friend, Hermeias of Atarneus
	330. Aeschines the orator settles for a while at Rhodes and had apparently given systematic instruction in rhetoric there
Philip II & Alexander	336. Death of Philip and accession of Alexander the Great
	334. Alexander marches through Asia Minor. The Persian fleet (then commanded by a Rhodian admiral) kept the islands from him
	333. Alexander does not punish Rhodes, as she had not openly supported the Persians. Alexander had ceremonially recognized the uprightness of the Rhodians by leaving his will in their keeping
	332. Rhodian ships support Alexander at 7-month siege of Tyre.
	323. Death of Alexander. **'Alexander had greatly advanced Rhodes, and her most famous age now began: she was no longer merely an equal of Chios or Byzantium, but the first naval power of the Ægean'**
	316. Flood at Rhodes
Death of Alexander Height of Rhodes' power	305/4. Great Siege of Demetrios Poliorketes. 6000 citizens and 1000 aliens bear arms at the great siege. He leaves with nothing of his own
	304-292. **Chares of Lindos builds the Colossus**, one of the 7 Wonders of the World. It took 12 years to build but stood for only 56.
	304. During his siege Demetrios is said to have spared the city rather than destroy even one of Protogenes' pictures. The besieger says he would rather burn his family portraits than such a masterpiece. **Protogenes was widely celebrated.** Later Apelles, Alexander's court artist, himself arrives and says he wants to buy Protogenes' unsold pictures for 50 talents - to sell as works of his own.
	330. Lindian Temple rebuilt
	330. Lindian Propylon finished. The bronze statue of the eunuch Combabos by Hermocles of Rhodes set up at Hierapolis in Syria
Conflicts between Alexander's successors	227. Rhodes shattered by a great earthquake. The gifts sent... by Ptolemy of Egypt, Seleucos of Syria, Hiero and Gelon of Sicily, Prusias, Mithridates and the other sovereigns of Asia Minor, Antigonos of Macedon and by independent cities without number showed the width of Rhodian influence. The rebuilding of the city after the earthquake was followed by a sudden development of the political power of Rhodes'
	220. Byzantines levy dues on the exports from the Black Sea to Greece. Rhodians declare war rather than negotiations fail and Byzantines soon concede. When Mithridates attacked Sinope (another commercial city) the Rhodians vote 140,000 drachmas to purchase supplies for its defence
	219. Demetrios of Pharos plunders the Cyclades. The Rhodians help drive him off. Some of the Rhodian ships fitted out for the war with Byzantium were sent to assist Knossos against Eleutherna, another Cretan city. Eleutherna replies by threatening reprisals and then declaring war against Rhodes
Philip V	208. The advance of Macedon under Philip V threatens more than just Rhodian trade. When the Macedonians march down into southern Greece, Rhodes joined Chios, Athens and Egypt in sending
	227. Earthquake destroys most of the city. The upper part of the Colossus breaks away at the knees and falls. Ptolemy offers 3000 talents to resurrect it. The rebuilding of the city is followed by the sudden development of the political and cultural influences of Rhodes
	227-168. All the sculptors and painters of the Rhodian schools appear to belong to this period of a little over 50 years (Parrhasios, etc.)
	220. Hiero and Gelon set up in the Deigma at Rhodes a personification of the 'Commons of Rhodes.' A masterpiece by Lysippos, a **'Quadriga with Helios of the Rhodians,'** is in the Temple of Helios in Rhodes
	212. Pictures and statues seized at the capture of Syracuse form the gift of Marcellus to the temple of 1st c. The 'Athene' at Lindos, the **Laocoön and His Sons** created by Athanadoros, Hagesandros, and Polydoros of Rhodes
	250. Rhodes was of some importance in ancient geography as the point of intersection of the primary meridian of Eratosthenes. 'The one passed through Merowê, Assouan, Alexandria, Rhodes and Constantinople; and the other through the Straits of Gibraltar and of Messina, Cape Matapan, Rhodes and Alexandretta Bay: both of them somewhat wavy lines when traced on a modern map.'
	250. c. Food and drink were not neglected on the island. Lynceus of Samos praises Rhodian cuisine, especially the 'alopex', the Thresher shark.
	220. **Apollonios**, commonly called the **Rhodian**, was born in Egypt, and probably at Alexandria itself, though Athenaeos claims him for his own birthplace. He was a noted teacher of rhetoric on Rhodes, as well as the writer of the fabulous story of Jason. It is known in its revised version and, 'in its new form it succeeded as completely as it had failed before: and now faultlessly polished and purged of all vigour it became a standard of

Theme	Events	Cultural notes
	envoys to arrange a peace. The Romans maintain a watching brief. 205. Philip makes peace, but still his admiral, Heracleides, sets fire to the dockyards in Rhodes. Philip disclaims act but does not punish his admiral. 201. The Macedonians cross into Asia Minor and begin to seize the independent cities. Macedonian squadrons attacked Chios and Samos. The Macedonian fleet is overtaken in the Straits of Chios and forced to fight. The allies, including Rhodes, although vastly outnumbered, 'were stronger in ships of the largest size and far superior in seamanship.' Under Theophiliscos, the distinguished Rhodian admiral, they destroy half Philip's fleet. The remains of the Macedonian fleet sail south. Only the Rhodian ships follow and they are defeated in an action fought off Lade, near Miletos 200. Philip secures the passage of the Hellespont by taking Abydos	Alexandrine taste and had some influence with the Roman poets. He also wrote epics on the founding of several cities, Naucratis, Alexandria, Cnidos, Caunos and Rhodes: but of Canopos he apparently wrote in choliambics, a metre sacred to sarcasm.' He has a claim, to this day, of still being the island's best-known literary figure
Steady growth of Roman influence in E. Med. Defeat of Philip and rise of Antiochus of Syria	199. Rhodian ships shadow the Macedonian fleet but leave early for the winter 198. The Romans, supported by certain Greek states, decide to take control and send Flaminius to Greece. 20 Rhodian ships join the Pergamene and Roman squadrons, and the combined fleet takes Cenchreae, the port of Corinth. With his power thus weakened at home, Philip, treats for peace 197. Flaminius utterly routs Philip at Cynoscephalae. Meanwhile Antiochus of Syria moves up along the south coast. The Rhodians see the danger of allowing his forces to unite with the Macedonians, and their envoys at Coracesion say he must not pass the Chelidoniae Islands by land or sea. Antiochus holds off and renews treaties between Syria and Rhodes. With news of the Macedonian defeat at Cynoscephalae the Rhodians see no further need to oppose the advance of Antiochus. Livy writes later, 'In the war with Antiochus, the Rhodians have performed many acts of outstanding courage on land and sea to show their loyalty to the Roman people and to help the whole of the Greek community; but they have never acted with more superb valour than in this crises, when, undismayed by the magnitude of the war that threatened, they sent envoys to the king, forbidding him to go past Chelidoniae'. 196. Truce with Antiochus. A Rhodian squadron helps Roman and Pergamene forces in putting down Nabis of Sparta. In the abortive negotiations for peace before Cynoscephalae, Philip offered to restore to the Rhodians the 'Peraea' (their cities on the mainland opposite). The Romans agree to honour this and the Carian cities that Philip had occupied were granted to the Rhodians, who now held most of them, recovered by their admiral Pausistratos	200. Lindian Stoa completed
Syrian War	192. Roman war against Antiochus begins in earnest. The Syrians recruit the great Hannibal of Carthage to fight with them. 191. The Rhodian squadron is too late to join the Romans in their defeat of the Syrian fleet off Cyssos, and merely join the blockade of Ephesus. Under Pausistratos they send 36 ships north. These are surprised at Samos through the treachery of the Syrian admiral Polyxenidas, a Rhodian exile. Only seven ships escape and Pausistratos is killed. Antiochus invades Greece but is held back by the Romans at Thermopylae. A rebuilt Rhodian fleet is involved with the allies after the naval Battle at Corycus	
Peace with Syria	190. Power of Antiochus wanes. Rhodians fight at Side and Myonessus, both wins for Rhodes and the allies 188. Peace of Apomea with Antiochus. Rhodes granted further territories in Lycia and Caria as a reward from Rome. But poor management by the Rhodians sees war break out between the	190. The 'Victory of Samothrace' made by Rhodian artist (Pythokritos?). The statue, 'its drapery windswept and swirling like storm-tossed waves', was a Rhodian dedication (as a fragmentary description reveals) for a victory over Antiochus III of Syria. It was found in

Campaigns against Philip and his son Perseus	Rhodes and these regions and strains Rhodes' relations with Rome. 185. Philip V restores Macedonian power 182. Pharnaces of Pontus captures Sinope. The Rhodians complain to Rome but nothing comes of it. 179. Death of Philip. Accession of his son Perseus 171. Eumenes of Pergamum's sacred embassy to the festival of Helios at Rhodes is turned back. Eumenes had been a former ally of the Rhodians against Antiochus. There are doubts over Rhodian allegiance against Perseus. Rhodes in danger of miscalculating her influence 170. Rhodes harbour dues reach a million drachmas a year 169. The Romans confirm treaty of friendship with the Rhodians and give them leave to export corn from Sicily. Rome begins her final push against Perseus. A surprise delegation from Rhodes arrives 'demanding' that the Romans and Macedonians make peace. Livy reports the Roman response: 'And so we now have the Rhodians as the arbiters of peace and war throughout the world!' It was a huge diplomatic blunder on the Rhodian side and one that was to have severe ramifications	1863 by French antiquaries in 100 pieces. 170. The famous carving on the Lindian Acropolis of a ship's prow
End of Macedonian War	168. Defeat of Perseus at Battle of Pydna. Rome cancels treaty of friendship with Rhodes and takes back certain territories in Caria and Lycia. Popillius Laenas lands on Rhodes to check on the Island's loyalty. 167. The Rhodian admiral sails to Rome to try and improve relations. Meanwhile the Rhodians put down a revolt of Caunos, Mylassos and Alabanda, fearing that if they lose total control of Caria and Lycia their other possessions would revolt or be seized by neighbouring states. In Rome the Rhodian ambassadors assure that they are loyal allies. They donate a tribute of gold. The Caunians revolt against Rhodes. At a battle near Orthosia Rhodes stamps her authority, keen not to lose prestige in area after Roman censure 166. But the Romans intend to weaken Rhodes and pressure Athens to make Delos a free port. This is a decisive blow against Rhodian marine trade 164. Harbour dues fall to 150,000 drachmas (from 1 million in 170 BC). The Rhodians press again for an alliance with Rome. Tiberius Gracchus supports them 156. Rhodes declares war on Cretan pirates but the campaign suffers reversals and Rhodes fails to gather other Greek support in case Rome intervenes 154. The Rhodians send some of the ships they had fitted out for war with Crete to assist the Pergamene fleet against Prusias of Bithynia. Prusias comes to terms with Rome	168. To appease the Romans for the great offence caused, the Rhodians set up the statue of the 'Commons of Rome' in their temple of Athene. It was 45 feet high
Wars with Mithridates	There follows a period of relative stability in the Eastern Mediterranean. The Romans are engaged in 'European' campaigns. But they suffer a series of defeats that in turn stirs civil unrest in Italy. The compass swings east again, however, with the rise of Mithridates and Rome unites to defeat him. When he is no longer a threat the Roman factions split again. Rhodes' geographical position, for two millennia her fortune, is now her undoing. Within 50 years her cultural and mercantile influences are gone 87. Rhodes supplies Lucullus when he seeks allies against Mithridates. The reputation of Rhodes restored by her resistance to Mithridates 85. Rhodian ships are victorious with Lucullus off Lectum and Tenedos	99. The Lindos 'Temple Chronicle' dates to this period. It was discovered in 1904 by Danish archaeologists, and is now in Copenhagen 143. **The Rhodian philosopher Panaetios.** 'The Rhodian Stoics all belong to the period of transition between the formulation of the Stoic doctrine by philosophers at Athens and its acceptance by generals and statesmen at Rome. Perhaps the ablest of them and certainly the most successful was Panaetios. The friendship of the younger Scipio Africanus gave Panaetios the opportunity of influencing Roman society. He was that general's sole companion on the embassy to the East and afterwards lived for years as an honoured guest at his house, which was then the meeting place of the ablest men at Rome. There he would dispute with them while Polybios looked on, and through them he made Stoicism the fashionable philosophy of Rome' 120. Apollonios Malacos the orator moves to Rhodes 100. **The famous grammarian Dionysios surnamed Thrax was a native of Alexandria, but migrates to Rhodes.** Of his many works there remains only part of his grammar, the ancestor of all grammars 88 & 81. Apollonios Molon was at Rome as Rhodian envoy, and was the first foreigner to address the Senate without an interpreter 86. Poseidonios of Apomea, head of School at

Civil unrest in Rome. Rhodes backs Pompey	84. At the peace, the Rhodians receive are rewarded by Sulla 70. Romans help Rhodes repulse Mithridates. Consulate of Pompey and Crassus in Rome 66. Mithridates defeated by Pompey 60. 1st Roman Triumvirate of Pompey, Crassus and Caesar. Pompey's power base lies in the East, and Rhodes sides with him in the build-up of tensions between the Roman generals 49. Pompey raises forces to oppose Caesar. Rhodian ships form one of his squadrons 48. Rhodian forces are with Pompey at the Battle of Pharsalos. Pompey flees to Egypt, where he dies. Rhodes finds herself on the losing side in the end-game of the Roman civil conflicts. In the Adriatic a Rhodian squadron of sixteen ships under Coponius sighted some of Caesar's ships crossing from Italy to Greece and went in pursuit. When the enemy had just made the harbour, the wind suddenly changed; and the whole squadron went ashore and broke up. This is the only case of the loss of Rhodian war ships through bad weather; and also the only case in which a Rhodian squadron was commanded by a foreign admiral. 47. Caesar chases the rebels to Egypt 45. Caesar becomes supreme commander 44. Caesar assassinated. Rhodians fit out ships for Dolabella	70. In denouncing Verres for carrying off works of art from Greek cities, Cicero instanced the 'Ialysos' by Protogenes, at Rhodes, as a work that it would be scandalous to carry off. A century later it was in the temple of Peace at Rome. Arguments over the rights and wrongs of removing works of art are not new	Rhodes. He was 'a traveller and historian and the best informed man of his day' 79. Caesar studies on Rhodes under Apollonios Molon, either just before or just after the impeachment of Dolabella. (Brutus and Cassius both studied rhetoric on the island) 78. After hearing the orators of Athens and Asia, Cicero comes to Rhodes to study under Apollonios Molon 67 & 62. Pompey visits Poseidonios on Rhodes 1st C. Among the Peripatetics, the Rhodian of note was Andronicus, the great editor of Aristotle. 'Theophrastos had bequeathed his own manuscripts and those of Aristotle that he had to Neleus of Scepsis. After keeping them for a century and a half in a damp cellar, the family of Neleus sold what the worms had left to Apellicon, a collector at Athens... Sulla carried off Apellicon's library to Rome, and there Tyrannion went to work on the manuscripts. Andronicus, who had probably met Tyrannion when that grammarian was studying at Rhodes, obtained copies from him and then brought out a complete edition, rejecting the spurious works and classifying and arranging the rest, which seem previously to have been arranged by chance or at best chronologically. This edition is probably the Aristotle of today'
Cassius loots Rhodes	43. 2nd Triumvirate of Antony, Lepidus and Octavian. Before the Battle of Philippi, Cassius loots Rhodes and leaves 3000 men there, 'and then went on his way to Philippi... Cassius had carried off all the Rhodian ships he could man and burnt the rest, and it no longer mattered what side Rhodes might take. The Rhodians never recovered from this blow.' Antony grants Rhodes several islands as some compensation for their losses: but these they governed so harshly that he revokes the grant 42. Battle of Philippi	43. The 'Quadriga with Helios of the Rhodians' is one of the few works not removed by Cassius. Pliny writes that there were still several thousand statues left in Rhodes after Cassius' looting. The island suffered less than the rest of Greece from the Roman passion for collecting	42. Before Cassius sacks Rhodes, Archelaos, in whose school Cassius had studied, was sent to plead with him for the city and made a lengthy speech 'with tears and all fitting gestures' but without result
The decline of Rhodes after Philippi	31. Antony defeated at Actium 30. Herod confirmed as King of Judaea by Octavian at Rhodes 6. Tiberius retires to Rhodes (but returns to Rome in 2 BC)	50. The famous painted panel with the rival lines of Protogenes and Apelles arrives in Rome. It burns in a fire at Caesar's House on the Palatine. The statue of 'Athene of Lindos' was taken to Constantinople, and stood opposite the statue of Zeus of Dodona at the entrance to the Senate	41. Claudius restores the independence of Rhodes in response to a speech delivered in Greek on their behalf by Nero, who was then a boy
To AD 1000	18. Death of Augustus 37. Death of Tiberius 44. Claudius withdraws Rhodian independence because they had crucified Romans 51. St Paul visits Rhodes 53. Claudius restores Rhodian independence. (Afterwards the island was 'several times forfeited for intrigues against Rome and then regained by services in war') 70. Vespasian places Rhodes among the Roman provinces 150. The celebrated 'maritime law' of Rhodes adopted by Rome. Antoninus Pius: 'I rule the land, but the law rules the sea. Let the matter be judged by the naval law of the Rhodians.' Salvinus Julianus, who flourished under Antoninus, provides the earliest (extant) report on the only principle of Roman naval law that is certainly Rhodian. This is the principle of general average: 'that if cargo be jettisoned to lighten the ship, all contribute to make good the loss incurred for the benefit of all.' This principle still obtains among all maritime nations; and probably much else of the naval law of to-day has come down from the Rhodians. Nothing is heard of these laws at Rhodes itself. The Jus Navale Rhodiorum is a forgery of the Middle Ages		100. Dio Chrysostom, a rhetorician of the Roman Empire, delivers 'a wearisome oration to the Rhodians' 157. Aristeides 'inflicts' on the Rhodians two long orations, one on the earthquake of that year 263. Melanthios of Rhodes appears among the Academics; and Antonios of Rhodes, who accompanied Porphyry from Greece to Rome on his first visit to Plotinos
Rhodes rebuilt after tidal wave and becomes a great	157. Earthquake and tidal wave: 'The sea went back, and	404. The statue of 'Athene of Lindos' marvellously escapes destruction during the Constantinople riots 653. It is said that when the Saracen raider Muawiyeh (Moabiah) occupied Rhodes they sold the remains of the Colossus for scrap. 900 camels were loaded with the bronze. The 20 tons of metal would not, however, load more than 90 camels.' Everyone has their own view on where the Colossus may have stood. It is strange that the many chroniclers of ancient Rhodes never firmly located it: what a shame. Torr was of the opinion that 'the Colossus stood in some public place	

Waning of Roman power. Rhodes vulnerable until protected by Byzantium	and then fires broke out that burnt on day and night. The Emperor Antoninus Pius rebuilt the city; and in a few years Aristeides could again call it the fairest of Greek cities. It was probably after this rebuilding that Pausanias reckoned the city walls among the finest he had seen' 269. Claudius Gothicus disperses Gothic fleet heading south towards Rhodes 330. Constantine Emperor in Constantinople 345. Earthquake on Rhodes 470. Arab raiders on Rhodes 515. Earthquake on Rhodes 620. Rhodes taken by the Persians under Chosrau Parwiz (Hosroes) 622. Byzantine fleet under Heraclius secures the island 672. Saracens first besiege Constantinople 678. Byzantine defeat of Saracens returns Rhodes to the Emperor's control 727. The Saracen fleet sails unopposed to Constantinople and captures Rhodes, briefly, on the way. The subsequent Byzantine victories restore Rhodes to the Empire until the arrival of the Knights of St John in 1309 807. Harūn-ar-Rashīd's (Seljuk) Turks make surprise attack on Rhodes	the lowest part of the city by the water. There is now a piece of very low ground near the south-west corner of the northern harbour; and perhaps the figure stood here on the site of the church of Saint John of the Colossus. The ludicrous medieval notion that it stood across the harbour would have been suggested by the two curious towers at the mouth of the southern harbour rather than by an ancient epigram'

Related 'Modern' dates

1099 [July]	Crusaders capture Jerusalem
1191 [April]	Richard Cœur de Lion at Rhodes with his English fleet for ten days
1204	Crusaders take Constantinople
1291	The Knights Hospitallers of St John of Jerusalem establish themselves on Cyprus, following their expulsion from Palestine
1309 [15 August]	Byzantine Rhodes finally surrenders on good terms to the Hospitallers. End of Byzantine rule on Rhodes and beginning of period of Knights' control (1309-1522)
1440 c.	Cyriac of Ancona visits Rhodes
1453 [29 May]	Fall of Constantinople to the Ottoman Turks
1480	The first great siege of Rhodes (May-August).
1522	Second great siege of Rhodes (June-December)
1523	New Year's Day. Suleiman enters the city as conqueror. End of Knights' rule, start of period of Turkish control, lasting until 1919
1821	Greek independence movement gathers momentum with uprising against the Turks in Peloponnese
1825 [April]	Byron dies at Mesolongi
1827	Battle of Navarino ensures Greek independence will become a reality
1831	King Otto I imposed as head of Greek state
1837	W. J. Hamilton looks for inscriptions on Rhodes
1853	The antiquarian and diplomat Charles Newton lives on Rhodes
1856	An explosion of gunpowder destroys the Church of St John outside the Grand Master's Palace. Much of the top (N/W)

	end of the 'Street of the Knights' is also badly damaged
1857	Cecil Torr born
1858	Biliotti and Salzmann excavate at Kamiros
1863	Earthquake destroys de Naillac tower. It had withstood all tribulations for over 450 years
1866	As a backlash to Greek Independence, Turks attempt forceful integration of Rhodes and the islands into Ottoman way of life
1868	Biliotti excavates at Ialysos
1870s	Biliotti publishes his finds
1880s	Torr visits Rhodes during these years
1885	Torr publishes *Rhodes in Ancient Times*. Theodore and Mabel Bent visit Rhodes
1886	Cecil Torr publishes *Rhodes under the Byzantines*
1887	Cecil Torr publishes *Rhodes in Modern Times*.
1902-14	Danes Kinch and Blinkenberg excavate at Lindos
1908	The Greeks of the neighbouring islands (but not Rhodes as yet) style themselves 'the Dodecanese' in defiance of the Turks
1912	The Italian-Turkish War and Balkan War. A congress (June) of Dodecanese island delegates meet in Patmos to establish a free Aegean state. Treaty of Lausanne (October). The Dodecanese to be returned to Turks
1915	Sir Alfred Biliotti dies on Rhodes
1915 [April]	Treaty of London confirmed that Italy should possess total sovereignty of the Dodecanese
1920	The Treaty of Sèvres. Venizelos obtains from Italy agreement to assign Dodecanese (except Rhodes) to Greece but the Italians never ratify

1922	On Rhodes, tourist visits to the island estimated at 700. Tourist 'infrastructure' planning begins
1924	2nd Treaty of Lausanne again confirms Italian control of Rhodes and Dodecanese
1925	The Cathedral church built on Mandraki harbour
1928	Cecil Torr dies. Tourist numbers given as 40,000
1931-1934	Further encouragement of tourism. The Hotel of the Roses, Kalithea spa, and other resorts are built/developed. Tourist visits registered as 60,000
1938	Italians restore Lindian Stoa
1940 [28 Oct.]	Metaxas says 'No' to Italian ultimatum. The Italian reconstruction of the Grand Master's Palace is completed
1943	Italian and German divisions on Rhodes. The allies gain and lose control of the neighbouring islands. Rhodes suffers greatly under British bombing raids. Jewish population of Rhodes expelled and transported. Few return
1945	Rhodes remains in German hands until the final surrender. Period of British control
1946 [June]	The Dodecanese granted union with Greece
1947 [May]	British command handed over to Vice-Admiral Pericles Ionnides of the Greek navy and the Dodecanese recognized as under Greek sovereignty
1948 [7 March]	Official union with Greece when King Paul I of the Hellenes arrives on Rhodes

221

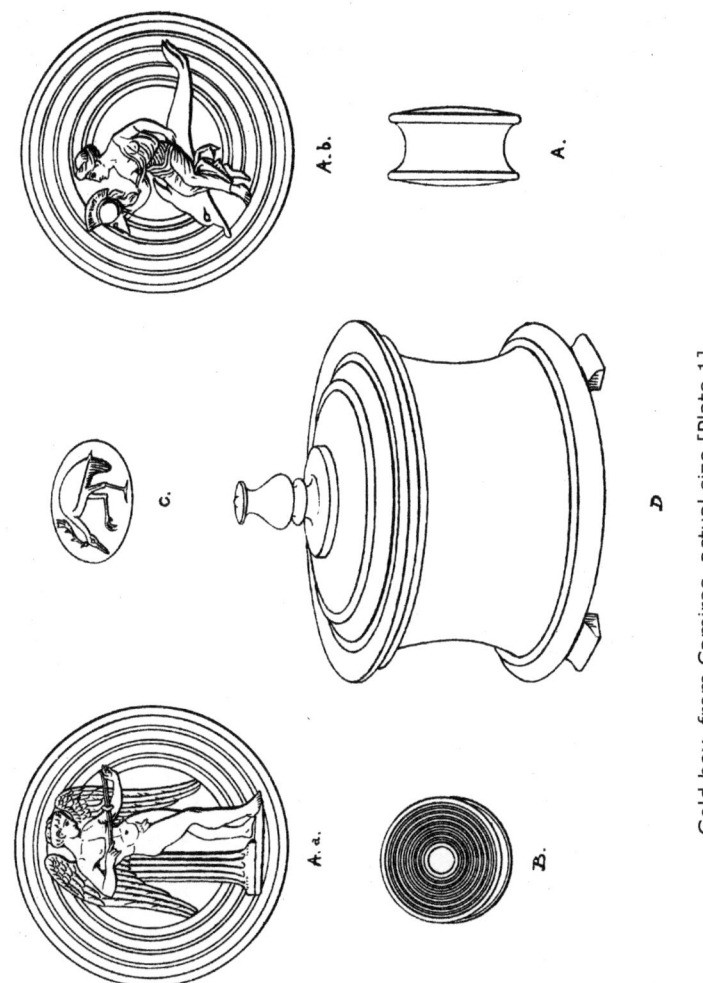

Gold box, from Camiros, actual size [Plate 1]

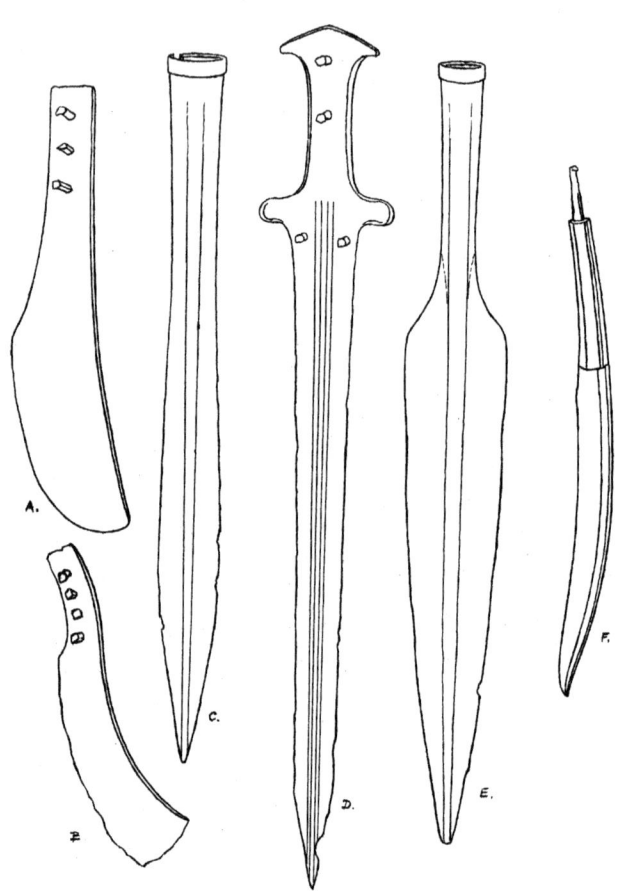

Bronze weapons, from Ialysos, one-third of actual size [Plate 3]

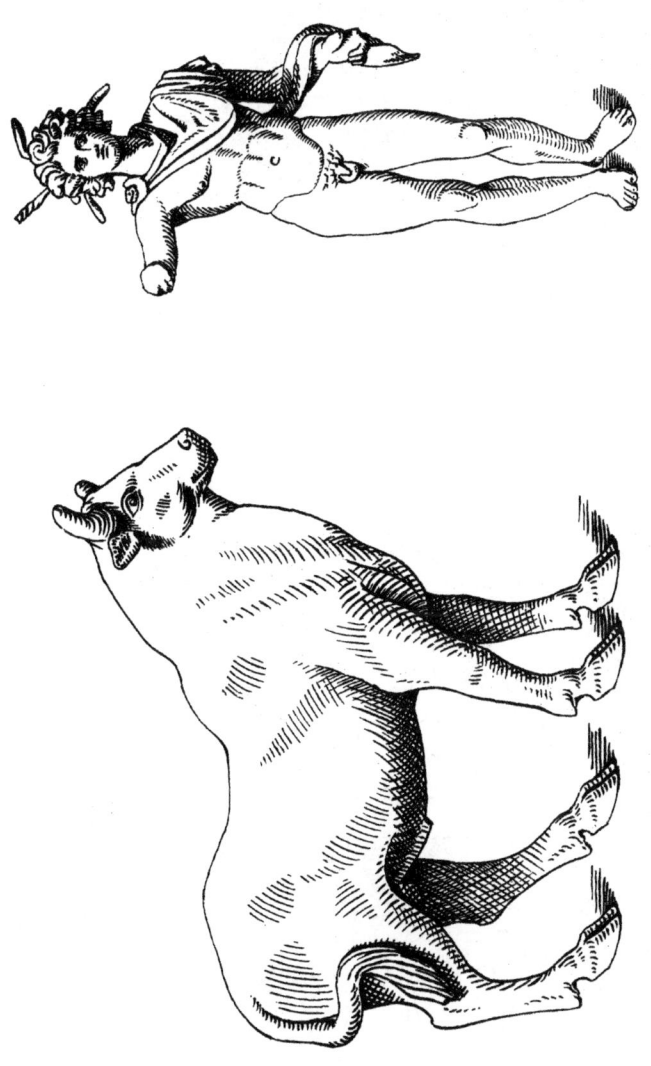

Bronze figure of a bull, from Rhodes and probably from Mount Atabyros, extreme height 6¼ in. [Plate 4]

A.

B. a.

Terra-cotta hydria, from Camiros, extreme height 13½ in.
[Plate 6]

A.

B. b.

A. a.

Cecil Torr on holiday in the Scilly Isles in 1907
(from the author's personal album)

The wide-bellied amphora, typical of the Rhodian vessels of the 2nd century BC, at the height of the island's trading influence around the Mediterranean.